STUART H

Stuart Heritage has written for the *Guardian* since 2009. His weekly column about his young son, 'Man With a Pram', ran in the paper's Family section between 2015–16. He is currently an *Esquire* columnist and has written for *Vanity Fair*, *Elle*, *Cosmopolitan*, *Red*, *Marie Claire*, the *NME*, *Shortlist*, *Time Out*, *The Times* and the *Radio Times*. He lives in Ashford, Kent.

STUART HERITAGE

Don't Be a Dick, Pete

VINTAGE

1 3 5 7 9 10 8 6 4 2

Vintage
20 Vauxhall Bridge Road,
London SW1V 2SA

Vintage is part of the Penguin Random House group of companies
whose addresses can be found at global.penguinrandomhouse.com

First published by Vintage in 2018
First published in the United Kingdom by Square Peg in 2017

penguin.co.uk/vintage

A CIP catalogue record for this book is available from the British Library

ISBN 9781784705213

Printed and bound in Great Britain by Clays Ltd, St Ives PLC

To all Heritages: past, present and future

Stuart is a pleasure to teach. He is unfailingly courteous and considerate. His ability, interest and effort have justly won him excellent marks. Well done, Stuart!

School report, 1992

Peter should not allow himself to be so easily led into foolish behaviour.

School report, 1997

CONTENTS

FOREWORD

The day I decided to write this book was also the day my younger brother Pete got a new job. That evening the five of us – Pete and Emily, me, my wife Robyn and our son Herbie – all went out for dinner, partly to celebrate his good news and partly so I could slowly start bringing Pete round to the idea of being the subject of a book that had the word 'dick' in the title.

He couldn't really grasp the point of it at first, so I tried to explain the tension in our inherent differences. 'We're opposites,' I told him. 'We're completely different in every way imaginable. It's almost inconceivable to think that we're even related.'

'I don't know,' my wife piped up, uninvited. 'You're both kind of exactly the same.'

Neither of us has really spoken to her since.

HUGGERS

Christmas 2014

'I think our house is on fire.'

My dad, by nature, is not a telephone person. He's a dad, after all. He knows the drill. If I call home and he answers, his first instinct is to hurl the phone across the room at the nearest bystander like it's a pinless grenade, because rather that than we inadvertently find ourselves trapped in the hell that is a meaningful exchange.

So, if Dad ever calls me, I quite naturally assume that there's an emergency. I grab my phone and instinctively scream 'OH GOD IS MUM OK?' into the receiver. Every single time. And every single time, Dad responds with:

1) An amused pause, and
2) A remedial-level IT query.

'How do you embed YouTube videos into emails?' he'll ask. Or 'How do you make things go bold?' Or 'My computer keeps making this "donk" noise . . .'

But I'm improving. This scenario has played out enough for me to know what to expect. My heart still races whenever he rings, but the historical likelihood is that he just wants to know which one the alt key is. So I pre-emptively tamp down my anxiety a little and, instead of answering with 'OH SHIT WHAT'S HAPPENED?' I've trained myself to force out a breezy 'Hi, Dad!' This is completely to my credit.

On Monday, my dad rang.

I'd been back in Ashford for three days. This in itself was an anomaly. People don't go *back* to Ashford. It isn't the done thing. People are born in Ashford, then leave Ashford as soon as they can, and never look back.

You're supposed to outgrow your surroundings. You're supposed to yearn for bigger and better things. That's why people move to London. It's the biggest and best thing around. It's a 24/7 swirl of light and noise and colour and excitement.

It's the place where, for centuries, people have met and shared ideas and helped to push humanity to the very limits of possibility. It's a perfectly realised, self-assured global metropolis. If you ever spent your youth running away from anything, the only sensible place to end up is London.

The centre of government? London. The centre of industry? London. The centre of finance and art and culture and recreation and fun? London. The centre of the world? You'd better believe it.

I wanted to move to London for the same reasons as anyone else. I wanted to make my fortune. I wanted to be around people who were like me. People who couldn't make it work in their scraggy little pockets of suburbia either. I moved to London because I wanted to reinvent myself. I moved to London because I wanted to breathe.

This was a mistake.

Jesus, though, London is the worst. To live in London is to begrudgingly make peace with its primary mode of transport; an expensive, sweat-drenched 150-year-old subterranean hell ride full of elbows and babies and backpacks, and thousands of people resigned to putting up with the sheer unrelenting misery of it all because it's still preferable to getting a bus.

To live in London is to fling all the money you ever earn at a cackling slumlord who charges eye-watering sums for a yellowing mattress wedged into an airing cupboard in a derelict bushmeat abattoir located in an area of Zone 18 that's colloquially come to be known as Stab Alley.

Worst of all, to live in London is to surround yourself with bellends. London is full – literally full – of giant thirty-something toddlers who boast about their own spurious accomplishments while ironically playing a vintage 1984 Professor Pac-Man arcade machine in the corner of a tatty upcycled pub that only sells a single small-batch IPA called BUKKAKE for £15 a bottle. They travelled there on a Swegway and they wear Pokémon backpacks and if you shouted the word 'Josh' at nobody in particular, the entire place would fall as still and silent as a Wild West saloon whenever a baddie walks in.

London isn't really a home for these people. It's a crèche. It's a hypersleep chamber that allows them to eke out their insufferable responsibility-free student lifestyle for a good two decades longer than any normal person should, because the thought of standing up straight and looking the world in the eye like an adult fills them with abject terror. London isn't a city any more. It's a biodome full of bastards.

Of course, I didn't actually tell anyone that I was sick of London. Because people who live in London don't just live in London. They love London. They're consumed by it. Institutionalised. It's like their collective amygdala has become clogged up with soot and sweat and exhaust fumes and rat faeces and they've grown incapable of critical thought. Tell someone who lives in London that you hate London and they'll look at you as though you've just shat vomit up Big Ben. Bitter experience has taught me that it's better to keep this sort of thing to yourself.

But then I met someone different. Someone who was more than just an empty bag of borrowed affectations. I met Robyn. Here's when I decided that we were going to get on:

One Tuesday night, we found ourselves in the middle of a three-hour queue for a pop-up hamburger restaurant located above a condemned pub in the arse-end of New Cross. There were dozens of people in this queue, each of them brimming with unbridled enthusiasm about the prospect of waiting for ever to be served a £20 hamburger in a room so suffocatingly packed that the most effective way to eat was to peck at it like a bird. Their excitement was palpable, even though the whole set-up felt like a relatively offensive cross between McDonald's, Alton Towers and post-Soviet Russia.

After about an hour and a half of being stuck in this poxy queue, Robyn whispered to me that she was getting sick of London.

This was exactly what I'd been waiting to hear. Like hostages blinking against the light on their day of release, we both came to the same conclusion. We didn't have to live here.

There are so many other places we could live, we said. Smaller cities. More polite cities. Towns where the air isn't speckled with grot. Tiny Scandinavian fishing ports. Huts in the woods. There was a whole planet out there, and it was ours to discover.

It became incredibly important that I stuck with Robyn. So I did what anyone else would do in my situation: I asked her to marry me. Then, just to be on the safe side, I got her pregnant. And then we started looking for somewhere else to live.

'What about the Outer Hebrides?' I asked, remembering the holiday we'd taken a couple of years earlier. The Outer Hebrides are quiet and beautiful and utterly detached from the rest of the world. We could move there, among all that open space. What a perfect place to raise a child. But then I remembered that I still worked in London, and I still realistically needed to be able to get to the office in less than six hours. With a heavy heart, we looked elsewhere.

That's OK, we thought. The English countryside is full of unspoilt little villages that we could be very happy in. All of them idyllic little chocolate boxes filled with ruddy-faced butchers and happy fishmongers and streets so safe that you could leave your front door wide open if you wanted to. But then I remembered that neither of us could drive, and we might as well have lived on Mars for how practical it'd be.

It's still not the end of the world, we thought, refusing to give in. There must be somewhere. So we logged on to Zoopla and set a very specific set of criteria. We wanted a home in a town that was under an hour from the office, and not eye-wateringly expensive, that had room to accommodate our new family. One result popped up. I saw it, and my heart sank.

Fucking *Ashford.*

Ashford, where I was born. Ashford, that did its best to flatten out all my charming idiosyncrasies. That scoffed at my hifalutin career ambitions and pointed me towards the nearest paper factory. That kept me cooped up and caged in and trodden down in my youth.

Ashford is a crap town. It's a vast, flat desert of estate agents and charity shops and Poundlands. It's a plain, grey, pointless little mound of vanished industry and narrow horizons and squandered opportunity. Its insignia, genuinely, is a lion with a castle for an arse.

And this – *this* – was the only place I could ever be.

The penny dropped. Without realising it, I had left home, found a nice London girl, clubbed her over the head and dragged her back to my lair. And while Robyn was being polite about the place – 'At least it isn't Bracknell,' she kept telling me in a voice pitched slightly too high to be sincere – I realised that I had no choice but to plant my tail between my legs, meekly acquiesce with fate and move there anyway.

Ashford isn't great, but our set-up does have its upsides. My son was born in the same hospital as me, which made me happier than I ever imagined. And it's been great for keeping my ego in check, too. In London, people sometimes stop me in the street to tell me that they enjoy my work. Here, though, they pretty much only stop me to tell me that they went to school with one of my cousins, and that my cousin owes them a fiver, and that I should get it back for them.

Most importantly, living here has given us an inbuilt support network. Raising a child is overwhelming and exhausting, so it's useful to have your family nearby to help out. Plus – and this is something that had long been nagging away at me – I wanted to be able to get to my parents quickly in case anything ever happened to them.

That was unlikely. My parents were getting on a little, but they were sturdy old buggers. They were workhorses, raised to graft. They didn't need me in the slightest but, by moving nearby, I could nevertheless assuage my anxiety that I'd be too far away to help if they ever did.

'Hi, Dad!' I breezed as I answered the phone.

'I think our house is on fire.'

'OH SHIT WHAT'S HAPPENED?'

He told me that someone had seen black smoke belching from my parents' bedroom window. The news eventually got to the lady next door, who managed to track down my mum at work. Mum called Dad to tell him, but he was fixing a boiler in Islington and wouldn't be able to get back for a few hours. So that's why he called me, to see if I'd pop over and figure out what was going on.

Welcome home, Stu.

Dad's tone was completely inscrutable. But then that's my dad. Last week he sent me – with no explanation at all – a Facebook video of a dog licking the inside of a baby's mouth. I don't know why. I've parsed the video again and again for hidden meaning. Is it somehow a coded message about my parenting skills? There was just this video, as weird and enigmatic as a serial killer's calling card. Maybe the dog represented the Middle East, and the baby the larger international community? I have no idea. If you have the slightest idea why a sixty-five-year-old man would send his thirty-five-year-old son a video of a dog licking the inside of a baby's mouth, get in touch. It's keeping me awake.

Before our conversation had even ended, I'd thrown on my shoes and started sprinting down the road towards my parents' little suburban semi – the house they'd lived in for nearly forty years on the outskirts of town, the house where I was raised – scanning the horizon for plumes of smoke. This was exactly the scenario I'd feared. This was exactly why I'd moved back home. In the moment, despite all the panic, I was suddenly grateful that I'd made the decision to return to this miserable little nothing town.

I reached the house just as the fire engines were packing up. The blaze had been extinguished, but the front door had been kicked off its hinges. The carpets were drenched, the windows were tinted with a thick smear of soot and the suffocating stench of smoke had permeated the entire house. The power had been cut off. It was a mess. It didn't look like our house any more.

I'd hoped that I'd be the first family member on the scene, so I could take stock and brace the others for what had happened. But Mum had beaten me home by a matter of minutes. She was standing in the middle of the living room, looking as small and frail as I'd ever seen her. A fireman in his thirties was doing his best to comfort her. By total coincidence, the fireman was also my cousin; my mum's older brother's youngest son.

I should probably point out here that this wasn't *such* a coincidence. My family is unimaginably huge, with dozens of cousins and second cousins spiking off in every possible direction all over the place. It's so huge, in fact, that one of my uncles claims to have once walked in on two of my cousins (who'd never met) having sex at a family wedding reception. Anyway, look, that isn't the point. The point is that I was pleased my mum had been met by a friendly face.

*

The fire itself sounded pretty spectacular. A neighbour had charged into the blazing house once the fire brigade had smashed the door in, and a few moments later rushed back out cradling Mum's two chihuahuas in her arms, to wild applause from a gaggle of rubber-necking locals.

The house was unrecognisable. The house that contained almost all my childhood memories had been ravaged. We were told that the fire had started in the bathroom, possibly thanks to a heated towel rail, and an open window had dragged the flames down a corridor and into my parents' bedroom.

The flames had smashed windows and sprayed glass out across the garden. It had buckled doors. It reduced the bathtub to a molten puddle in the middle of the floor. The smoke had painted everything – walls, ceilings, furniture, mirrors – a thick tarry black. And yet, by some strange quirk of nature, the six-inch chocolate Santa that my mum had been keeping on the floor three feet from the path of the fire miraculously managed to remain completely intact.

Confronted with all this chaos, I wasn't sure what to do, other than to awkwardly reassure Mum that it wasn't her fault and try to pitch in with all the tangled logistics spread out before us. I just stood there, sad and scared and useless, but I figured that was OK, because it's not like they give you a guidebook of appropriate reactions for when your childhood home burns down or anything.

And then my little brother Pete arrived.

Pete and Mum wrapped their arms around each other. It was an instinctive exchange of spontaneous affection and it bolstered Mum's spirits no end. And, after seeing how effortlessly they were able to comfort one another in a moment of genuine crisis, I was struck by a powerful realisation:

Oh, I see, I thought. You're huggers now. That's how things work, is it?

I had not hugged Mum when I got there. Hugging seemed like a relatively low priority at the time, to be honest. I never even thought we were that much of a hugging family. Certainly we'd never hugged very often before. We hugged at my wedding, but only because everyone else was hugging and we all silently came to the conclusion that we'd look like a pack of brittle lunatics if we didn't join in. And even then, when we did, it felt weird and alien.

I'm definitely not a hugger. The etiquette of a hug throws me every single time. The only coping mechanism I've found to get around a hug is to narrate it. If I can draw attention to how awkward I am at hugging, then it means I can drag my hug companion down with me. I don't have to be the only one who feels stupid about it. If I can narrate my hugs, I make everyone else complicit in my awkward failure. 'I THOUGHT THIS WAS GOING TO BE A HANDSHAKE,' I scream at the hug initiator, or, 'THIS IS ALL WELL AND GOOD BUT I SHOULD REALLY APOLOGISE FOR MY SWEATY BACK.' It's certainly a defence mechanism of some description, but it has to come from somewhere. My theory is that I got it from my family. And this is the real reason why I didn't hug my mum that day. She had it bad enough as it was, without having to put up with her fat son bellowing 'OOH HOO AREN'T YOU BONY?' at her mid-embrace as well.

But now Mum and my little brother were hugging, as plain as day, and all because her house had been destroyed in a fireball. Neither of them was even shouting 'HAHA WELL THIS IS AWKWARD' at each other. Something was up, and it didn't seem fair. A memo had clearly been circulated in my absence, telling everyone that it was OK to hug each other now. And I'd been kept out of the loop. I turn my back and move to the big city for five minutes, and my family all suddenly turn into a load of fucking huggers without telling me.

Hand on heart, this whole hugging thing was much more galling than the fire. How the hell did Pete know the right thing to do in the heat of the moment? I'm the favourite son, after all. That's how this works. I was always the favourite son.

I was the one who did well at school. I was the one who went to university. I was the one who remembered birthdays and knew what people wanted for Christmas. I was polite. I was thoughtful. I was the one who volunteered at the local old people's home and spent my afternoons gardening for blind pensioners. That's prime favourite-son stuff. Jesus, it's practically textbook.

But Pete? Pete was a nightmare. He screamed and swore when he didn't get his way. He got into fights. He was an inveterate truant. He threw tantrums. He was riddled with scabs. I, meanwhile, was so clear-skinned and fresh-faced that I could have advertised anything from Milky Bars to an issue of the Hitler Youth's in-house magazine. That's what you want from a son, isn't it? A well-behaved pin-up, not an inert scabby lump with a grudge against the world.

And yet, here was Pete handling the situation like a pro while I just twonkishly stood around next to them. That son of a bitch. I'd get him back for this. I'd get him back for this if it killed me.

Clearly, something had changed while I'd been away. All the things I'd done since I left home at nineteen – getting a degree, living abroad, starting a family – were supposed to cement my reputation as the reliable, successful one. I had thousands of Twitter followers, for God's sake. I'd been on an array of Channel 5 talking-head clip shows. Didn't that mean anything to my family, the recently homeless idiots?

I'm not saying that I expected the red-carpet treatment on my homecoming, but I wasn't anticipating such a painful demotion. And, make no mistake, that's exactly what this was. All that time I was away, Pete had insidiously decided to become the son to rely on. He was the one my parents could turn to when things took a dive. And, worst of all, he'd done this by becoming a hugger. Low blow, Pete.

As Mum – and, later, Dad – slowly began to go about the crushing job of packing up whatever clean clothes they could find in order to embark on a joyless three-month stint in a nearby Holiday Inn, things became clear in my mind. While I'd been away – even though I'd only been an hour and a half up a motorway – I'd lost my place within the family unit.

The bad news was that my parents no longer actually had a home. The worse news was that I'd been supplanted as the favourite son. And what really stung was that the kid who did it was a *dick*.

A week after the fire we discovered that a local newshound had somehow beaten everyone to the punch and taken a dramatic picture of smoke billowing from the top-floor windows of my parents' house. Much to my mum's annoyance, the photo made it onto page five of the *Kentish Express*. I tried to buy the photo from the paper, because I thought I could get it turned into a snazzy jigsaw puzzle and give it to her as a late Christmas present. It didn't work out. Probably for the best.

THE MIRACLE CHILD

I've always felt a little sorry for Pete. But let's not go overboard. I'd feel sorry for anyone who had to follow in my footsteps.

I was a miracle baby. My parents got married in 1971. They met at a youth club a bus ride away from each of their villages as teenagers. Dad was twenty-one when they married, all his hair still intact. Mum was twenty, and so young-looking that for years after their wedding travelling salesmen would knock on the door and ask if her parents were in.

For seven and a half years, my parents struggled to conceive a child. They tried and they tried – visiting hospitals and speaking to doctors with an increasing sense of desperation – but every new hope led to a dead end. Nothing worked.

The years came and went, and eventually my parents resigned themselves and quietly decided to submit to the bittersweet agony of watching everyone else in their lives get pregnant and have babies around them. There was no other choice. Test-tube babies and IVF were still brand-new technologies. If you couldn't have kids in the seventies, then you probably couldn't have kids. So my parents consoled themselves the only way they knew how. They got a couple of cats.

But then, in the dying breaths of 1978, completely out of nowhere, Mum got pregnant. After years of heartbreak, it was finally happening. The thing they wanted more than anything was, at long last, going to be theirs. My parents started to plan like crazy. They picked names. They bought clothes. They thought about building an extension on the back of their little two-bed semi, all to give this unexpected bundle of joy a life that was better than their own.

He was born, this perfect little boy, and he was tiny. They called him Paul. My dad could cradle him in the smallest crook of his arm. Finally, they had what they'd wanted more than anything else in the world, and six weeks later it was taken from them.

My older brother Paul died of sudden infant death syndrome, or cot death. I can only imagine what this must have done to my parents, and how they found the strength to get through each new day afterwards. I overheard my mum talking about it to her friends once, and I remember snatches of the conversation. About how judged she felt by everyone. About how the local GP had visited, and told her in no uncertain terms that it was absolutely not her fault.

I didn't give Paul an awful lot of thought growing up. When you're a kid, you tend to accept whatever circumstance you've been handed. The trauma of my parents losing a baby – especially a baby who died before I was born – was just A Thing That Happened. I simply assumed that the scenario was universal. Everyone has a garish avocado-coloured toilet. Everyone has a front door that needs to be slammed shut in the summer because the latch sticks. And everyone's got an older brother who died before you could meet him.

Now that I've become a father myself the whole thing just seems unimaginably horrific. If I'd been through anything that even remotely resembled what my parents went through, I'd have gone to bed and stayed in bed and just allowed myself to be liquefied by circumstance. Not my parents. They're made from sturdier stuff than me. They might still only have been kids at the time, but that didn't stop them. They got back on the horse and powered through.

In retrospect, you could argue that they were a little too eager to get back on the horse. Paul died in October 1979. I was born ten months later. Ten months, for God's sake. I mean, sure, it's a cruel and callous thing to judge the actions of grieving parents. But at the same time, Jesus, Dad, keep it in your pants.

This is how I came to be. Born to two parents who'd spent a decade trying to have children, and who'd suffered one of the greatest losses imaginable in the process. I was everything they'd ever wanted. See? Miracle baby.

From my behaviour around my own son in the first few months of his life – watching his chest rise and fall at night to make sure he was still breathing properly, fretting over every last pimple and rash – I can only guess at how over-cautiously my parents must have treated me as a newborn. After all, if you're given a second chance at something, you'll do everything in your power to keep it from slipping through your fingers again.

But you can't remain on full alert your whole life. Standards slip. You come to learn that, rather than being delicate porcelain flowers that perpetually need to be wrapped in cotton wool, babies are actually amazingly robust.

For Robyn and me, this slacking of parental standards came pretty fast because we're both quite lazy. But for my parents, it came with the arrival of Pete. Because when you have a Pete in your life, that's where all your energy goes.

THE MONSTER

Peter Heritage was born in October 1983, twelve days after the first ever branch of Hooters opened in Florida. Squatter and less blond than his miraculous older brother, Pete didn't fit so easily into the world. He didn't fit anywhere. In fact, he almost crippled my poor mum.

Pete weighed in at eight pounds and thirteen ounces at birth, close to twice what I weighed. That's four kilogrammes. That's the weight of an adult cat. It's a figure my mum still quietly repeats to herself sometimes, as if she's trying to convince herself that she actually managed to push this ferociously gigantic clump of boy out of her body. These roles would continue through childhood. I – six weeks early and so small she barely even felt me coming out – would cause her no trouble at all. Pete, meanwhile, will for ever be the boy who destroyed her life from the vagina up.

Family stories about Pete's early days make him sound like a monster, albeit one of those sad monsters who inspire pity while they're screaming into the night and setting fire to orphanages. Pete cried constantly. His whole body was covered in eczema for most of his infancy. As a result, barely any photos exist of him as a baby. In those that do he's angry and blotchy. Many of them are out of focus, like he's trying to swipe the camera out of the photographer's hand. He's still got a chip on his shoulder about this lack of presentable baby photographs. It's a chip he'll sometimes use as a weapon.

Pete didn't crawl until he was eighteen months old. His first steps came several months later. He never exhibited any interest in speaking, choosing instead to communicate in tortured screams. My mum claimed his slow progress was a sign of laziness. I'm not so sure. My son was on his feet and propelling himself around at ten months and, as nice as it is to be able to boast about this relatively early crossed milestone, there's still a part of me that would immediately trade the whole thing for an extra eight months of rest. I daydream about rest. If we'd had a Pete, I would have had eight extra months of not babyproofing everything. Eight extra months of not having to navigate a complex series of stairgates whenever I wanted to enter a different room. Eight extra months of being able to keep cups of hot tea on side tables without worrying that they'll be yanked to the floor, scalding everyone in sight. However, I suspect that Pete wasn't really a late developer. I suspect that he was simply picking his moment to pounce.

Because, when Pete did finally choose to start propelling himself around, he found himself with almost two years' worth of extra energy stored up inside him, and I'm convinced this is what has powered him through the rest of his life. The moment Pete's motor skills kicked in, there was no stopping him. Keeping him under control was like trying to use chopsticks to fill a hot-water bottle with a swarm of flies. Pete was a force of nature. He was wayward and erratic. He was, basically, a gigantic pain in the arse. I mean this literally.

One of my first memories of Pete is the phase he went through as a toddler when he ran around pinching women on the bum. Where this creepy behavioural tic came from is anyone's guess – perhaps his one true formative experience was a Sunday-afternoon television broadcast of a *Carry On* film – but for a good few months Pete was relentless. He'd run up behind a woman (and it was almost always a woman, rather than a girl his own age), clamp his stubby little fingers down on her arse, then run away screaming with laughter. It was as if, instead of a regular kid, my parents had given birth to the lead character in a Shane Richie West End musical about the legend of Spring-Heeled Jack. I vividly remember the time when Pete – on the cricket pitch that our garden backed on to, in front of my parents and a couple of my cousins – screamed in out of nowhere and pinched my Auntie Helen's bum. Nobody really knew what the correct response to that was supposed to be, because children aren't really supposed to aggressively molest their own relatives. Still, you live and learn.

Had Pete grown up in South Korea, this would have been perfectly normal behaviour. In my twenties I spent a couple of years teaching English to Korean toddlers in Seoul, where I was exposed to an abomination called the '*dong-chim*'. Roughly translating to 'shit finger', a *dong-chim* is performed by clasping your hands together, extending your two index fingers like a double-barrelled pistol, taking aim and charging at full pelt towards someone's arsehole. And I mean their arse*hole*. The aim of a *dong-chim* is to slam your fingers right into someone's winking bullseye, because that's the bit that hurts the most.

I must have been unwittingly *dong-chimmed* dozens of times over the course of my career. And these kids, believe me, are like little fucking radars. They know exactly where to aim, and they home in on it like bloody falcons. And it really does hurt. It hurts so much that one afternoon I went home and googled '*dong-chim* anal prolapse' because I was scared that one of the kids – specifically the beefy one with the sloping forehead who seemed genetically doomed to a life of criminal muscle – would somehow *dong-chim* me so hard that my intestines would *piñata* out of my bumhole like a drop-down Millionth Customer banner in a 1970s supermarket.

If Pete had been raised in this environment, he wouldn't have been seen as a ridiculous sexual deviant in the making. No, he'd have been crowned as the all-time Harry Potter Quidditch champion of non-consensual anal fingering.

*

But really, it was the eczema that defined Pete's early years. He'd cry because it itched, so he'd scratch it, but that would only make it more livid, so he'd cry even more. My parents tried everything. They put him in mittens to keep him from scratching, but he tore them off. They slathered him in lotions and creams and ointments, but he rubbed them off. They even tried cranial osteopathy, Mum dragging the pair of us on an hour-long bus trip to Tenterden once a week to pay a man she couldn't really afford to try and help ease the pain my brother was in.

Then they tried altering his diet. For a huge chunk of his childhood, the food that Pete was allowed to eat was incredibly restricted. Almost entirely consisting of items bought at Holland & Barrett, it was a nightmare of miserable, taste-free, fun-free health food for him. Milk was out, unless it was a special occasion, in which case he was allowed a thimbleful of thin, watery, see-through skimmed muck.

Meanwhile, I, the miracle child, I could eat whatever the hell I wanted. This was masked from Pete, of course, in an absurd cloak-and-dagger ritual that involved me pretending that I was eating a small bowl of dry Rice Krispies when actually I was chowing down on a small mountain of chocolate buttons like a goddamn champ. And, clearly, Pete could tell that he was missing out on something. He wasn't an idiot. He had the mental capacity to understand that he was being treated like a second-class citizen. It's just a shame that he didn't have the mental capacity to tell that it was all for his own good.

This made Pete resentful of anyone who got to eat normal food, setting one of his key character traits in place: wild indignation whenever anyone else had something he didn't.

All he ever wanted was for everyone to have exactly the same amount of stuff, right down to the number of chips they were served for tea. Not that this extended both ways, of course. If anyone ever gave him anything, that meant that it was his, and there was no way on earth that he was going to share it. It also meant that, since he had something and you didn't, this was indisputable proof that he was better than you. But, if he caught anyone with more than him, he'd throw himself to the ground and thrash around like a beached shark, all in the spirit of fairness.

Here's an example. Once a year, in our sole overtly religious act as a family, my mum would gather the pair of us up and take us to the church a couple of streets away.

Along we trooped every Christmas Eve to the Christingle service, where we'd gently cup a candle-studded, ribbon-wrapped orange in our hands and, in the crisp chill of the draughty church, sing carols and hear stories of suffering and kindness from within the local community. But then one year the vicar told a story about a boy called Peter who had a lot of toys, and Pete threw a tantrum because he thought the story was about him, which meant that we'd all somehow been keeping this enormous stockpile of toys away from him, and in a wanton act of retaliation he tore open his sacred orange and ate it in front of everyone. That was the Heritage family's last Christingle service.

The most nefarious instance of Pete's fury happened at my infants school. It was so subtle that I didn't even realise it had happened for years.

I was in my first or second year, which meant that Pete must have been about two. Walking from our main assembly hall one day, a teacher – not even my teacher, a new woman I didn't recognise – slapped her hand down on my shoulder and pulled me to one side. I'd seen this happen a few times before, and it was usually down to a minor breach of uniform standards: a pupil's shoelaces were undone, or they weren't wearing their tie.

But the teacher didn't look angry. If anything, she actually looked a little concerned.

'Stuart,' she whispered, softly enough so that only I could hear, 'is everything OK at home?'

'Yes,' I replied shyly.

'Are you sure?' she asked, a little more urgently. 'It's OK to say if it isn't. Nobody can hurt you here.'

This stopped me in my tracks. Nobody can hurt me? What on earth was this woman bibbling on about?

'Stuart, listen. I want you to tell me what happened to your face.'

In that moment, I understood the cause of her concern. My entire face was covered in a grid system of tiny scratches so completely comprehensive that I couldn't have possibly inflicted them on myself. Imagine applying a moisturising facemask out of tinned pilchards, going to a cattery, finding the biggest, meanest, most socially maladjusted beast there and calling it an arsehole. My face looked like the aftermath of that. In retrospect, the teacher was probably well within her professional care of duty to worry about me.

'Oh, this?' I replied with an obliviousness that I'm now aware comes off like genuine stupidity. 'That's just my little brother. Sometimes he scratches my face. That's just what toddlers do.'

Then I wandered off and instantly forgot that this temporary disruption to my school day had ever even taken place. This moment remained an unexamined memory until one day, maybe fifteen years after it happened, when it suddenly struck me:

Hang on a minute. They thought I was being *abused*.

My teachers must have all got together and discussed the state of my face. Worse, they must have all come to the same conclusion. Stuart's parents were beating him up. Oh, sure, they look nice enough at the school gates, but who knows what really goes on behind closed doors? Actually, now they came to think of it, of course Stuart's being abused. Look at the size of his dad's eyebrows. They're Bond-villain eyebrows. If Stuart's dad isn't beating him up, then he's almost definitely developing a satellite capable of controlling the global nuclear stockpile. I mean, look at him, with his big bushy eyebrows.

They must have decided to play it cool. They weren't going to get the authorities involved just yet, and they certainly weren't going to make any calls home, but they were going to test the waters by asking me what all the scratches were about. Maybe they thought I'd collapse, crying into their arms, revealing between frantic gulps of air that my mum jabbed me in the face with red-hot knitting needles every night before bed because I didn't wash the dishes properly.

Instead, I'd just told them that my baby brother was a bit of a twat.

This realisation – that Pete had spent his early years clawing at my face so violently that my school almost called social services – was huge. Potentially, it's second only to the realisation (which we really don't need to go into) that hit me five years after my grandmother's death while I was lying on a sunlounger on holiday: that this wonderful woman with the kindest heart imaginable had given her poodle an unutterably offensive name. I think she named him after the dog from *The Dam Busters*, and she just really liked *The Dam Busters*. Anyway, look, we don't need to get into that.

This was Pete all over. He'd noticed – possibly wrongly – that I was getting preferential treatment, and he'd chosen to enact a violent knee-jerk revenge on me. The kid thought the whole world was out to get him the whole time, and he could only succeed by clawing and scraping until all his enemies had been vanquished. He was a Shakespearian tragedy wrapped in scabs, a barely contained ball of spite.

This is not how it was supposed to go. Admittedly, as someone raised as the elder child, with zero experience of having an older brother myself, I might not be the best person to make this statement. But, still, it needs to be said: being a younger sibling looks like a piece of cake.

I was the one getting slammed in the face by life over and over again, because I was the one who had to go through everything first. I was the first to go to nursery school, to primary school, to secondary school, to college. I had to fumble through each new institution blind, figuring out the rules on the fly.

And I had to forge my own tastes in a vacuum, discovering my own music and films. This is why the first cassette I ever bought was a Curiosity Killed the Cat compilation. If I'd had an older brother, he'd have slapped it out of my hands in the record shop and gently eased me towards The Fall. That's what big brothers are for.

I was the first to go off-piste with an independently chosen haircut, for crying out loud. Pete could simply look and learn as I struggled with the desperate limitations of being born with my mum's fine hair and my dad's slightly conical skull. I didn't have the luxury of sitting back and watching. If I'd had an older brother to observe, I wouldn't have tried to grow my hair out, only for it to curl up at the ends so violently that I spent three years of my life walking around like a giant letter W. I'd just have shaved it off, like he did.

I had to do all this stuff first. I was the one shoulder-barging all these doors open. All Pete needed to do for a quiet life was ball himself up, roll into my slipstream and enjoy the ride.

That's it. That's all he had to do. And, to this day, I'm staggered that he didn't. I hacked out the path for him, setting the best examples I possibly could by charming my elders and working hard and winning good grades, only for him to lumber in a few years later and dynamite my beautiful trail to smithereens.

Take primary school. A few weeks after my academic journey began, I was introduced to the peculiar tradition of the Harvest Festival. In most schools, these things operated as a jumped-up food bank, with pupils bringing in cans of soup and packets of rice that the school would later hand over to charity.

Not at Willesborough County Primary Infants School, though. Not at my weird little out-of-the-way parochial English countryside school, with its mandatory weekly country-dancing lessons and its maypole and its menacing oak tree logo and its whole general Wicker Man vibe that couldn't have been any more pronounced if we'd been taught PE by a naked Swedish woman with deer antlers stuck to the side of her head.

No, at Willesborough County Primary Infants School, the Harvest Festival included something called the Harvest Festival Parade. This mainly involved getting all the kids together and making them walk around the school three times, presumably in the hope that the almighty god Woden would grant us a bountiful crop of tinned peas and Cup-a-Soups. And, just to make this meaningless gesture even more needlessly ceremonial, the students first had to pick a King and Queen of the Harvest.

In a secret-ballot-type coronation worthy of the Vatican itself, each child had to tell the teacher who they wanted to be the King and Queen of the Harvest. When the votes were counted, it was declared that I had won. I was King of the Harvest. I think my Queen's name was Kelly or Jennifer or something. Anyway, shut up, this isn't about her. My point is that I started my schooldays with a coronation, and Pete didn't.

A few years later, my charisma had become so undeniable that I was given my first speaking role in a school performance. Fittingly, I was picked to play Jesus. 'Come with me and you'll be a fisher of men!' I boomed at a disciple, because, evidently, even at this young age I had the inescapable charisma and deep authoritative voice of the actual Messiah. My heady career reached yet new heights when I was cast as the lead in the end-of-year production of *The Nutcracker*. This, admittedly, is less impressive than it sounds, partly because I was essentially playing a food-retrieval implement, and partly because I spent the bulk of the play standing under a Christmas tree by myself. But, still, it was the lead role in a play. I think, in his corresponding production, Pete landed the role of Sixteenth Sheep (Non-Speaking).

So there I was, blasting away at the upper limits of my ability, introducing the Heritage name to the good people of Ashford and paving the way for my younger brother to waltz in effortlessly after me. Only it didn't really work out like that.

*

To confirm a few of my suspicions, I recently made the pair of us take an online left-brain/right-brain test. My assumption was that the results would show me to be slightly more right-brained, favouring curiosity and creativity; Pete would be slightly more left-brained, favouring logic and systems.

I was half correct.

According to the test, I am 62 per cent right-brained. This is exactly what I expected. It means I'm a little bit dreamy and a little bit woolly, but not to the extent that I should buy a ton of pashminas and become a secondary-school drama teacher.

Pete, though, is 94 per cent left-brained. Ninety-four per cent. My kid brother craves facts and logic so relentlessly that he might legally qualify as a Terminator. Only 6 per cent of his brain is devoted to light and art and creativity. If you gave Pete an easel and set him down in front of a house, you'd return half an hour later to see the canvas covered in Zoopla-derived property valuations for the surrounding region, all written out in a neat Courier font. Ninety-four per cent. Ninety-four.

Pete and I have vastly different skill sets.

Pete's great love is sport; I'm a bit more indoorsy. Pete is naturally dexterous; I'm almost two-dimensionally uncoordinated. I like reading; Pete has read a maximum of fifteen books in his life, and all of those were ghostwritten footballer autobiographies. As a child I liked watching new films; Pete would watch *The Karate Kid* over and over again until he knew the whole thing off by heart. I'm passive enough to go along with anything so long as it lets me have a relatively quiet life. Pete needs to know exactly why anything new is directly relevant to him, or else he'll rebel from it as violently as possible.

We're so different that Pete was never realistically going to be able to live up to my shining example. One look at our school reports bears this out. Mine are consistent throughout my entire childhood – Stuart is intelligent, but lacks confidence – but, when read in order,

Pete's unfold like some sort of dreadful dawning realisation. It's like watching an episode of *The Twilight Zone* when an astronaut slowly learns that his co-pilot has exploded planet Earth in his absence.

His academic journey begins unremarkably enough. As a nine-year-old, his report read, 'Peter is a surprising boy. He often gives every impression of not listening to what is being taught, then some time later, he will recall the facts and offer well thought-out opinions.'

Two years later at secondary school, signs of tested patience start to crop up. 'This report reflects what Peter can do when he exerts himself, but also clearly shows that he should do this more often!' his form tutor wrote in Year Seven. By Year Eight, after they'd been around Pete long enough to know what he was actually like, they'd grown exasperated enough to baldly state things like, 'Peter *must* improve.'

When Pete reached Year Nine, his reputation had solidified enough to allow his form tutor to write, 'Peter seems to be a little selective in deciding which lessons he will approach with his best efforts,' which I know from my teaching days is code for, 'Pete is lazy and misbehaves and I hate my life a thousand times more whenever he's in it.' Then, in Year Ten, it all comes out. 'Peter needs to make more of an effort if he is to reach his potential,' writes his geography teacher. 'Peter could improve his performance if he made a little effort,' snaps his business studies teacher. 'It is a pity he did not submit his Module One coursework after three months of preparation,' wails his French teacher. 'His uniform is spoiled by his stubborn attitude towards trainers,' said his form tutor. 'Peter is extremely idle,' states his science teacher.

I don't know if this is still a thing, but we had to part-write all our secondary-school reports. They formed something called a National Record of Achievement; a document of our academic career that the government wanted us to use in lieu of a CV, presumably because they didn't want any of us ever to get a job. My self-assessments, as a rule, show an unsettling lack of confidence – my Year Eight PE entry just reads, 'I like PE. I am average' – while Pete's sound like things that Pete would still say today if you sat him down and pressed him on a subject. By Year Seven, he'd already mentally checked out of learning any foreign languages, arguing, 'I find French hard because it is in French.' This is exactly the sort of insane hermetic logic that Pete still utilises to this day when he's spoiling for a fight.

This pattern held throughout our childhoods, both in and out of school. I tried to learn how to play the recorder and guitar, but Pete could never be bothered. I was a member of the Cub Scouts and the St John's Ambulance Cadets, plugging away week in and week out, not necessarily enjoying it but going along anyway out of a sense of duty. Pete, meanwhile, went along a couple of times, threw a wobbly because he couldn't see the point of it and got to stay at home.

I had a paper round with a local newsagent. By no means could I ever be confused with paperboy of the year, but I always showed up on time and I always got the job done. Over time I proved myself to be reliable, a highly sought-after trait in a paperboy. When I retired, and Pete inherited my round, he was always late and his work was sloppy and he was fired after a few weeks, the words 'Why can't you be as good as your brother?' ringing in his ears on the way out.

That's probably the phrase that Pete heard the most. 'Why can't you be as good as your brother?' I thought I was making it easy for him by being such a high achiever, but all I was really doing was setting an impossible standard that he couldn't hope to emulate. After all, he was walking in the footsteps of a miracle child.

We wouldn't be friends if we weren't brothers. I'd sneer at his laddy interests and he'd think I was a ponce. I like nice quiet pubs; he only goes to places if they promise some sort of Sky Sports megatron. He can drive; I rely on public transport. My life is spent trying to mould myself into whatever situation I'm in, while he breaks his neck trying to force the world to fit around his needs. I'm the brain, he's the brawn. I'm the favourite son, he's the disappointment. Under no circumstances would we ever be friends. Of that I am completely certain.

THE WASP JAR

There's a story in our family that cannot possibly be true. I've examined it from every angle and it's just too neat, too absolutely pristine in its construction, to ever be able to exist in real life. But I'm going to tell it to you anyway.

It is the mid-1980s. Something has happened in our house – maybe a toy has been misplaced or a game has been lost or a television has been switched to an undesirable channel – and it has caused Pete to throw a tantrum. *Another* tantrum. Another vast, hinge-rattling, planet-destroying tantrum that's culminated in a furious slammed-door bedroom retreat. Around the house, the rest of the family stagger about like they've just blundered into a nuclear blast. My dad, having possibly been goaded into it by my mum, decides that something needs to be done. Pete might only be about four or five years old, but he's still old enough to be reasoned with like an adult.

Dad climbs the stairs and enters Pete's bedroom. He sits down at the foot of the bed and attempts to talk some sense into my brother, who's still hurt and seething about whatever perceived insult just took place exclusively within the confines of his own mind.

'Look, Pete,' my dad says. 'Enough is enough. You can't behave like this any more. We live in a normal, decent society. If you want people to like you, you have to start doing some of the work yourself. You have to be likeable.'

'I have to be . . . *like a bull*?' my brother responded. Dad didn't bother to correct him. And this, the story goes, is how Pete Heritage came to be Pete Heritage. See? I told you it was too neat. It has to be bullshit.

But at least it fits within the broader narrative. Pretty much until he hit adulthood, and even sporadically after that, Pete was the single angriest entity in the known universe. He was angrier than every single warlord and dictator, living or dead, combined. You could have put a million wasps in a jar, shaken it for half an hour, thrown the jar into a nursery classroom at nap time and the ensuing melee would still have only been about a tenth as angry and chaotic as my little brother.

Everything in his life – the eczema, the lack of childhood photos, the academic indifference, the having to compete for space with a boy whose reputation as the favourite son was quickly becoming canon – had conspired to plant a seed of dissatisfaction within my brother's heart, and all he ever wanted to do was lash out at everything around him to make up for it.

To better demonstrate this, let me take you on a quick guided tour of my childhood home – the house my parents still live in, the one that caught fire – so I can point out the pockmarks left by Pete's endless flare-ups. I'll let you in through the back door. I'll do it quickly, so you don't see the garden where I once accidentally invited the local paedophile to a paddling-pool party. That's a long story, and nobody really comes out of it looking particularly great, and now I sort of wish I hadn't brought it up. Anyway, hey, wow, get a load of this back door.

What a handsome back door this is. It's a wooden stable-style affair with only a small square window of thick rippled glass to let any light in. Now, look closely at that window. See how it's only held together by strips of yellowing Sellotape? That's because one day Pete ran the length of the garden, his brain a mess of noise and fire, and punched it. He punched it once, and it cracked from the centre outwards like a spiderweb, and then he had to contritely tape it up. Conservatively, this must have happened twenty-five years ago. Nobody can even really remember what caused Pete's absurd little outburst. And yet the crack and the tape are still right there; a monument to what happens when you tell Pete that he has to do something he doesn't really want to.

We now find ourselves in the kitchen. For about a decade from the mid-nineties, my family had a spaniel called Barney. Barney was good at doors. Velociraptor good. Barney was an open-the-fridge-door-on-Boxing-Day-and-eat-all-the-leftovers dog, which necessitated a sort of slapdash bolstering on the part of my parents. We fitted child-locks to the cupboards. We drilled holes into the units so that a metal bar could be slotted across the fridge whenever we had to leave him alone in the house. And, for the door separating the kitchen and living room, we had a plank of wood that we'd wedge against the handle to keep him out of the rest of the house at night.

This plank of wood holds great sentimental value for me, because it once caused Pete to try and stab me. Ladies and gentlemen, allow me to tell you the Knife Story.

The Knife Story takes place one afternoon after school in either 1994 or 1995. My mum is out, and my brother has his friend Craig over. For reasons I've chosen not to remember – but almost definitely were not my fault – Pete had somehow worked himself up beyond all comprehension. Not even Craig could placate Pete's stuttering bouts of planet-consuming fury. Pete was incandescent, pretty much to the point of actual vibration, and in the middle of this storm he clomped off into the kitchen to – I don't know – start a fight with a kettle or whatever.

Seizing my chance, in a moment of what can only be described as divine inspiration, I shut the door behind him and wedged the plank against the handle. Pete was trapped. Now, it's important to remember that I only did this out of a basic sense of civic duty – I only had Craig's safety at heart – and not because I'm a petty arsehole who gets a weird kick out of making bad situations even worse. However, it sent Pete spiralling out into even more splenetic fits of hysteria. 'HEEEEEEEEEEEEE!' he kept screaming, like the world's most lividly deflating balloon. 'HEEEEEEEEEEEEE! HEEEEEEEEEEEEE!'

Now, if this had happened in a film, the screaming would have carried on underneath an exterior shot of my house, then another shot of startled birds flying out of a tree, then a shot of the world obliviously turning on its axis deep in space. But it didn't happen in a film, so here's what actually happened: without warning, a carving knife shot out of the gap under the kitchen door, stopping with a loud thump about two inches from where I was standing.

Pete was trying to stab me to death, feet first.

I know for a fact that he was trying to stab me to death, because he kept telling me that he was trying to stab me to death, in a voice so loud and high and hoarse that it made him sound like a broken Leo Sayer android being fed through a mincer. 'I'LL KILL YOU!' he screamed between pointless, heartbreakingly impotent stabs. 'I'LL KILL YOU! HEEEEEEEEEEEEE!'

This by itself was funny enough. But what made it my all-time favourite memory of Pete is the fact that, at literally any point of this insanity, he could have stood up from his crouchy little stab position, opened the back door, walked around the house, come back in through the front door, calmly stabbed me through the heart and then performed a brief ceremonial dance covered in my blood. That's all he needed to do.

But Pete was too angry, too far along a burning path of blinding, paralysing anger, to realise any of this. The poor boy was red-zoning with fury, and the fury had turned him stupid and, instead of doing anything constructive, he'd set his heart on knifing his way through the bottom of the kitchen door, like Jack Nicholson in *The Shining* if Jack Nicholson had been born a Borrower. This limp-dick rage – combined with the fact that all I needed to do to avoid the stabbing was simply shuffle backwards a couple of inches – might still count as the most hilarious thing I've ever seen.

(Not the funniest thing I've ever *heard*, though. That involves a friend's younger brother attempting to give himself a blowjob with the nozzle of a vacuum cleaner, then being caught by his mum, and then wetting himself out of fear directly into the vacuum cleaner. Alas, that is not my story to tell.)

Weirdly, I have no recollection of how the Knife Story ends. I know for certain that I didn't get stabbed, and I can't remember wrestling a knife out of anyone's hands. Perhaps Pete just hyperventilated and collapsed in the kitchen and woke up calmer. Maybe I should ask Craig.

We now come to the living room; the scene of more tantrums and meltdowns and fistfights than I care to remember. Over the years, Pete's anger became so incendiary that we all just figured it'd make sense to simply let him win any game he ever played. It was better, after all, to deliberately mis-hit a few buttons on a Sega Master System than put up with another hour of his wildly indignant yelling. So that's what we did.

Incidentally, if you do ever find yourself trying to throw a game in the company of a furious win-at-all-costs demon child, I recommend that you steer well clear of board games. Not only will the dice take most of the decision-making out of your hands, which will in turn make it much harder to deliberately lose, but they usually have loose pieces that – in the event of an accidental win on your part – will inevitably be flung at your face like buckshot. Even something as benign as, say, Ludo can be turned into a weapon in the hands of a practised sore loser. I suspect that this is the primary reason why we never had Pop-Up Pirate as kids. Things were bad enough as they were without introducing Pete to a game exclusively consisting of swords and a kind of spring-loaded maritime bazooka.

I probably knew better than to let Pete win all the time back then, too, but even then I preferred the quick fix of a peaceful afternoon to the hassle of mopping up another shit-spill. Clearly, this is a catastrophic way to raise a child. Let a kid have its way all the time and, by the time it turns into an adult, it'll be insufferable and entitled and of no use to society whatsoever. I sense that Justin Bieber's family, for example, *always* let him win.

I'm certain that Pete's childhood tendency towards sore-loserdom, and my tendency to placate it by rolling over, has coloured our personalities into adulthood. Just recently, we were talking about an elderly relative who – in the long and grand tradition of elderly relatives – enjoys mouthing off about politically sensitive subjects. I told him that my approach to this sort of behaviour is to put my head down, quietly mumble a series of non-committal responses and wait until she runs out of breath. Pete, meanwhile, pointed out an incident in which – two seconds after she started to carp on with some dreadful guff about immigrants – he argued back with full-blown aggression, because her world view was different from his and it was intolerable for him to think that hers was more correct.

'That's the big difference between me and you,' he told me. 'I'm not afraid of confrontation. You should write chapter seven of your book about that.'

I mumbled in vague agreement. But guess what? I'm actually writing chapter four about it instead. Fuck you, Pete. You're not the boss of me.

The living room is also where my mum invented her legendary catchphrase, the one she liked to drop for close to two decades whenever she grew too tired to stop us fighting: 'You can both kill each other for all I care.'

I used to hate this phrase. As far as I could tell, a parent existed exclusively to prise apart warring siblings. If Pete and I were rolling on the floor, tearing lumps out of each other because I wanted to watch *Blue Peter* and he wanted to watch, I don't know, a cartoon about a funny cow, it should have been the responsibility of the adult in the room to break us up.

But telling us that we could kill each other, with the specific implication that it'd be much easier for her to raise one powerful and victorious child than two needy and argumentative children, just seemed like bad parenting. Decades after Pete and I stopped physically fighting, opting instead for the classic passive-aggressive simmering that's served our family so well for generations, I realised that her approach – the hands-off, kill-or-cure competitive approach that favoured only the strong – was the exact same one that Heath Ledger used in *The Dark Knight* when he was trying to carve up Gotham City's organised crime syndicates. Mum was wasted in retail. She'd have made an amazing supervillain. It's a wonder neither of us ever had our eyes stabbed out with a pencil.

However – again – now that I've got a kid of my own, I can completely see her point. You can't be the parent who solves everything for their kid all the time. Not only would it exhaust you beyond words, but you'd end up raising a useless fleshbag incapable of doing anything for themselves. Sometimes, kids have to be left alone to figure things out for themselves. Sometimes it's better to just snap a snooker cue in half and let them whale on each other until one of them is dead. Legally, I'm required to inform you that this last sentence was a metaphor.

We now sweep upstairs to the bathroom. For many years, this room contained a genuinely distressing avocado-coloured bathtub. The bathtub was never perfect. Not even for a second. While he was fitting it – during the part of the seventies when basic taste flew out of the window and got mangled in a jet engine – my dad had allowed his younger brother-in-law, my Uncle Vince, to help out. Before the thing was even plumbed in properly, Uncle Vince accidentally smacked it with a hammer, and for twenty years there was a small and perfectly round circle of cracked enamel right between the taps for all to see.

This little blemish nagged away at my dad. He'd wanted the bathroom of his dreams, but the unwitting actions of someone else had taken it from it, and a replacement was simply too expensive even to contemplate. So my parents scrimped. They saved. Then, at some point in the mid-nineties, they finally scrabbled together enough cash to pay for a brand-new bathtub. This one was white, and made of hammer-resistant plastic. It was beautiful. It was sleek and tasteful and installed without as much as a scratch. It had been two decades in the making, but finally my dad had achieved peace. Everything was exactly as it should be.

Then, six weeks later, Pete – driven mad by the early surges of puberty – grabbed a pumice stone and carved his name into it.

Nobody can really say for sure why Pete carved his name into the bathtub with a pumice stone. I'm sure that, if I asked him today, he still wouldn't be able to come up with an adequate excuse for this weird outburst. It was a compulsion. Pete saw something pristine, and he felt compelled to mess it up a little. As a punishment, my parents told him to to French-polish the scratches out of the bathtub with the same pumice stone, so perfectly that nobody could even tell he'd done it in the first place. This took him a full day of seething and blinking back angry tears, and by the end it still looked rubbish. At one point, I even climbed into the bath and helped him scrub, because – and I really hate having to underline this subtext so explicitly – I am a wonderful person with a kind heart who has never done a thing wrong in his life.

Next to the bathroom is my old bedroom, where I once accidentally head-butted Pete so hard that he ended up with a nosebleed. We can skip that room. In fact, you know what? We can skip the rest of the house. You've seen enough. Tour's over. Move along.

*

There are many, many other examples of Pete's rage. There was the time when he rugby-tackled me from behind on the first floor of Littlewoods while we were out shopping for school uniforms, and started punching me in front of everyone because, for some inexplicably insane reason, he didn't want to leave. And then there's the whole Blobbyland incident. You'll probably need some context for this.

For almost the entire duration of the eighties and nineties, the king of Saturday-night television in the UK was Noel Edmonds; a weird sort of egomaniacal, slime-obsessed man-elf who wore jumpers that looked like migraines and truly believed that the universe owed him a livelihood. With the benefit of hindsight, his show *Noel's House Party* now comes off like a forerunner to the final twenty minutes of *There Will Be Blood*. Each episode would see Edmonds alone in his giant mansion in the fictional village of Crinkley Bottom, surrounded by the possessions that had long since ceased to entertain him. Here he would plot elaborate schemes of cruelty and humiliation against his many foes. Celebrity guests of the day – your Mr. Motivators, your Vicki Michelles, your Freddie Starrs – would inevitably be led to a vast Perspex torture chamber and – while Edmonds hopped from foot to foot like some sort of demonic Rumpelstiltskin figure – they'd be doused with gallons of a faux-toxic sludge called Gunge.

In 1992, in the second series, Edmonds realised that he could humiliate his contemporaries by creating a *Candid Camera*-style prank character called Mr Blobby. A pink-and-yellow man-blancmange with a voice that sounded like a chorus of devils vomiting in hell, Mr Blobby posed as the star of a fictional kids' show in which celebrities would demonstrate the skills that had made them famous. Blobby would deliberately infuriate these celebrities to the point of nervous breakdown, before removing his head and revealing that he was Noel Edmonds all along and ho ho ho you've been comprehensively undermined on television ha ha ha. Mr Blobby was a sensation. People couldn't get enough of him.

The Great British public adored Mr Blobby so overwhelmingly that Noel Edmonds and his business partners decided to maximise upon it by creating the nightmare that was Blobbyland. Blobbyland was a cash-in, a too-quickly-expanded series of tacky attractions that existed purely to transform our fleeting love affair with a desperately ephemeral one-joke mascot into piles of cash. People would be excited as they walked through the gates of this nightmare, then the excitement would turn into disappointment, then the disappointment would fester into anger at being so brazenly hoodwinked.

I spent my fourteenth birthday in Blobbyland. On 16 August 1994 I woke up in a Somerset holiday camp, my dad taught me how to shave, I listened to the Crash Test Dummies album *God Shuffled His Feet* on cassette three times in a row (which clearly wouldn't have happened if I'd had an older brother) and then we all drove to Mr Fucking Blobby Land.

My parents, confronted with this bleak maze of fibreglass and nothingness, gritted their teeth and tried to make the best of it. I, being a freshly minted fourteen-year-old, followed tradition by being sullen and distant. But Pete? Pete shouted at the family and ran away.

Pete was spoiling for a fight the entire time. His running away felt inevitable, like the grand culmination of a diabolical plan to screw up everyone's day. And, intentionally or not, it worked. His mood grew worse and worse throughout the day, and then he simply disappeared. My parents and I spent the rest of our trip searching for Pete among the park's fibreglass mushrooms and ripped-off and horribly disillusioned clientele in an increasing state of distress, which at least took everyone's focus off how shit-awful Blobbyland actually was. So at least there's that.

We searched the place for two hours, too worried that Pete had been abducted to properly take in the park's threadbare delights, until my dad eventually suggested that we return to the car. I was terrified that this meant we were leaving Pete behind. My parents attempted to win my favour by buying me a Seltzer – a short-lived carbonated drink that came in a see-through plastic can – but that turned out to be so disgusting that it somehow managed to beat the disappearance of my little brother and the all-encompassing shittiness of Blobbyland to become the greatest disappointment of my fourteenth birthday. I realise I'm getting off-track here, but it needs to be reiterated that Seltzers were awful and I'm glad they failed.

Pete was waiting for us by the car, incidentally. Dad was right all along. Pete ran off, got scared, and went back to the one place to which he knew we'd eventually return. To this day he claims that he didn't actually run away – he says he just walked around to the other side of a tree and we wandered off without him – but that's bollocks. Pete ran away, and Seltzer is a terrible drink that must never be brought back to the mass market, not even as a joke. Those are the two main things I want you to take from this.

MEET SHAGGER

Letting Pete get his own way was a bad idea. Every time I deliberately lost a game of Double Dragon to save myself from another tantrum, every time I let him be Player One because he wanted the molecule of imagined prestige all to himself, every time I bit my tongue when he was spouting another torrent of angry nonsense into the sky, I was helping create a sense of entitlement within him. I was reinforcing the notion that Pete should get everything that Pete wants. This is a dangerous notion to have, especially when you hit adolescence and hormones start kicking in.

What Pete wants, Pete gets.

There was a period of Pete's life when Pete wanted to have sex. Let me introduce you to Shagger.

As a family, we only discovered the existence of Shagger by accident, via his friend Craig. Now, Pete and Craig have been close friends since their very first day of primary school. Back then they were inseparable. They always sat next to each other in class, and they'd always spend their afternoons and weekends together. They were as close as close could be. Craig was around for all the big events. He witnessed everything our family could muster up; fights, reconciliations, hard times, better times. He was there when Pete tried to stab me in the foot, for crying out loud. He was part of the family. He was comfortable around us.

Maybe a little too comfortable. One day in our living room, when they were in their late teens, Craig dropped his guard and referred to Pete as 'Shagger' in front of my mum. If we're going to be accurate, what he actually did was refer to Pete as the first syllable and a half of 'Shagger' in front of my mum, then screech to a halt, pause in abject horror for about forty-five seconds, and then pull a face that made him look like he'd happily accept the welcoming arms of death.

But by then it was too late. Shagger's cover had been blown, and Mum wouldn't shut up about it. 'Do you KNOW what his nick-name is?' she'd rhetorically ask friends and relatives whenever the subject of Pete came up, purely so that she could then shriek the word 'SHAGGER!' at the top of her voice in mock disgust like a pearl-clutching Victorian. Later, in what would mark the lowest point in their relationship, she'd call him 'despicable' for having that nick-name. He probably deserved it.

I wasn't really around for the genesis of Shagger. I left for university when he was fifteen, and communication was little harder back then. Facebook didn't exist. Mobile phones weren't ubiquitous. If I wanted to send anyone an email, I literally had to go into a special room on campus and queue up for a computer until one became free. So Pete and I drifted apart for a little while. But what flourished within him in my absence has taken on the timbre of legend.

When I *was* around, I noticed that girlfriends were becoming more frequent, along with a slow adoption of the term 'my bitches' when-ever he was discussing women. Then, out of nowhere, I came back and he'd emerged from this chrysalis as full-fledged Shagger. He'd forged this new identity so completely that it was how people actually referred to him. Even within his band of horny teenage boys – surely the horniest subset of human beings on the planet – he was unstop-pably horny enough for that to become *his actual name*. For a point of comparison, I don't like anything enough for it to become my name. I mean, I enjoy eating biscuits, but start calling me Mr Biscuits and I'll cut your bloody tongue out.

Shagger came out of nowhere, and I had absolutely no clue who he was. I think I met him twice, though, just fleetingly. I was working in Seoul when Pete turned twenty-one, so he flew out to spend a week with me. Our time together was relatively sedate for the most part – we saw some sights, I exploited Pete's hatred of foreign food by innocently plying him with *kimchi* and *soju* until he threw a tantrum and, in a fit of mutually misguided optimism, we went to see the Halle Berry film *Catwoman* together.

We did, however, have one big night out. Knowing that he'd enjoy it – and knowing that it'd save me from hearing any more rants about how much he hated foreign food – I took Pete to Itaewon, the district of Seoul where all the Westerners tended to congregate.

Now, Itaewon is generally not a fun place to be. In 2004, at least, it felt like the campsite at the end of the world. The area was built up around an American military base that had been there since the end of the Korean War, which meant that all the bars were permanently full of aggressive GIs, all blowing off the sort of steam that tends to build up when you're trained to kill people and then sent somewhere where you never get to kill people. The GIs had a curfew and, if the curfew wasn't observed, they'd be dragged back to base by the swarm of white-helmeted military police officers who'd flood each establishment at exactly 1 a.m. each night.

This gave the place a weird heightened tension, a sense that everyone was cutting loose as hard as they could because they knew that their freedom was about to be snatched away from them. I've only seen debauchery like Itaewon in one other place, and that was on a ferry full of pensioners that went from Estonia to Finland, and I'm still too traumatised to talk about that.

Itaewon was one long road at the bottom of a hill. There were two roads leading up and away from it – Homo Hill, which contained all the gay bars; and the self-explanatory Hooker Hill – but that was it. That was where all the madness had to be contained. The place attracted a throbbing swarm of undesirables; soldiers, teachers, dropouts and fringe Koreans who wanted to rub up against the worst impulses of Western culture for the night. Frankly, I never liked Itaewon much. But I had a feeling that Pete might appreciate it.

I don't know if he did or not, but Shagger had a ball. We got to a bar, ordered a couple of drinks, and then Pete vanished. He just ran into the crowd and stayed there for the night. I'd hear him going 'Weeeeeeey!' from time to time, and he ran up to me twice – once to tell me that he almost got in a fight for banging into a soldier's broken arm, and once to aggressively force me into a hug – but that was it. I spent the rest of the evening sitting at the bar, talking to a Canadian girl about Nick Drake and Murakami, because I am easily as much of a cartoon as my brother, and a worse one at that because I'm far easier to beat in a fight.

Where did Shagger go? I never really found out for sure, but there are clues. His birthday present from me was a digital camera, and a memory card that only held about thirty photos. To combat this lack of space, we landed on a workaround. He'd take the camera out with him every day and then, at night, he'd upload all his photos to my laptop. I still have those photos.

According to the metadata from that night, he took two blurry photos of himself with his arm around a girl at 1.47 a.m. What happened between them I don't know, but Pete looks very happy.

Soon afterwards I threw him in a cab to take us home, and the journey was one of the tensest I've ever been on. Pete felt sick, and he kept belligerently shouting about how sick he felt at the driver. In the end, inevitably, Pete threw up and we were charged a vastly inflated fare and booted out miles from home. Pete then sat on the pavement and continued to throw up down himself, and his vomit was full of noodles and a mysterious substance so pink that his favourite T-shirt was indelibly stained.

The second time I encountered Shagger was a few years later. We were at a family wedding with my parents, held in one of those weird multi-room venues that can host several receptions at a time. Who knows why Pete did what he did that night? Maybe he was bored. Maybe the fact that we'd booked a hotel had thrown off his sense of reasoning. Maybe he's just a boundaryless dimwit. Nobody can really say for sure.

But at the reception, once we'd eaten our dinner and listened to the speeches, Pete vanished. He just ran into the crowd and we didn't see him for the rest of the night. We later discovered that he'd been darting between three or four different wedding receptions, searching out girls that he could feasibly pull. He can't have been particularly successful because, by the time we came to leave, his efforts had been blasted up into a feverish last-ditch madcap effort to secure some – any – form of transient connection with a stranger. My dad watched this unfold, and he still talks about it sometimes.

'I've never seen anything like it,' he'll say. 'The determination of the boy. If he saw a girl getting into a taxi – even if she had a boyfriend – he'd just jump in next to her and try his luck. If she turned him down, he'd brush it off and start again with someone new. It was relentless. There was no stopping him. No shame whatsoever. It was astonishing. Astonishing.'

To this day, I swear that this was the moment Dad started to take Pete seriously as a person. After all, if he could be this determined in the pursuit of something as ephemeral as a snog, he could achieve anything he wanted in life.

This whole period of his life is a mystery to me. But, if I was really going to dedicate an entire book to the subject of Pete, I decided that it was only fair to roll up my sleeves and plunge my arm down the clogged U-bend that is Shagger. I'd only ever had the briefest of encounters with this ridiculous-sounding party boy and his permanently broken moral compass, but his friends had seen the lot.

That's something I have to give to Pete. The friends he has, he keeps. While the chapters of my life can easily be demarcated by the friends I had (and inevitably lost contact with) over time, Pete's are in it for the long haul. And Craig's haul has been longer than anyone else's. I knew what I had to do.

I sent Craig a Facebook message asking if he fancied meeting up to go through some old memories. He quickly replied, suggesting that he bring Pete's old flatmate Mike along as well. I'd only met Mike a couple of times before, but he's been in Pete's inner circle for over a decade. Between the pair of them, I knew I could get to the bottom of this void. We arranged to meet up in a local café that Sunday. And to my surprise, given the subject matter, our time together was delightful.

We were all adults now. The three-year difference between Craig and me that seemed like such a gulf in our teens had vanished to nothing now that we were all in our thirties. Mike's married. Craig's got a daughter. Aside from Craig's repeated tendency to refer to Pete as Shagger in the present tense, our chat felt as though they were talking about another life entirely. Their recollections kept meandering off into wistful cul-de-sacs about how they never got to go out any more, and how all Craig really wanted to do was bring up his little girl as well as possible. They were telling old stories, but they were happy to tell them.

'Even at a young age, the pressures of school never really affected Pete,' Craig explained. 'He'd be more concerned about what his masturbation material would be. He was into all that way before anyone else at school. He was so open about it, which has never changed. And in my mind, I was like, "I dunno, I'm not really there yet."'

'He's so confident about it,' Mike chipped in. 'No disrespect, but he's a bit of a loner. And that's not a negative thing at all. But I think that's why he's so open about it, because he literally does not care what you think.'

Over the course of the conversation, a theme started to emerge. Pete, it turns out, is extraordinarily single-minded. There were stories about his superhuman persistence with women, about his ability to break down even the most stubborn would-be romantic partner until they'd fallen for him. His trick, according to Mike, was nothing but out-and-out bullshit. 'His old chat-up line was, he used to stare into their eyes and go, "I can see myself falling in love with you. I can see us setting up a life together." And they'd fall for it.'

There were stories that corroborated what Dad had seen at the wedding reception, about Pete's weird indifference in the face of rejection. Stories about Pete immediately bouncing back and moving on after being turned down by girl after girl in a club, where most normal people would at least experience a moment of sadness. Craig and Mike were talking about Pete with a sort of incredulous awe. Not even his nickname – which, after all, is so crude that he might as well have called himself Captain Chlamydia – could apparently dent his chances.

'I remember going back to the house, and we brought two girls back,' Mike said. 'Pete goes, "I'm going upstairs." So I said to one of the girls, "Go upstairs to see Pete," and she said, "No, I've got to work tomorrow." "Go on, it'll be all right, we can set an alarm for you." "No no no." "He's a nice guy, just go upstairs and Shagger will set an alarm." And she paused and went, ". . . Shagger?" And her face. It was so awkward. But she went.'

I am a great compartmentaliser. One of the best. Everything in my life is very neatly fenced off from everything else, and one of my greatest fears is that one day all the fences will vanish and order will be lost and that will be the end of it. Talking to Craig and Mike, and learning about this side of Pete that I didn't fully know about, represented a vanishing of the fences. Before, Shagger had just been an abstract punchline. But now he was being fleshed out, and the details were starting to make me feel uneasy. But at least this had to be as bad as it was going to get, right?

Nope.

'Tell him about the Bang Folder,' Mike urged Craig.

Oh Christ.

Apparently, they explained, Pete's phone once contained something called a Bang Folder. For anyone who doesn't know what a Bang Folder is – like me until pretty much this very second – it is a list of different telephone contacts that you can text at the same time.

'But why's it called a Bang Folder, Stu?' you're asking, because you're exactly as naive as I was until ten seconds ago, when my entire notion of good and evil came raining down on me like burning wads of molten lead.

The reason it's called a Bang Folder, Reader, is because you text the word 'Bang?' out to all these contacts at once whenever you fancy having a grotty, impersonal bunk-up with a relative stranger you last saw three months ago in a crap nightclub at 2 a.m., fifteen seconds before she blasted eight pints of Bacardi Breezer into the overflowing bowl of a broken toilet. Pete's Bang Folder, I'm told, had twenty numbers in it.

'It always worked!' Craig yelled. 'Two or three would always text back "yeah". It was brutal. That's why he got the name Shagger.'

Oh GOD.

'He sort of got his name from foam parties, where he'd just disappear into the foam with a girl, and then come up boasting,' Mike added, except he said something other than 'boasting' and I'll never tell you what because I'd quite like my brother to be able to find work once this book comes out.

This is my theory: whatever the hormone is that determines sexual behaviour, Pete accidentally ended up with my share. In contrast to him, I am extraordinarily buttoned up. I was a late bloomer. I've ended up in a relationship with 95 per cent of the people I've ever kissed. You could count the number of sexual partners I've had on your fingers, and still have enough free to unwrap and eat a Mars bar. I'm shy and awkward and self-conscious, to the extent that I don't even like taking my top off to go swimming. I am, in short, the Anti-Shagger. If I were to have any sort of folder in my phone, it'd just contain pictures of cakes and reminders to have afternoon naps sometimes.

Mike said, 'If he had a poor night at the club, he used to just walk around outside at kicking-out time, at two o'clock in the morning, just going, "Hot tub back at mine? Hot tub back at mine?" He'd always say, "Mike, there's always a percentage. There will always be a percentage who'll want to come back."'

Staggered, I asked Craig and Mike if they behaved like this too.

'I certainly wasn't confident with girls back then,' Craig said. 'Were you, Mike?'

'To be honest, it was Pete and his friends who forced me into it. Sort of like, "If you're going to live under this roof, we're going to expect a lot more from you."'

'Pete's nights out were not the same as ours,' Craig clarified. 'Because he was on a mission. I spent more time on my nights out talking to the guys than I did girls. Because that was where my head was at. But Pete would be chasing, chasing, chasing until he'd give up and go, "Ugh, let's go and get a KFC." And that was the night he got arrested.'

Right. Good. Finally. I'd been waiting for this to come up. Pete's arrest. At the height of his Shaggerdom, Pete started to compulsively streak whenever he got drunk. Three drinks and, whoomph, he'd take all his clothes off. His Facebook page is a handy illustration of this – for a few months early in 2010, his profile picture was a photo of him in his pants trying to hump a snowman.

I'm telling you this because, one day, Pete got drunk and streaked in front of a policewoman, who immediately arrested him for public indecency. It was quite a big deal at the time, not least because the arrest gave him gigantic visa headaches when he later decided to travel to America.

According to Pete, though, I'd got the whole thing wrong. Early on in the stages of putting this book together, Pete asked me the kind of thing I was going to write about.

'Probably that time you got arrested for flashing a policewoman,' I said.

He couldn't correct me quickly enough. 'I didn't get arrested for flashing a policewoman!' he yelled. 'My junk was tucked between my legs because I was pretending to be a woman!' It's a subtlety that was probably lost on the arresting officer when it happened at 2 a.m. outside an Indian restaurant – how was she to know that Pete was actually just subverting traditional gender dynamics in a pointedly satirical way? – but one he feels the need to make clear nonetheless.

I'd hoped that Craig and Mike would act as witnesses for me, providing me with an independent account of what exactly happened. So I pressed Craig to tell me more about his arrest. This is what he told me:

'KFC was always really busy back then. You'd usually have to queue for about twenty minutes to get served, and Shagger was just like, "Urrrgh, I can't get any women," so he started climbing up the KFC sign. This policeman's gone, "What are you doing, mate?" and Pete's gone, "I'm climbing the sign!" The policeman goes, "Well, get down," and Pete goes, "Urrrgh, all right then." And this is Pete being Pete. The policeman went, "Why were you doing that?" and Pete's going, "Well, I dunno, I'm just having a good night out." The policeman goes, "Do you want to be arrested?" and Pete goes, "Well, it's up to you really, I suppose." So that's really why he got arrested. For talking back, for his ignorance.'

Holy shit, this was a completely different arrest. I had no idea that Pete had been arrested twice. Jesus. I think Mike saw how startled I was at this news, because he quickly jumped in to reassure me.

'Fundamentally, he's a very, very nice person, though. He'd do anything for you, of course he would.'

'Of course he would,' Craig agreed. 'One night I got arrested for, like, shooting this policeman with an air rifle. I got given my court date, on a Friday. But the night before was the last night of all-you-can-drink for fifteen pounds at the club. The solicitor had already briefed me, saying, "Look, bring your personal effects, because you could be getting four months for this." I didn't know the guy was a policeman, by the way, and actually I was only trying to shoot his bike tyre as he cycled past. But he followed me back and did some kung fu on me, and armed response turned up. I'm not proud of it. So Shagger was like, "Let's get our priorities straight. Fifteen quid all-you-can-drink. Let's get down there. Your last night of freedom." I was like, "Easy, Pete, I don't think it's that serious." So we went out that night and I got absolutely shitfaced, and then I had to roll up to court the next morning. But then Shagger came along with me, in the suit and tie, to be a witness in the dock. I had to go and work in Oxfam for a year. Shagger would come in and see me sometimes. So, he's nice. He's a nice person. He is.'

'It's like having a big Labrador, isn't it? It has a lot of faults, but you love it anyway,' Mike added.

KING OF ASHFORD

Until recently, my brother's Twitter bio was 'King of Ashford'. Had anyone else written this, it would have come across as self-deprecating, or at the very least self-aware. But this is Pete. Pete called himself 'King of Ashford' because he honestly believed he was the actual King of Ashford.

He'd worked out all his reasoning. By his calculations, he'd earned the title because by then he was the manager of the town's biggest shop: a giant department store positioned on the edge of the town's biggest shopping centre. Not only did this role afford him dominion over scores of employees, but it also gave him a seat on a number of committees. He got to say how his shop was run, he got to say how the shopping centre was run, and he got to say how the town itself was run. He had numerous tendrils of influence spread far and wide throughout the council, and his office was in a location so elevated that – if the weather was decent and the time was right – he could see the exhaust fumes from the A2042 shrouding the distant branch of Pets at Home in a mysterious yet beautiful fog.

'See?' he'd smile upon explaining all this, with all the misplaced Emperor's New Clothes satisfaction of a tinpot demagogue. 'King of Ashford.'

*

School tended to happen around Pete rather than to him, with every new fact bouncing obliviously off the top of his inelegantly curtained head on the few occasions he actually bothered turning up. Once he left school, he spent a couple of years aimlessly bumbling around, taking a course at the local sixth-form college that had something vaguely to do with computers. He didn't know what he wanted, or where he wanted to go. And then came Pete's first big change – he got a Saturday job.

This would be an unusual fork in the road for most people. For instance, I hated my first Saturday job, in a sort of proto-Greggs outfit called the Three Cooks. I had to wear a hairnet. I had to load dishwashers and wear hairnets. I hated the place, so violently that I used to fantasise about ramming my hand into the bread slicer – a great, whirling nightmare of sharp edges and perpetual slashing that could quite easily cause any number of fatal injuries – just because it'd let me take off my hairnet and go home a bit early. To me, a Saturday job was a reminder of all the things I didn't want to do. It was a hell that would trap me unless I worked hard to crawl out from underneath it. It was Ashford.

But Pete's first day in his Saturday job, working in a discount clothes store on the outskirts of town, was a revelation. Suddenly, out of nowhere, a fire was lit underneath him. He found himself in a world of systems and logistics that finally made sense to him. He didn't have to read or study or write to get anything done. He could just enact a change in the heat of the moment and see its immediate knock-on effect.

So he worked his way up the greasy ladder. The Saturday job became a full-time job. The full-time job became a spot on a management training programme. That became a management position in a failing shop. Once he'd shored up the losses there, his reputation as a firefighter was sealed and he started being flung about the region; the hot new thing who'd solve problems and reverse declining sales patterns wherever he went. He was applying himself, just as all those teachers had exasperatedly asked of him in his reports year after year, and it was paying off.

Brimming with this new-found sense of purpose, Pete aggressively started moving between companies, clawing his way up to bigger and bigger shops. A high-street fashion shop. Another discount clothing shop. Before anyone knew it, he'd become a branch manager of a department store, then the branch manager of the department store in his home town, then he ended up managing two stores at once. And then he wept, for there were no more worlds to conquer.

This put Pete at a crossroads. Circumstances had conspired to present him with two options.

OPTION ONE: Leave the UK and move to Moscow for six months, to open and run a gargantuan new branch in Europe's biggest shopping centre, all of it forged in his own image.

OPTION TWO: Walk away from shops altogether, and take a job at head office.

One option seemed like a culmination of his entire career, the chance to act as an ambassador for his company in a strange new land, to enforce his might upon a veritable army of servants desperate to learn from him via a translator who worked for him and nobody else. The other seemed to me like the chance to be a cog in the machine. One option offered the possibility of updating his Twitter bio to 'King of Moscow'. The other, murky head-office anonymity.

He chose anonymity. And now he's no longer the King of Ashford. In a way, his abdication was a sad event, because it meant that he had to pass his title down to the next most deserving candidate: possibly the weekend supervisor of Poundland, or the street performer whose entire shtick involves wearing a clown mask and banging a hairbrush against a bucket. But, in another way, it's no real surprise. Pete moved on to bigger and better things. This is what Pete does.

So Pete now finds himself with a job that he loves, and that I have repeatedly failed to understand. He's in charge of gift vouchers. All the gift cards his department store sells, and all the gift cards you see for that store in other shops, are now under the strict supervision of my dipshit little brother. It's a weirdly narrow field of work, and one that doesn't necessarily utilise his greatest talents. You can't bark orders at a gift card. You can't threaten a gift card with unemployment if it doesn't do its job properly. You cannot – as Pete has done with customers in the past – chase a gift card out of a shop, across a shopping centre and over a road before eventually rugby-tackling it to the ground on a riverbank because you caught it surreptitiously pulling clothes off racks and ramming them into an empty suitcase when it thought nobody was looking.

But gift cards are apparently a huge industry, and it presumably has plenty of room for improvement. This is another one of Pete's key skills. He sees opportunity where everyone else can only see dead ends, and he always makes good on it. This is why, one year from now, I fully expect to see him enact a sequence of Machiavellian back-room machinations that:

a) secure him a place as the chairman of the company, and
b) inspire him to make a series of bold acquisitional moves that take control of all the supermarkets in the United Kingdom. In short, Pete's face will be on every pint of milk I ever buy, and my nightmare will become real.

In the past, whenever I've described Peter Heritage to people who've never met him, I've found it helps to tell them that he would easily win *The Apprentice*. Because he would, in a heartbeat. In fact, I even know exactly how he'd win it.

WEEK ONE: Pete nominates himself as team leader, and forces his team to name themselves the Dwayne 'The Rock' Johnson Bantz Ladz All-Star Legends. He draws upon his fifteen years of retail experience to power them through their task of selling sweets to tourists or whatever.

WEEK TWO: The phone rings at 5.15 a.m. Pete is the first to answer because he's already been frantically doing pull-ups on a banister, into a mirror, while licking his lips, for the last hour and a half.

He draws upon his fifteen years of retail experience to power his team through their task of selling soap to tourists or whatever.

WEEK FOUR: Pete's first loss. The unconventional task – upcycling lavender baskets in a pop-up east London haberdashery – ends in disaster when Pete decides that the whole thing is bollocks, kicks over all the lavender, punches another candidate in the side of the head and then scratches the phrase 'PETE FUCK GOOD' into the side of an antique chair with his teeth. However, Pete survives the boardroom because he calls the rest of his team 'cunts' and Lord Sugar secretly starts to recognise a little of himself in him.

WEEK EIGHT: Another candidate attempts to oust Pete by blaming him for the failures of the team. Pete responds by shouting the entire lyrics to 'Keep Your Shit the Hardest' by DMX right into his face so loudly and insistently that Lord Sugar – having already secretly identified Pete as his unofficial successor – fires the rest of his team for gross insubordination. He decides that Pete should be the only candidate to enjoy that week's reward, and Pete is happy because it just involves looking at a picture of Bobby Charlton for three hours.

SEMI-FINAL: The job interview. Pete sails through every round with flying colours, surprising everyone with his comprehensively watertight preparation.

THE FINAL: Pete's suggested product – 'A Manchester United-themed sambuca bar where all the staff have big old tiddies' – goes down horribly among the fancy London millionaires assembled by Lord Sugar. However, by this stage Lord Sugar has started not only to call Pete 'son', but also to dress and talk like him, so his victory is secure. The series ends with Lord Sugar and Pete wearing sequined suits and top hats, and rapping 'It's Murda' by Ja Rule into a low-angled fish-eye camera while money cascades down around them.

My theory about Pete is this: to him, the world is entirely binary. There is good and there is bad, and in between is a vast chasm of nothingness. And something always – always! – has to win. Present Pete with a pair of shoes, give him ten minutes and you'll return to see him deeply in love with one shoe and ready to violently renounce the other as the worst piece of shit that has ever been made.

This is why Pete likes football so much. Because, really and truly, and however you look at it, football is pointless. Football is just a bunch of millionaires who you'll never meet engaging in meaningless busywork for an hour and a half while the adults get on with more important things. What happens if one team wins a game of football? Nothing. Nothing happens. Nobody dies. The losing team don't get set upon by lions. Everyone still gets paid. Football is an abject waste of everyone's time. You'd be better off spending your life blankly applauding a random number generator.

But for some reason, this speaks to Pete. Real life is nasty and lumpy and ambiguous and complex. But football gives Pete one afternoon a week to retreat into a world where people are only either winners or losers. In football, you're one thing or another thing, and nothing in between. All of life's interesting nuances and subtleties are planed off and, for a couple of hours on Saturday afternoon, everyone is either a champion or a failure.

Politically, Pete veers right. I was lucky enough to see the moment he started veering right, in fact. It was in the run-up to the 1990 conservative leadership election. Pete was only about seven at the time, and he knew nothing of policies or ideologies. But he saw the Conservative logo – a bold design of an arm thrusting a torch skyward – and decided that he liked it. And if he liked the Conservative logo, his reasoning went, it must mean that he also liked the Conservatives.

Pete was just getting into football and wrestling by then, and those were his only two real points of reference when it came to demonstrating his enthusiasm for anything. So his chosen method of showing off his new-found zeal for political analysis involved putting on a red nylon Halloween cape, waving a cut-out of the logo in his hand, and bombing up and down our living room chanting 'MISSUS THATCHER! MISSUS THATCHER!' as if she'd just scored the winning goal in the last minute of the FA Cup final.

Pete just loves a winner. The Conservatives have been in power for the bulk of Pete's life, and Pete loves the idea of being on the winning side. I know this makes him sounds like a thoughtless, heartless glory-hunter with no real morals or principles to speak of, but then again he does support Manchester United despite living just about as far away from Manchester as an English person can without toppling into the sea.

(Pete has urged me to point out that he has never voted conservative. This is because he hasn't actually voted once in his entire life.)

In a way, I'm a little jealous of Pete's all-out clarity of mind. I haven't enjoyed Pete's burning, all-encompassing rocketship-to-the-moon career ambition, either. I have enjoyed no such career jetstream. Where Pete sets his targets on a goal and bulldozes a direct line towards it, I'm never even certain what my goal is. I initially thought that I'd be a scriptwriter, until I studied scriptwriting at university and realised that most of scriptwriting just involves sitting in a dark room and trying to spout the most insufferably smug bullshit about *Battleship Potemkin* that you can think of.

So then I thought I'd write gags for TV shows. This was also a bad fit, because it turns out that everyone who works in entertainment is pathologically insecure about losing their job, and brimming with barely contained bitterness because they feel their talent is somehow being wasted on a substandard product.

Clearly I'm talking about myself here. One series I worked on was a topical Channel 4 comedy show that ran nightly from Monday to Friday each week. Usually you'd be lucky if more than a couple of jokes made it onto the show. One night, however, nobody's jokes made it onto the show because – in an arse-achingly dismal 'Ooh, wasn't the past great?' moment of genuinely vapid nostalgia – the host scrapped the whole segment at the last minute in order to rap the *Fresh Prince of Bel-Air* theme tune in its entirety on air. Worse, it got the biggest response of the entire series. This was the night I stopped wanting to write gags for TV shows.

So that's how I ended up doing this. I get to write whatever I like and – unless my editor decides to spite me by replacing chapter ten with the lyric sheet to the *Hangin' With Mr. Cooper* theme tune – I get a decent amount of control. Plus, what job could possibly be more secure in the age of the Internet than professional writer? I can see no problems with that in the future, no siree.

I've also been a barman, a sunglasses salesman, a candlestick salesman, a short-order cook, a market trader and a teacher. And I was a model for a Korean hip-hop clothing catalogue for one afternoon in 2004, too, but there is no way on fucking earth that I'm ever admitting that to you.

This means either that I'm a restless spirit, drifting along on the winds of serendipity and trying to make the best of wherever it takes me, or that I wouldn't know how to pull my finger out of my bum if I had a gun to my head. Whichever one it is, I guarantee that Pete doesn't have this problem.

I recently asked him if he had a backup career in his pocket, on the off chance that the gift-card business ever went under. He was perplexed by this question; partly because the gift-card business will never go under, because the world is full of people who can't be arsed to put any real thought into Christmas, but mainly because this is the job he wanted and therefore is the job he has. Still, I pressed him on the matter and, eventually, he told me that he'd join the army.

This makes perfect sense. Everyone has a role in the army. Everyone has a purpose and a rank, and everyone always knows where they stand in relation to everyone else. Plus you get to run around, and fire guns, and drop the pretence that food is anything but baldly utilitarian fuel designed to keep the body functioning during extended periods of activity. It's as though the entire concept of the military was invented exclusively to give Pete something to do when gift cards stop being a thing.

I do not have a backup career. It definitely isn't the army, because my second-biggest fear as a child was that they'd declare World War Three and I'd be enlisted. For a while I thought I might be a baker, were it not for the simultaneous and inescapable facts that it looks like gruelling physical work and I've never baked a loaf of bread that hasn't to some degree resembled an exhibit from the Museum of Massively Deformed Vaginas.

Maybe a zookeeper . . . except I don't really like animals or being outdoors, and I'm not really that jazzed about the idea of being around people, and I can't drive so there's no realistic way I'd ever even make it to the poxy zoo in the first place. But, yes, sure, a zookeeper. I could be a zookeeper.

If you ever want to see the spoils of our different approaches to life, you just have to look at where we are now. Pete is the capitalist's capitalist. He'd managed to put together an impressive property portfolio before I'd even settled on a career. He drives a sleek black BMW, which might just be the love of his life. He runs and swims and cycles for huge distances every single day. His television is so colossal that I get motion sick just watching the news on it. His kitchen is spotless. He has all the free time in the world to play video games.

Me? I've never owned a house in my life. The one I live in now is a terrace, sandwiched between an angry Polish family and a couple who wake my son up every night because they sound like bludgeoned seals whenever they have sex. I have a gym membership that I don't use because I'm either working or looking after my son, and my very occasional slivers of free time are spent buying new trousers because I keep getting too fat for the ones I already own. This paragraph, hand on heart, is one of the first I've written for this book where I've actually been wearing outside clothes, and that's only because my landlord just came over to fix my toilet door.

This isn't how things were meant to go. I've read our school reports. Pete was genetically predetermined to be the slacker. I was the sensible, hard-working one. I was the one with prospects. I had all the pep and drive. I went to university, for crying out loud. I was the very first Heritage ever to go to university. Pete didn't. He realised that the whole thing would be a colossal waste of his time, so he threw himself into work instead, and he drove himself as hard as he could, and now he's got the goods and the position and the status to show for it.

Things just weren't meant to turn out like this. Pete can talk about cars and contracts and kitchen designs and margins and growth projections and building materials like it's the easiest thing in the world. Meanwhile, I'm the one still fumbling around in the dark.

That's our biggest difference. If Pete would theoretically win *The Apprentice,* then I'd theoretically get banned from *Sunday Brunch* for accidentally making a focaccia that looked as if it urgently required the aid of a pessary.

A CONVERSATION WITH PETE HERITAGE ABOUT THE FIRST THREE CHAPTERS OF THIS BOOK

In retrospect, telling Pete about this book was a mistake. I should have just written the thing, edited it, published it, popped a copy through his letterbox and then run off to spend the rest of my life hiding underneath an upturned rowing boat on a beach in Guam. That way I wouldn't have to deal with any of the fallout.

But I told him, and he wanted to read it, and that presented me with a dilemma. If I showed him everything upfront – if I told him that I'd been sneaking around talking to Craig and Mike, or that I'd made the time he tried to stab me in the ankle a key part of the story – he'd have made my life miserable until I died. No, I needed to work up to all that stuff.

So instead, I landed on a compromise. Although the book was half written at this point, I'd only show him the first few pages. The pages where he gets to come in and hug my mum and look like the hero. That'd butter him up, wouldn't it? So I invited him to my house, made him lunch, let him read the first three chapters and discussed it with him over a game of Streets of Rage 2. This is a transcript of the ensuing conversation.

*

'Do you want lunch, Pete?'

'Fuck yes, I want lunch. What have you got?'

'Quiche.'

'Quiche is bullshit. There's not enough meat and I don't like pastry. Quiches are poncey and you're a ponce. Where are Robyn and Herbie?'

'Nando's.'

'That just about sums it up, doesn't it? Fucking Nando's. Am I Player One?'

'No. This is my house. I'm Player One.'

'But I'm always Player One.'

'Look, just tell me what you thought of the first three chapters.'

'Well, the biggest issue I had was your take on Ashford. I think you're very harsh on Ashford. Look, I want to show you something. I took a photo of exactly where I was when I read your first chapter. Look at this.'

Pete grabs his iPad and shows me a photo of some idyllic woodland, glinting beautifully in the sun.

'This is literally where I was when you said how shit Ashford is. Look how pretty that is.'

'Where is that?'

'That's a five-minute walk from my house.'

'That's not fair, though. You live near the woods.'

'And you situate yourself near the town centre because you can't drive. You fucking only see Lidl and the train station and that's it. That's why you think Ashford's all grey and shit.'

'And you felt it was your duty to say something?'

'Yeah. I mean, don't get me wrong, it's got its chavvy element and its bad areas, but I was out in the countryside this morning, walking the dogs in the countryside. Lovely. My second bit of beef is around the whole fire thing. You've missed a whole massive— How do you pick up the apples?'

'The A button.'

'You've missed a massive point. Hang on, I'm going to pick up this knife. Stabby stabby. All you talk about is the fact that I hugged Mum, right? But don't you remember anything I did afterwards, while you just stood around faffing? I went through the fucking paperwork in Mum's hellhole of a cupboard, which frankly should have been set on fire . . .'

'Wait a minute, I called the Gas Board for her.'

'I don't remember you doing shit. I called the insurance company, explained what happened, became the major incident contact, arranged for emergency people to come around and do shit like board the doors up, I arranged their accommodation that they lived in for the next six weeks, I arranged to get their evening meals paid for them. So I had the emotional consideration to give Mum a hug, but also a whole practical aspect that you haven't acknowledged. And I kept thinking, "Oh, he's going to come to that in a minute, he's going to come to how I bossed the situation," and you didn't.'

'Is this what this is about? You think I didn't praise you enough?'

'Definitely. I did a lot. And what did you fucking do? You had everyone around for dinner and made, like, fucking *lemon roulade* or something.'

'Yeah, it was nice. It brought everyone together.'

'That's great, but I'd arranged to get their meals paid for them for the next three fucking months, so it was unnecessary.'

'It wasn't unnecessary! If something's gone wrong, you don't want to go and sit in a fucking Travelodge by yourself being all sad, Pete. You want to be around your family and have a lovely meal. A lovely chicken-and-chorizo stew. I'm cooking another one of those tonight, by the way.'

'Why didn't you cook it for lunch, then, instead of giving me half a fucking quiche?'

'Becau—'

'Now, the rest of the book. You're right in most ways, actually. But I think there were times when you used to play up to this favourite-son thing, and I distinctly remember getting the blame for your shit by default.'

'Like what?'

'I can't remember. I remember really thinking it once, though.'

'What, that I'd do something wrong and you'd get the blame because you were the shit son?'

'Just if something bad happened then by default it was going to be my fault. Do you remember when we went to fucking Noddy Land or some bollocks?'

'Mr Blobby Land?'

'That's it. I bet you're going to fucking write about how I ran away when we went to Blobbyland, aren't you.'

'Probably not.'

'But I didn't fucking run away! I swear, right, I really remember this clearly. Really remember this clearly. I was the other side of a fucking tree. I was looking at something on the other side of a fucking tree. I swear on my fucking life. I was the other side of a tree. And then, when I walked around to find you, you'd all fucked off.'

'No, no, that's not how it happened at all. You were in just a shit, angry mood. You were being argumentative and starting fights with everyone, and then you just walked off.'

'Yeah, to the *other side of a tree*. Granted, it was a big tree. But it was still the other side of a tree. I remember it really clearly. Really clearly. And I fucking walked around everywhere looking for you. I went back to the car looking for you. That's where I found you. I went back to the car to look for you, and you weren't there, so I was walking back to the park, and saw you all going to the car. So you'd obviously fucking given up looking for me.'

'What's all this got to do with me being the favourite son?'

'Because I got the blame. I'm on the other side of the tree, and everyone fucks off and leaves me, and somehow I've done this awful, awful thing, but even though everyone was supposedly looking for me so hard, they didn't bother looking *on the other side of this fucking tree*.'

'Is that the only example you've got?'

'Well, there's also the Baked Potato Situation. Have you written about that?'

'Hand on heart, I have not written about the Baked Potato Situation.'

'Well, you probably should do, because it just about sums everything fucking up.'

In accordance with Pete's wishes, I will now write about the Baked Potato Situation.

A couple of years ago, Pete had to move back in with my parents for a few months, sleeping in his old bedroom. It was, in fairness, a tricky time for everyone. Pete was a little all over the place, and Mum and Dad had long since stopped expecting to live with their kids. By this point the three of them hadn't lived together for over a decade, and a great deal of tension stemmed from their clashing ideas and routines.

Chief among these were my mother's dietary habits. Pete, an inveterate health nut with a holiday on the horizon, only ate lean meat and Creatine. Mum, as she's always done, would serve a baked potato for tea on Monday to accompany Sunday's leftovers. Pete hates baked potatoes. Every time my mum gave him a baked potato, he'd flood me with texts about how much he hated baked potatoes and how much they made him want to kill himself. Photos of baked potatoes and declarations of suicide. That's all I got from him for a month.

Around this time, a report came out investigating the stresses that occur when older parents are forced to live with their adult children. So I wrote a column for the Guardian *about the subject, using Pete's hatred of my mother's baked potatoes as a hook. Really, the baked potatoes must have only accounted for about a tenth of the article, with maybe another tenth given over to the weird way that my mum sprinkles granulated sugar on crumpets. Which, I still feel justified in mentioning, because that genuinely is quite a weird thing to do.*

The morning the column was published, Pete sent me a text.

Haven't read it yet, but the first thing mum said to me was, 'How many times are you going to text Stu about suicide today? Doesn't make me feel very good about myself.

I called my mum straight away. And, in the worst possible way, she was upset rather than angry. She was honestly as upset as I've ever heard her. I could hear her choking back tears during our call. And, of course, she was right to be upset. All my mum has ever done for us was the best she could, and now her two sons were yucking it up about her weird attitude to food in a national newspaper.

Her reaction made me feel terrible. I'd hurt my mum and it made me feel like the worst piece of shit who ever walked the earth. I couldn't go and see her to straighten things out, because I still lived in London at the time, so I did the next best thing and spent the entire fee from my column on flowers for her. That lunchtime, after the flowers had been delivered to the shop she worked in, Mum phoned me again. She cried and I apologised and everything got quite intense, and by the end of the call we were good again.

Pete sent me another text that evening.

Good save with the flowers, brah. That's why you're favourite son and I'm a cunt.

He followed this with a photo of some faeces in a toilet, captioned 'TAG SOMEONE WHO SHITS LIKE A TONKA TRUCK' and that was that.

However, Mum recently told this story to one of my uncles, and it became apparent that now – instead of being the story of how her terrible older son wrote horrible things about her in a newspaper – it had somehow become the story of how her terrible younger son intruded on her life and disparaged her cooking, and how her brilliant older son bought her some flowers to make up for it.

So that, in a nutshell, is the Baked Potato Situation. I shall now return you to the scheduled conversation, which picks up exactly where we left it.

'I was trying to get in shape for Bali, though, wasn't I? And, to be fair, I looked red hot when I went to Bali. Red hot. I've got a picture of me at the gym with my top off from back then, and I might make you put that in the book because I looked so red hot in it. Did you just die?'

'Yeah.'

'Then you're a fucking idiot. Anyway, the Baked Potato Situation was a classic example of, yeah, OK, I didn't handle it fantastically, but I was just venting to my brother. You expect to be able to do that, and it not become an issue. But you stitched me up.'

'I didn't stitch you up. I texted and asked you if I could write about it.'

'The thing is, though, that when you talk to Mum about Baked Potatogate now, you come out of it smelling of fucking roses, just because you bought her some fucking flowers.'

'Do you know what that is? That's doing something wrong, and then realising that you did something wrong, and then trying to fix it.'

'If you'd just gone, "Oh, you know what, my brother, got his back, don't worry about that, I'll just keep that shit to myself," then it wouldn't have gone any further and we wouldn't be talking about it two years later. Anyway, listen. The third chapter. Actually, I don't massively disagree with it. But I do think it's bullshit that you thought being the oldest was harder.'

'It was, though.'

Pete adopts a feeble-old-man voice, specifically to mock my perfectly valid claims.

'Ooh, nobody lent me any tapes, and that's why I ended up liking the Wonder Stuff!'

'Yeah, all right, shut up. Do you really think you had it harder than me?'

'Definitely. You had no comparison. I was always being compared to this golden boy. I wasn't any fucking good at school. Or paper rounds. Did I really write that bit about French in my report, by the way?'

'Yes. Word for word.'

'Did I tell you about the French test I did? They gave us French dictionaries, and we had to think of a sentence and use the dictionaries to translate them. My sentence was: "This test is stupid and you can stick it up your arse." I got a . . . what were those things you got at school when you misbehaved?'

'The opposite of a merit mark? I don't know.'

'You probably never had one, did you, you ponce?'

'You know what, though? Your school reports weren't actually that bad.'

'Yeah, they all mainly said that I was nice but lazy.'

'I was a bit disappointed about that. I wanted them to be a big part of that chapter, but they weren't quite severe enough to work. I should have made some up.'

'Making stuff up is the fucking theme of the book, isn't it?'

'I haven't made anything up! I might have embellished the Christingle story a little bit. But almost everything else is true. Do you know what an unreliable narrator is?'

'Fucking you're an unreliable narrator.'

'That's the point of this chapter. It's so that, if I start getting out of line, you can come in and tell everyone that it's bullshit.'

'Well, I think it's like, in the third chapter, it's kind of right, and I don't disagree with most of the stuff you say about me in it, because I really was lazy. But I just think your perception of *[adopts feeble-old-man voice again]* "Oh, it's so tough living with these expectations, being a wonder child". . .'

'I didn't say it was tough. I just said that you had it easy and you fucked it up. All you had to do was copy me.'

Pete farts.

'It was much harder being the young one.'

'I don't think so.'

Pete burps.

'Listen, I was ill.'

'You weren't ill, Pete. You had a bit of eczema.'

'I've still got the fucking scars.'

'Have you?'

'Well, I've still got scars from chickenpox.'

'Yeah, but not eczema.'

'It was the combination of the two. Pause the game. Look at this a minute.'

Pete pulls up his T-shirt and shows me the smallest dimple I have ever seen, two inches under his right nipple.

'That is an invisible tiny spot.'

'No, wait, look.'

Pete holds the bottom of his T-shirt in his mouth, then moves towards the window for better light with which to examine his scarred torso. He spends six seconds searching as hard as he can, then triumphantly spins around towards me, pointing at another dimple.

'That's the same one, isn't it?'

Pete then spends another fourteen seconds – I know this, because I went back and timed the recording – biting on his T-shirt and looking for more of these deadly disfiguring scars that have made him so unbearable to look at. He spins around yet again and points at another, even smaller, even more invisible, dimple.

'PROOF!'

'That makes two. You've got two tiny scars.'

Pete sits down, furious.

'I've got more than that. I'm only choosing to show you two. Fucking hell. What else are you writing about? I bet you're going to fucking write about the Knife Story.'

'Well, I'm probably going to have to tell the Knife Story.'

'That's fucking bullshit, don't do that.'

'It's not bullshit. It's funny. Don't you want me to write about the Knife Story?'

'I don't care, you can write about whatever you fucking want. I just wish I'd fucking connected with it.'

'You wish you'd stabbed me?'

'Yeah, then you'd really have something to fucking write about.'

'Why are you making out it was my fault?'

'Because you must have done something to provoke me.'

'You were just in a really angry mood. We should ask Craig.'

'Oh no, keep Craig out of it.'

'Why? He was there too. He can be our independent witness.'

'Nah, keep fucking Craig out of it, because he's a dick and he'll just fucking say whatever makes me sound most like a cunt. Pretty much what you're already doing.'

'I should write a chapter about how angry you are.'

'I'm not angry.'

'All right then, about how angry you were as a kid.'

'I'm not angry.'

'You were as a kid. You beat me up a lot. Well, you didn't beat me up. We had fights.'

'Well, yeah, but you must have been angry too if we were fighting. Why weren't you angry? If there were fights, why weren't you angry?'

'Because I . . . fucking . . . because you were uncontrollable! You were this uncontrollable little boy. I never did anything. I'd say, "Oh hello, Pete," and you'd just run at me and try to beat me up.'

'Hahahaha. You know why I did that? Because you were a fucking DICK.'

'Did you just laugh and fart at the same time?'

'I wasn't that bad, was I? I mean, we had a few fights.'

'We had loads of fights. Remember when you scratched my face up?'

'I was a toddler then, you pussy. I was beating the shit out of you, and I was three years younger than you. At that age, you were probably double my size. That sums up our relationship. I kicked the shit out of you because I'm superior.'

'This is way further than I've ever got in this game.'

'Actually, I think it was a bit of a vicious circle, me being naughty.'

'What, you were naughty, so you got told off, so you acted worse?'

'There were definitely times when I – granted, it would have been my fault in the first place – but there were times when I couldn't do anything right.'

'Like what?'

'Like fucking I don't fucking know. But I do definitely know – and I can't back it up with specifics – that there were times when whatever I did was shit, and I'd get the blame for everything, so you think, "Well, fucking what's the point?" Vicious circle. What's that?'

'Is it an Alien egg?'

'It's got a turkey in it.'

'So you think if Mum and Dad had hugged you more, you'd be better behaved?'

'Maybe. I don't know about that because, despite what you wrote, I'm not a hugger.'

'I know. I was so surprised when you hugged Mum.'

'Well, you know, I was fucking upset about the fire as well!'

'Yeah, I suppose.'

'I'm surprised that you didn't hug her, though.'

'Yeah, and it feels dumb that I didn't. I didn't think to do it at the time. But now I kiss her goodbye and everything, every single time I see her, so we're making up for it.'

'I'm not a kisser. If there needs to be a hug then I'll have a hug. But I don't want to be all "Oh, I'm going now so I'll do a little weird air kiss on your cheek."'

'It's not a little weird air kiss, it's a nice—'

'People at work do that. You know how people like kisses? Certain people you know will be fucking kissers. Little air kisses. Mwah mwah. What's the point? What else are you writing about? Are you writing about me being a champ?'

'I might. Ideally, what would you have as the next chapter?'

'Just about me fucking training like a legend for Ironman.'

'Just about you training?'

'Yeah, let me write about my training plan and stuff. Like a diary. "Today: great swim session. Swam intervals."'

'For a whole chapter?'

'Yeah. You could just take some extracts from Mudmanpete.com.'

'I'm not linking to your website in my book, Pete.'

'What else are you writing?'

'I'm thinking about doing a chapter about you and Herbie.'

'Oh, what's that gonna be?'

'What do you think it's going to be?'

Pete, once again, does the feeble-old-man voice.

'"Errr, he's shit with Herbie! He throws him in the air and shouts at him a lot!" Correct?'

'Look at that! That's just a fat bloke with a gun.'

'Listen, I'm fucking good with Herbie. It's him that's shit with me. I'm surprised you haven't talked about the fact that Mum and Dad were so desperate for me to be a girl, by the way. They've always been desperate for a girl. They had three boys and now they've got a grandson. They're desperate for a girl. They both are. I was a disappointment from the start. I wasn't a girl, I was fat.'

'You weren't a disappointment because you were a heavy baby.'

'You said I ruined Mum from the vagina up!'

'Do you think I should keep that bit in?'

'I dunno. It's a bit weird.'

'Yeah.'

'So is this going to be a whole chapter, this conversation?'

'I think so.'

'How are you going to do it?'

'I don't know yet. I might just write it out.'

'What, you're just going to transcribe everything we've talked about?'

'Might do.'

'Jesus, Stu, that's going to be so fucking boring.'

AN INDEPENDENT VERIFICATION OF THE KNIFE STORY BY PETE'S FRIEND CRAIG, WHO PETE WANTED TO KEEP OUT OF THIS

'Your family dynamic was always really odd to me. You weren't around a lot, because you were at university. But your parents used to let Pete talk back, and that's where that chip started growing on his shoulder. I remember that you'd always eat stuff that your dad had grown in the garden, and Pete would be like, "What's for pudding? What's for pudding?" If he wasn't happy with the answer, he'd be like, "Cuh, what's this?" Then he'd go, "Craig doesn't even like this, do you?" and I'd be like, "I do, I do." Even if I didn't like it, I'd eat it around someone's house, just to make everyone feel comfortable. But Pete would go on and on. You dad would be like, "Wind it in, Pete," and your mum would be really kicking off at him, and he'd be, "Shut up, shut up, come on, Craig, let's go to my room." It was like an American family.

'The knife thing, if I remember rightly, we were playing skittles on your landing. We used to put skittles at one end, next to your bedroom door, and throw balls at them. And I think Pete was on a good score or something like that, when you just opened the door and kicked all the skittles over.

'You were just being a big brother. Not in a nasty way. You used to take the piss out of Pete in front of me a lot. Being a big brother. And Pete was all, "Ugh, get off, Stu."

'Anyway, we come downstairs and I think we were waiting for dinner. But then, like you said, he was just getting angrier and angrier, and you two were arguing about something. God knows what it was. I can't remember what it was, because it was so long ago. This was probably twenty years ago.

'So Pete was getting angrier and angrier, and I was like – as a guest round somebody's house – just backing away. Your dog was sensing that something was up, so he was backing away and all. Then I remember you locking him in the kitchen with that bit of wood you had. And then I remember him just going *batshit*. Like, I've never seen him like that.

'And you were leaning against the door, and all of a sudden this big bread knife came shooting out the bottom and we heard, "Argh, I'll kill you! I'll kill you!" And you were still taking the piss like, "What are you gonna do, kill my ankles?" and by now I'm standing way back like, "What. The fuck. Is going. *On*?" Like your brother was going mad, everyone's going mad, the dog's going mad, and I was like, "*I have no idea what's going on here*."

'I was up by your dining table. I thought it was funny, the way you two were. I thought it was hilarious. But then he calmed down and he was like . . . he was spitting, he just couldn't process what had happened. And he wouldn't talk to me about it. He was just like, "Nnnng, he's such a dick, that Stu."'

'So the whole thing was my fault? He only got angry because I kicked his skittles over?'

'No no no, not at all. It was just Pete being a div.'

IRONMAN

The most terrifying man I've ever met tends owls for a living. When I was a kid, he'd tour around the local youth groups; ostensibly to show children his wonderful owl collection, but mainly to freak them out so comprehensively that they'd be doomed to spend the rest of their lives waking up at 3 a.m. screaming the word 'OWLS!' into balled-up fistfuls of damp duvet.

This man – a big, red-faced rural type – had lost his hand in an accident. Quick thinking on everybody's part meant the hand could be surgically reattached with relative ease but, as a result, he was left with three side effects. Those side effects were:

1) reduced movement in the affected hand,

2) a complete lack of feeling in the affected hand, and

3) a sporadic tendency to become the most singularly morbid human being in the history of mankind.

And he knew exactly how to combine these three things to startling effect.

He needed to, because you need to assert your authority very quickly in situations like this. If you've ever been a Cub or a Brownie, you'll understand the rebellious energy that these places tend to crackle with. They're full of kids who mistakenly think they've somehow got one over on their parents, when actually their parents just want two hours alone to drink or have sex or watch *Taggart*. However, this energy does not do well when introduced to a large collection of easily spooked flying claws. One wrong move in a room full of owls and it'd be massacre time.

So, over the years, the owl man devised a plan to keep kids in line. I've seen his schtick two or three times now, and it's always exactly the same.

First our hero will introduce himself. But he'll do it quietly, deliberately talking underneath the group. He'll tell us his name, and his job, and that he's going to teach us about his owls. Then comes the twist.

Over a still-murmuring thrum, he'll hold up his damaged hand. He'll explain exactly what happened to him, showing us the reattachment scars around his wrist. And then – and he'll modulate this bit depending on how much noise his audience is making – he'll drop his chin and growl, 'This hand is dead.'

The next part still makes me queasy. To demonstrate exactly how dead his hand is, he'll raise it up high above his head and hammer it down on the nearest available surface with a sickening crunch. 'DEAD!' he'll scream.

Don't mistake this for an authoritarian palm-slam, by the way. It's not Jack Nicholson banging the table in *A Few Good Men*. No, this is an ugly, awkward crash that lands on the outer knuckle of his little finger. Imagine you're holding a fish by the tail, and you want to kill it against a wall as quickly as possible. That's the sort of movement this is, and it makes such a violent combination of bangs and cracks that every single child in attendance, no matter how badly behaved, will immediately fall silent in order to blink or faint or swallow back the mouthfuls of vomit that have involuntarily shot up from the depths of their gut.

'It's DEAD!' he'll scream again. Only then can our hero resume showing off his owl collection, safe in the knowledge that he's got us all in the palm of his increasingly obliterated hand.

But he's not done yet. Oh no, not by a long shot. 'Your dad,' he'll ask a little later on, guilelessly Columboing us all into a corner, 'drive on the motorway, does he?'

A few of us, by this point, might have foolishly regained enough courage to force out a meek nod. 'How fast does he drive?' he'll ask, homing in on the nodders like some sort of hellish bloodhound.

'Suh-seventy miles an hour?' they'll hesitantly reply, suddenly aware that they've walked right into his trap.

'Seventy miles an hour,' our hero will slowly confirm. 'You know what happens when you drive a car at seventy miles an hour?'

Silence.

'At seventy miles an hour, you create a slipstream of fast-moving air above your car. You know what happens if an owl flies into this slipstream?'

Silence.

'It yanks them down onto the road. They smash into the ground and they break their necks and they're dead. DEAD!' Then he'll smash his hand into a wall so loudly that everyone flinches again, because a good showman never lets a gimmick go to waste.

Now, this would be a perfectly acceptable place for him to stop, but clearly we weren't quite as irreparably traumatised as he wanted us to be, because there was still one last gruesome curtain to rip back.

'If your dad drives at seventy miles an hour,' he'd gravely intone, numb red hand dropping to his side in mock defeat, 'he's a *murderer*.'

This stuck with me. To this day, if I'm ever in the car with my dad and he's doing anything above sixty, I'll spend the bulk of my time with my toes curled up in my shoes, frantically worrying that we'll suddenly pass a load of dead owls, bulldozered together into a giant pile on the hard shoulder.

Anyway, the story always reminds me a little of Pete. Only in this scenario Pete is the car and I am the owl. Because, when Pete gets excited about something, I'll inevitably get caught in his slipstream and end up breaking my neck on the tarmac.

*

Let me tell you something about the phrase 'Winners never quit'. It's bollocks. Quitting is amazing. All my favourite people are quitters. Bands that gave up at the height of their powers rather than lumber on dumbly towards irrelevance. One-and-done authors, who put everything they had into one book and then disappeared. America, the greatest social experiment in the history of the world, is a country full of quitters. Almost every single American is a descendant of a quitter; a founding father who arrived on the east coast and, at some point during the exploration of his vast and unexplored new continent, thought, Fuck it, this'll do, before downing tools and setting up shop on whatever nothingy scrap of wilderness he happened to be standing on.

I am a quitter.

God, though, I love quitting. I could spend my entire life saying no to things and I'd be the happiest boy who ever lived. My biggest problem, in that respect, is that I'm for ever shackled to Pete. And Pete never gives up, ever. It's the worst.

I did two Tough Mudders thanks to Pete. I never even wanted to do one of the bloody things.

A Tough Mudder, for those of you lucky enough to have never encountered one, is an obstacle-course race. It's a half-marathon, dotted with stuff that you have to climb over or crawl under or wade through. There are dozens of similar events all over the country, but the Tough Mudder stands out because it makes the most noise.

Pete was the first to hear about Tough Mudder. He saw a video online, where a load of burly topless men all roared in slow motion together. They sprinted through mud in slow motion together. They hurled themselves at netting in slow motion together. Then they embraced and stood in front of billowing flames and looked up and away like heroes in a Soviet propaganda cartoon, in slow motion, together.

Pete saw this video, and immediately wanted to do a Tough Mudder. He showed me, and I immediately did not.

I take the blame for what happened next. I should have set some ground rules. I should have said no once, as firmly as I could, and then just got on with my life. That's what you need to do with Pete.

What I did instead was prevaricate. I hemmed and hawed and told Pete that I'd think about it, because I didn't want the bother of confrontation. Anyway, I knew that he'd forget about it in time.

He did not forget. Pete does not forget. I should really tattoo 'Pete does not forget' on my forearm. It'd save me so much hassle in the long run.

The barrage of texts was endless. He started with a simple Fancy it? before escalating quickly through Up for it?! to MUDDER MUDDER MUDDER which was followed, at something like 3 a.m. that night, by MUDDER FUCKER!!! This is what you get for not taking a hard line with Pete. This is the hell you create for yourself. I looked around and saw my choices narrowing to two options: either I agree to do this bloody race, or I'm kept awake by dozens of exclamation marks for the rest of my life.

So, begrudgingly, I committed. Pete texted back the word BOOM!!! in reply, and that was that. But there was one problem. Pete was already race fit, and I – to put it especially mildly – was not.

Pete has always been physical. He constantly played football growing up. He ran as a teenager, to the point where his knee eventually gave out. He joined a gym as early as he possibly could, and grew so burly that – at a national managerial meeting early on in his career – he startled his superiors by accidentally ripping through the sleeve of his shirt with his bicep during a meeting. This used to be his favourite story, but it's recently been replaced by one in which he went on a company awayday to a falconry centre and outran a hawk. Anyway, Pete loves fitness is my point.

I am not Pete. I like sitting down. My biggest thrill as a child was the day my mum let me copy a Christmas cake recipe onto a sheet of paper with the family typewriter. I played a little football at school, but that's because the only real options for school lunchtimes were either playing football or sitting alone in a classroom, and the latter would have singled me out as enough of a weirdo to warrant a beating. And, even then, I only played on the proviso that I could go in goal, because that would require the least amount of running around.

My parents eventually made me join a gym, because this profound lack of physical activity had warped my posture to such an extent that I ended up being crippled by migraines. They gave me two choices: either start doing exercise or go and visit an osteopath. I went to the osteopath a couple of times, but the thought of stripping down to my pants in front of a stout Polish lady was too much for my prudish teenage sensibilities to take. So the gym it was.

But I hated going to this gym so much that, on more than one occasion, I'd take my gym gear out of my wardrobe, spray it with water to make it look as if I'd been sweating, dump it in the laundry bin for my mum to discover and carry on watching telly. The gym's not there any more, by the way. It's a strip club now.

I've tried to maintain some level of regular physical activity as an adult, not because I enjoy exercise, but because I work from home and I eat a ton of food all the time. Until relatively recently, I even hired a personal trainer to gear me up into staying fit; partly because I needed the motivation, but mainly because it was £50 a week that I wouldn't get to spend on KitKats. My sole reason for exercising is because I'm trying to stave off obesity. Pete's reason is because he wants to succeed at everything all the time.

And I mean everything. Commitment to a cause has never been a problem for Pete. He's always laser-focused on one distant goal or another. A decade ago, back when he was Shagger, that goal was becoming some sort of immortal Ultimate Lad figure. But then he discovered fitness, and now we're dealing with a different Pete altogether.

This Pete exercises as hard as he can every single day.

This Pete is almost completely teetotal.

This Pete counts calories as though his life fully depends on it.

This Pete once told me that he'd bring snacks to my house for New Year's Eve, then turned up with a chopped-up stick of celery in a plastic zip-lock bag.

This Pete, if he sees you eating or drinking anything that isn't a chopped-up stick of celery in a plastic zip-lock bag, will snatch it away from you and read the nutritional information as loudly and disparagingly as he can in a bid to shame you into eating as healthily as he does.

This Pete, following a recent supermarket trip, had to witness the pathetic sight of me attempting to conceal a bottle of fruit juice from him, all because I couldn't face hearing the 'Why Fruit Juice is Literally the Worst Thing You Can Possibly Drink, It's Just Like Drinking Poison, Why Can't You Only Drink Water Like I Do?' lecture for the thousandth bloody time.

So there was already no chance that I'd ever be able to keep pace with Pete during the Tough Mudder. But, alas, it was too late. I had agreed to it. My fate had been sealed.

At least I wasn't alone. Pete had assembled a crack team of friends and cousins to participate with him. To bolster my side of the arrangement, and to help me prepare, I enlisted the help of my trainer Gus. The first thing Gus suggested was to leave the confines of my gym at the height of winter, pour a bucket of freezing water over my head and go for a 10k run. This whole endeavour, it quickly transpired, was going to be a giant pile of shit.

Our warm-up race, if you can even call it that, took place in the woods in Dorking. Our team consisted of me, Pete, Gus and our cousin Craig. It was only a seven-kilometre run, but there were hundreds of obstacles separating the start and the finish. There were ditches and hills and banks and streams and climbing frames all over the place, and the penultimate obstacle was a lake that we had to wade through. Only, because this took place in February, they had to break up the surface ice with a hammer before anyone was allowed in it.

The race was horrific. Pete shot off ahead right from the very start, engaged in a berserk alpha male battle with our cousin, who at least had a burgeoning midlife crisis as an excuse. Then Gus took the middle ground, and I was left lumbering along behind. All there was separating the lake from the finish line was a heavy cargo net that we had to crawl under, and I remember being so completely exhausted by that point that a man had to crouch down and slowly instruct me to move each individual limb to get out from underneath it.

We finished, we were handed hot drinks and foil blankets and – because we are all insufferable dickheads – we took a series of victory selfies.

'Get in a tent! Now!' cried a volunteer steward. 'Do it now, or you'll get hypothermia!'

Stupid jobsworth, we thought, and took more selfies.

Five minutes later, Gus got hypothermia. He was in the middle of getting changed, and he suddenly just stopped moving. I asked him if he was OK, but he wouldn't respond to his own name. Something was up, so I called the same steward over. Tutting, she led him to the heated hypothermia tent, where she wrapped him in more foil, put him in a sleeping bag and laid him down near a heater. It was a bit scary, so after fifteen minutes I went to check up on him. 'Twenty more minutes,' they said. My ride home was being treated like a chicken dinner.

And this was just the warm-up.

The actual Tough Mudder itself took place in Winchester that July. My training had mainly involved thudding around Crystal Palace park and listening to podcasts every morning. I hated it. Running made me too sore, it made me too hot, it blistered my feet beyond all recognition. And yet I persevered, because a part of me still held out hope that I might trip on a rock and break my leg and end up too injured to race. What can I say? I'm an optimist.

I was barely in shape come Mudder day, but I quickly realised that it didn't matter. Far from being the hardest race in the world – which is how it bills itself – it turned out that the Tough Mudder is actually just a well-oiled marketing machine. It's a receptacle for weekend warriors, for people who want to pretend that they're in the army but can't get time off from work to go abroad and get shot. It's a haven for the sort of men who enjoy taking off their tops and pretending that life is one long stag party. It's Pete's kind of deal, basically.

Here's how a Tough Mudder works. You pay anything up to £180 to go, and then you pay £10 a pop for any spectators you want to bring. You drive there and you pay between £15 and £30 for parking. You walk to the registration tent and pay another £5 to leave your changing bag there. Then you exhaust yourself doing the race itself, drink a free pint of gruesome luminous alcopop, pay over the odds for a gristly burger-van burger in a too-big bun and then you go home. The course itself is far from easy, but you're left with the realisation that the hardest obstacle of all is getting through it with any money whatsoever left in your bank account.

As our race began, Pete and his pals all ripped off their shirts in a bizarre Hulk Hogan-style bonding ritual and zoomed away into the distance. I plodded along in the middle of the pack, slow enough to be overtaken by a ton of people at the start, but steady enough to grind past most of them again halfway through, once they'd given up and had resorted to walking the rest of the course.

There was one bright spot in the middle. Just as my spirits were wavering, we ran into an obstacle that required you to partner up and piggyback each other along a stretch of the course. And, having just about caught up with him, I chose Pete as my partner.

Once I was on his back, and we were diligently making ground together, I could just about understand the point of Tough Mudder. It's really all about camaraderie. It's about brotherhood. You don't take part in a Tough Mudder to win. You take part to feel close to your fellow racers. You take part to show that you're there for each other. During this obstacle, bobbing up and down on Pete's back like a kid on a donkey at the seaside, I finally got it. We'd been through a lot together, he and I, and we'd butted heads time and time again for every possible reason. But right there, at that precise moment in time, I don't think I'd ever felt so close to him, or as proud of him.

Then it was my turn to carry him and I fucking hated him again, the lardy fucker.

Looking back, the end of that Tough Mudder should have signalled the end of my running career. For most of our party, it was. They'd focused everything on those twelve miles and, once it was over, they were out. I envy that lot. Because, between the violent enthusiasms of Pete, our cousin and Gus, I found myself being pulled forward by a momentum against which I was completely helpless. They wanted to do more races, which meant that I had to do more races. No arguments.

Over the course of the next year, I ended up being dragged along to a handful of smaller events. A cross-country 10k in a hop farm. A half-marathon nightmare of hills and blind leaps in an army training camp. It slowly started to take over my life. And I was only an occasional weekender. Pete and our cousin, trapped in an eternal willy-swinging competition to the death, were racing every single month.

But my training continued and, two months before our second annual Tough Mudder, I was in the shape of my life. We took part in a race in Wiltshire, and for the first time ever, I managed to run without difficulty. I made it all the way to the end in fairly decent shape, and I even managed to beat the others up a couple of big hills. I felt unstoppable, which is always a bad thing for me. Feeling unstoppable means that I can coast. It means that I can exercise less and eat more and fairly quickly end up in no fit state to run for a bus, let alone a finish line.

Christ, I hated that second Tough Mudder. I hated it right from the outset, when one obstacle – advertised as a full-body dip into ice-cold water – actually turned out be a tepid skipful of barely diluted sheep shit. I hated the heat. I hated the queues for the obstacles. I hated that the reward for booking early was getting to complete a whole extra stretch of course, as if being made to push yourself even closer to the brink of vomiting exhaustion was somehow an adequate compensation for agreeing to take part in this piece-of-shit race in the first poxy place.

And then someone kicked mud in my eye.

By accident, obviously. I was trying to crawl out from underneath this bullshit obstacle that keeps fucking electrocuting you, and a guy came running up to help me, and as he stopped a gritty glob of mud flew out from the toe of his shoe and dug deep into my eyeball. I washed my eye out, but it kept streaming, and then my nose started running, and suddenly I couldn't see or breathe. Right then, after about thirty feet of suffering, I was struck by a thunderbolt of realisation.

I didn't have to do this.

The race wasn't compulsory, and I clearly wasn't having fun. What are they going to do if I stop? I thought. Ban me from Tough Mudders? So I stopped. I stopped running, and I swerved the rest of the obstacles, and it was brilliant. I quit, and quitting was brilliant.

I like to think that I quit doing Tough Mudders because Robyn was pregnant. I like to think that I was thunderstruck by the sensation that Tough Mudders and their ilk were for lost souls, for people with nothing going on in their lives, who had to pay through the nose to experience a modicum of suffering because they had no higher purpose. I, meanwhile, was about to become a father. I was about to be given custody of something that would mean more to me than I did. Being a father was my calling. Being a father was my higher purpose. I didn't need to put myself through this foolishness, because I had something bigger and tougher and more profound ahead of me.

Which is bullshit, obviously. I stopped doing Tough Mudders because I'm lazy. But, still, it's a nice thought.

*

Eventually the entire group fell away from Pete. One by one, just like me, they all realised that life is short and activities should be enjoyable, and paying hundreds of pounds to run through suspiciously coloured mud (and then get diarrhoea for a week afterwards) wasn't in the slightest bit enjoyable. Even my cousin's midlife crisis ended up hopping along to the next stage, where you get a tattoo and pretend to enjoy grime music. Before long, Pete was left out on his own.

So he did more races by himself, but they no longer scratched the itch they once did. And then he thought about running a marathon, and he ran a marathon, and he still felt unfulfilled. So he decided to do a triathlon, even though he couldn't swim. He started filling his evenings and weekends with swimming lessons, gradually progressing from being the slowest person in the pool to the second-slowest, and then the third-slowest, and working on his breathing, and fine-tuning the efficiency of his stroke, and plugging away with everything he had until he could finally hold his own, and then he did a triathlon.

And then he did another one. And another one. And then he did one with his swimming instructor, and swam faster than her. And then he signed up for Ironman.

Ironman is insane. It's fully insane. First you swim. You swim for two and a bit miles. It's ridiculous. It's such a stupid distance to swim that, if I ever found myself on a capsizing boat two and a bit miles from shore, I guarantee that I'd just give up and drown.

After that, you climb out of the water and ride your bike for 112 miles. Which, again, just sounds annoying. I own a bike, and I don't think I've even ridden it for 112 miles in total. I rode it a bit when it was new, then I gave up because my trousers split open at the crotch when I got on the saddle, and I was wearing bright red pants, and I had to suffer the indignity of riding home while flashing my junk like it was the Eye of bloody Sauron to a succession of horrified dog-walkers.

And then, after all that – after doing more exercise than most mortals in a year, all in one go – you run a marathon. It's obscene. The two responses I had from anyone when I told them that Pete was doing an Ironman were either 'Cool!' or 'Why?' and I don't think I can really be friends with the first lot.

But still, this is a serious business, and Pete knew that it would be the hardest thing he'd ever do for fun, so he wasn't taking any chances. The day he signed up, he made a training plan, and then put the training plan on a spreadsheet, and there wasn't a day between that point and the race when he didn't know what exercise he'd be doing. He started eating healthily too, to the point when he spent the bulk of my mum's last birthday dinner laboriously telling everyone how great it is that he only drinks water in restaurants now.

But his training wasn't completely without difficulty. His bike was the first thing to buckle under the pressure of training. As his routes grew ever longer, taking him out in huge loops to the deep countryside, a chain would break or a fork would splinter or a pedal would come loose, and Pete would be left with no choice but to call my dad and beg to be picked up.

He had the bike fixed, but it broke again. And again. Though he'd never admit it, there was the slightest chance that he'd have to compete in this aggressively elite athletic event using my bike. Which I made myself, out of wood, and is so insufferably hipsterish from top to bottom that I can't rule out the possibility that it was ever once a ukulele. Pete wouldn't be seen dead on it.

This was around the time that I decided to write this book. I was writing it about Pete, and deep down I felt bad – but not too bad, clearly – about the front cover calling him a dick. So, because I am a good and true person who lives to serve his fellow man without personal agenda, I told Pete that I'd buy him a new bike with my publishing advance.

Pete resisted, and then resisted again, and then a part of his bike broke off in Hastings, and Dad had to come and pick him up, and he took the bike to a repair shop, and the repairman whistled through his teeth for a solid hour, and then Pete relented. Fine, he said. If I was absolutely sure it wasn't a problem, he'd like to accept the offer of a new bike.

So he picked out a bike on the Internet – a berserk specialised triathlon bike that looked like what you'd see if you tried looking at the reflection of a normal bike through a shattered mirror – and showed it to me. It was beautiful, he said.

'There is one condition to all this,' I warned him.

'What's that?' he asked, absent-mindedly.

'If I'm going to buy you a bike, you have to put a sticker on it that says "I love Stu".'

'Yes, sure. Whatever. Buy the bike and you can do anything you like,' he replied. But it wasn't sinking in. Pete was lost in his own little world, imagining what life would be like on this new carbon-fibre beast of his. I can't say this for certain, but I strongly suspect that his entire internal monologue at this point consisted of nothing but sirens and fighter-jet noises.

I ordered a sticker online. The bike was black so, in an effort to be tasteful, I kept the sticker black, with the words 'I love Stu' written in muted cursive. However, I did this in such a rush that I completely ignored both size and quantity, and a fortnight later I received three sheets of inch-long 'I love Stu' stickers. I counted them. There were ninety in total, each of them completely unsuitable for bike-defacing. By the way, if you ever want a tiny 'I love Stu' sticker, just ask me. I can barely move for the fucking things.

So it was back to the drawing board. This time, I was taking no chances. Size be damned. Taste be damned. When the finished article arrived, I told Pete.

'What?' he spluttered. 'You really made a sticker?'

'Yes,' I replied. 'I said I was going to make a sticker.'

'But my bike is so beautiful,' he protested. 'It's *beautiful*. Is it a big sticker?'

'It's quite big.'

'Is it a black sticker?'

'Um . . .'

It was not a black sticker. Second time around, I'd decided to really swing for the fences. This thing was huge. It was almost – but not quite – too big for the frame. And it was pink. It was hot pink, for maximum contrast, with 'I LOVE STU!' stamped on it in colossal letters. Yellow letters. Bright yellow Comic Sans letters. The whole thing looked as though Mr Blobby had prematurely ejaculated on a birthday cake. It was – and remember I've got a son – the single most beautiful thing I have ever created. Glowing with pride, I took a photo of it and sent it to Pete.

My phone pinged instantly.

Get fucked, the reply read.

The Heritage family reticence to verbally express pride in each other is well known and deeply entrenched. We are proud of each other, but for some reason we can never actually bring ourselves to say it. You could say that this reticence is a good thing, because it gave Pete such a gaping inferiority complex that he had to complete something as stupid as an Ironman to prove his worth. However, I'd argue that it's actually a bad thing, because it gave Pete such a gaping inferiority complex that he had to complete something as stupid as an Ironman to prove his worth.

But there are exceptions. When the day of the Ironman arrived, my parents and I crowded around our phones and computers, compulsively refreshing the page that updated his split times throughout the day. Then, once he was in the later stages of the marathon, we found the live stream of the finishing line and watched it on TV. We watched it for over an hour, and it quickly became quite hypnotic.

As runner after runner staggered towards the finish line, the French officials would repeat the same thing again and again. 'You are . . . AN IRONMAN!' Over and over, several times a minute, until their accents became impenetrable and the phrase dissolved into white noise. 'Yeu are . . . AN EYERONMAN!' 'Yu er . . . ANNIAMAN.' 'HYURIAMAN.' For over an hour.

Then we heard a different noise. A deep, guttural roar. 'I am . . . AN IRONMAN!' it went. Then it got louder. And louder.

Oh Christ.

The live-stream camera cut away before our suspicions could be confirmed, but subsequent finish-line photos made it abundantly clear. That was Pete, shouting that he was an Ironman at the top of his voice as he crossed the finishing line. He was shouting so loudly that he drowned out everything else. So loudly that every artery, vein and capillary in his body jutted sharply out of his skin. It was the Peteiest way imaginable to end a race like that.

Amazingly, he did the final marathon – after a two-mile swim and a 112-mile bike ride, in 32-degree heat, in August – in four hours and twenty minutes. Faster than I could run a marathon in perfect conditions, in the shape of my life, downhill. It was amazing, and we were all bursting with pride for him. So proud that, for once, we actually told him.

Everyone told him, in fact. His Facebook page was laden with expressions of pride, from everyone he's ever met, for days. When I met Craig and Mike to discuss all the gruesome stuff he got up to as Shagger – most of which I didn't even include in that chapter out of basic decency, by the way, like the time he passed a car with a 'For Sale' sign in the window, decided that the owner was pretty and then texted her until she had sex with him – the conversation quickly veered off into impressed astonishment at his achievements. 'I mean, who signs up for an Ironman if they can't even swim?' Mike kept asking, incredulously.

Obviously I was proud too, but it seemed like another sign that I was no longer the favourite son. Sure, flat-out physical exertion for twelve straight hours is an impressive achievement. But how many people told me they were proud of that sticker I made? None, that's how many, even though it's the most beautiful sticker the world has ever seen. People are such wankers.

VANS

Like me, you probably spend a lot of time thinking about the Many-Worlds interpretation of quantum mechanics. This interpretation, you'll remember, exists on the assumption that every possible outcome to every decision ever made has already happened, with each outcome inhabiting its own parallel universe.

So by this regard – to pick the most careworn example – there are several million different parallel universes in which a different one of Alois Hitler's spermatozoa ended up being implanted within the depths of Klara Hitler's ovum one evening in July 1888, and created a baby who was bright and curious and empathetic and not hell-bent on extinguishing the entire Jewish race. We just happen to live in the universe that had the worst possible outcome to that particular ejaculation, because we live in the universe that produced Adolf Hitler, and all the billions of knock-on repercussions he wreaked on the human race.

The Many-Worlds interpretation says that a different universe must exist in which every losing political candidate had their moment in the sun. There's a universe somewhere where every failed job interview went amazingly. There's a universe where New Coke was, and still is, a raging success. There's even a universe somewhere where – and I realise that this is a stretch but, if my understanding of the Many-Worlds interpretation is correct, this is a mathematical certainty – Mark Chapman shot at John Lennon and missed, and John Lennon was so spooked that he shut himself away from society and went to live in a cave, and he decided to subsist on plants and creek water, but he didn't realise that the cave was immediately downstream from a facility that processes nuclear waste, and the irradiated water altered his DNA, and he became a terrifying ultra-strong fire-breathing *kaiju*, and he went on a berserk city-trashing rampage so nightmarish that the UN was left with no choice but to genetically alter Ringo Starr in a similar manner and set him loose in Lennon's path, thereby creating a zero-sum Mega Shark Versus Giant Octopus scenario featuring two lovable yet ferociously super-powered mop-headed pop singers.

I consider myself to be an expert on the Many-Worlds interpretation. This is because I've seen the film *Sliding Doors* exactly one and a half times, and also I've read most of a Wikipedia entry on it. It definitely works the way I said. Definitely. There's no need for you to check.

However, there is one aspect of the theory in which I am resolute: I guarantee that a parallel universe exists where Pete Heritage ended up becoming a white-van man. And, in this parallel universe, Pete is the happiest chap in the entire world.

Now, I probably don't need to remind you that Pete is actually pretty great at the job he's actually got. Unlike me, he's a natural leader, and he enjoys nothing more than exerting his will on a group of people powerless to disagree with him. He's single-minded and restless and determined enough to make a success of himself however he wants. I've lost count of the times I've sat back in admiration and watched him bludgeon his way through an impossible situation with the sheer blunt-force trauma of willpower alone. In that regard, I'm pleased he's only in charge of some gift cards and not, say, the nuclear codes.

But still, deep down, the boy was born to be a van driver. Cut him and he bleeds a mixture of diesel and pulped-up copies of the *Sun*. To prove my point, let's quickly scroll through some of the things that Pete loves more than anything else:

- Driving vehicles
- Listening to TalkSport
- Shouting at motorists
- Spending so much time on his own that he involuntarily develops what he believes to be a series of bulletproof arguments about the way that the world should be run, even though they're all so deeply flawed and illogical that they universally fail to stand up to even a modicum of uninvited scrutiny
- Going 'Weeeey' at stuff

In the nineties, when I was becoming a teenager and Pete was just about to hit double digits, my dad decided to embark on a side job growing and selling potted plants. He borrowed a piece of land from his sister-in-law's brother-in-law, erected a polytunnel on it and set about growing enough pansies and petunias to sell at market each week.

I was Dad's assistant in this endeavour: his scruffy little urchin helper, earning a fiver for every twelve-hour shift I took flogging geraniums to the good patrons of Canterbury Indoor Market (which then became a Laserquest, then a supermarket, and is now a dreadful-looking student nightclub called Chill), and sometimes Pete would reluctantly tag along with us. The only way we could transport the plants to market each week was either in the boot of Dad's estate or inside a massive, unwieldy wooden homemade trailer that we left unsecured in front of our house and which ended up being routinely nicked by drunks on the way home from the pub. One day, Dad decided that we needed to increase the number of plants we took to market. And he had just the answer. A friend of his was about to sell his white van for scrap. He said that Dad could have it, if he wanted, for £30.

My dad is a fine man in many regards, smart and strong in a way that has passed me by completely. But, that said, he does have a fairly pronounced gullible streak. There was a time we still talk about, when a man in a B&Q car park offered to sell him a state-of-the-art DVD player from the boot of his car, and it wasn't until he got it home – after much gathering-round and pomp and ceremony – that he discovered he'd actually been sold a fifteen-year-old VCR with all its cables snipped off. He was also strung along by a *Reader's Digest* competition once until we ended up drowning in encyclopaedias and increasingly bewildering verbal instructions from the chairman of *Reader's Digest*, delivered on cassette tape as if they were important state secrets. Also, most gullibly of all, he paid £30 for this piece-of-shit van.

And I don't want to single this out as Dad's silliest act, but the van didn't work. It just did not work. It was covered in rust holes big enough to fit your fist through. It came with a creepy clown-face on the bonnet – two giant unblinking eye stickers and a leering, red, wonky mouth sticker – that made it look as if Pennywise from *It* had assembled a rubbish version of the A-Team on the cheap. Dad rightly felt that this face didn't quite align itself with the brand he was trying to develop, so he pulled the stickers off. But the stickers took the paint off with them and, instead of being known as 'the market traders with the funny clown van', we were subsequently referred to as 'the market traders with the nightmarish rapey-looking van that looks like it has been painted with a mural of that time when a deranged serial killer escaped from hospital, broke into a circus, locked all the clowns up in an animal cage together and set it on fire while he danced around and masturbated'.

Plus, you know, the thing *didn't work*. My family once booked a stall for a show held at the Kent County Showground in Detling; a vast expanse of land on top of a steep hill with a motorway at the bottom. It was only when we – me, Dad and Pete – were leaving the showground at the end of the day, and we were barrelling down this steep hill towards the motorway, that the engine suddenly cut out. My memory of what happened next has long been locked behind a firewall of terror, but I seem to remember it consisting of the van freewheeling at speed towards a blur of fast-moving perpendicular traffic, and Dad frantically turning the key in the ignition over and over again, and the engine finally kicking in seconds before it could leave us stranded sideways in the middle lane of the M20 – a sitting duck of rust and flesh and unsold petals – and Dad warning me never to mention any of this to my mum.

(It only seems fair to point out that I have inherited Dad's gullible streak wholesale. The first time I ever went to Berlin, for example, I noticed that the streets were lined with all these glamorous women in skimpy outfits. A guy I was with told me that they were part of a new citywide initiative to help tourists – that they were effectively hired to give directions to befuddled holidaymakers – and it didn't click that they were actually prostitutes until long after I'd phoned my mum and girlfriend to breathlessly tell them about Berlin's amazing civic-minded progressiveness. I was twenty-nine years old.)

Perhaps this explains why I'm not all that keen on vans. But Pete? Oh, you should see him down at the van-hire place. He's like a pig in poo. A van-hire centre is a spiritual homecoming for him; it's the place where he gets to pick out the chariot of his destiny. It's where he can kick wheels and whistle at prices and make the sort of impenetrably van-related small talk with the rental people that'd immediately make my testicles retreat quickly into the upper regions of my torso. This, you see, is where Pete Heritage gets to *be*.

It doesn't matter if the van doors don't close properly, or if the suspension is noisy, or if the glove compartment pops open whenever he hits a pothole. That van is Pete's throne, high up above everyone else. The more rotations the steering wheel needs to get around a corner, the better. Up there, bouncing around in the badly upholstered driving seat, swatting away the length of window sealant that might not ever have been attached properly, Pete is king of his own domain. Driving a van is a man's job, and Pete is a man.

*

The nearest I ever came to being a white-van man – which, bearing in mind that I cannot drive, is pretty bloody far from being a white-van man – was the fortnight of work experience I did at a removal firm in Folkestone when I was fourteen. Soft-handed ninny that I am, I turned up for my first day in a *suit*. A thick, ill-fitting burgundy suit from Burton that my mum had taken me out especially to buy for this occasion. I wore this, at the height of summer, to a warehouse full of removal men. In *Folkestone*. My card was marked the second I arrived. Over the course of the fortnight, at various points, I was mocked for not knowing what a crankshaft was, mocked for liking girls' music (Oasis), accused of sniffing the secretary's seat every time she left the room and forced to watch helplessly as three of my co-workers gaffer-taped my rucksack to the ceiling of the warehouse.

This was clearly just good-natured ribbing on their part, the sort of blokey initiation ceremony that'd eventually single me out as one of their own. But it very obviously wasn't for me. For two whole weeks, all I wanted to do was run back to my ivory tower, pull up the drawbridge and spend the rest of my life doing pencil drawings of moonbeams and unicorns while listening to obscure French jazz.

My work experience put me off ever wanting to use the services of a removal company. This is partly because I saw what terrible taste in pornography most long-distance removal men have – in 1994, at least, it almost exclusively consisted of thin-papered European magazines full of morose Belgian housewives with permed mullets and the sort of voluminous pubic hair that you could quite easily whip up into a dreadlock – but mainly because I saw what removal men do to your stuff when you leave them alone with it. One of my colleagues had been attempting to make a giant Union Jack for the back of his cab out of whatever red, white and blue knickers he was able to swipe from his customers. Another always headed straight for the photo albums because, creepily, he'd come to learn that most British women are too embarrassed to complain if they discover that all the naked photos they kept of themselves had suddenly gone missing. It was all just a little bit too grim for me.

Fortunately, I don't have to use removal men, because I've got Pete who jumps at the excuse to hire a van and live out his elaborate white-van man role-play fantasy.

And I always help him move too. I'm not always a great friend. I can be aloof and stand-offish, and I'll go for years on end without seeing some of the people I'm supposedly closest to. I don't text. I don't stay in touch. I don't have any traditionally male interests. I don't drive. I can't stand sport. Two-day hangovers have ruined drinking for me. I have a baby who needs to be in bed by seven, and my idea of a good time currently consists of falling asleep in front of the telly fully dressed at half past eight at night. Who'd want to be associated with a dreary old fun-sponge like that? I would not be friends with me.

But I do have one redeeming quality. If you're moving house, and you need a spare pair of hands, I'm there. If you need a fridge-freezer carried down three fights of stairs, I'm your man. If you need someone to grab the underside of a sofa while you choreograph an elaborate series of Tetris pirouettes in order to get it over a banister, through a door and into a van, I'm here for you. My spacial awareness is dismal, my ability to organise barely there at all, but a day of unthinking gruntwork is the least I can do for you. There's a camaraderie that comes when you help a friend move house. A fraternal bond that acknowledges the strength of your relationship without ever making it explicit. To help someone move house is to prove yourself trustworthy, and there's no greater compliment than that. If you ever want to test the integrity of your connection with an adult male, ask them to help you move.

Despite our constantly clashing personalities, and our different interests, and our utter failure to really grasp each other's lives at all – Pete and I help each other move. Like, a lot.

Our family home is our family home, and it's always been that way. My grandparents bought it long ago, then my grandfather died there and my parents moved in. That was forty years ago, before Paul or me or Pete were born, before anything caught fire, and then they never moved out.

Since we moved out, however, we've both lived in many different places. Since the age of nineteen, I've never lived in the same place for more than two years. Before I moved back to Ashford, I bimbled around renting homes wherever the wind took me. I lived in three similarly awful student houses in Bournemouth, then moved back in with my parents, then lived in a minuscule bedsit in Korea, then moved back in with my parents, then lived in a flat that was too near a train line, another flat that was too far away from a train line, then a windowless room in a converted south London church, then finally a ninety-year-old flat on top of a hill that overlooked the South Circular and inexplicably kept filling up with ladybirds. All this time, the dream of home ownership has eluded me completely.

Pete has never rented anywhere in his life. Relentlessly business-minded hardass that he is, he has scaled the property ladder as though he's just realised it's on fire. Straight from home he managed to buy a flat in Ashford with his friend. Then he scaled up to a three-storey townhouse with the same friend – this is the house where he installed a hot tub to help facilitate his Bang Folder acquisitions, even though his garden was exactly the size of a hot tub – while he rented out the first flat in a quickly abandoned attempt to forge a bold buy-to-let empire. Then he sold that townhouse, bought a house with his girlfriend, sold that house, moved back into the first flat, then sold that and finally bought a beautiful new house that he's fitted out exactly as he wanted.

Pete had the foresight to make his money work for him, leapfrogging with every move to somewhere bigger and better. But what have I got to show for my approach? A succession of partially refunded security deposits and an inescapable feeling of stasis, that's what. Still, at least we both know that we can count on each other if we need to move in a hurry. This has been quite useful in the past, but I'm getting to that.

ROBYN

As weird as it was for me to leave London and move back home to Ashford, it must have been a thousand times weirder for my wife. Realistically, it was never outside the bounds of possibility for me to one day go and live closer to my family. But her? Never. This town wasn't in her orbit. It didn't show up on any of her maps. And why should it? For someone to move here, completely of their own accord, with no sort of familial pull whatsoever – *here*, for God's sake, with its lack of ambition, withered-on-the-vine high street and lions with castles coming out of their arses – simply defies all sense of logic.

In my twenties, during a time when life's bungee rope had snapped me back to Ashford, I spent a year working in a sunglasses shop. My manager was Scottish. And I could never fully trust her, because she'd come all the way here from Glasgow, entirely by choice. *Here*.

'Why here?' I'd ask her.

'Why not?' she'd reply.

'No, but I mean why here? There are so many other places you could have gone.'

'I know. I just felt like it.'

'But it can't be because it's pretty, because it isn't pretty.'

'No.'

'And it can't be because it's cheap, because there are plenty of cheaper places to live.'

'No.'

'Do you know someone who lives around here?'

'No.'

'Did you think you were actually moving to Canterbury?'

'I know the difference between Canterbury and Ashford, Stuart.'

'But I mean, you've seen the place, right?'

'Oh, aye. We visited before we moved down.'

'Please just be straight with me. All I want to do is help you.'

On and on this went, every single day, during the gaps between customers. And, remember, this was in a designer sunglasses shop in Ashford. The gaps between customers were huge. One day a man came in at 11 a.m., bought a replacement cleaning cloth for his reading glasses, and that was it. That was the only thing we sold the entire day. The shop isn't there any more.

So, strapped of anything better to do, I kept interrogating my boss on this insane decision of hers, and she kept giving vague 'When you know, you know' non-answers, and by the end of it I'd convinced myself that I should tread carefully around her because she was clearly a Mafia snitch who'd been forcibly relocated under a government witness-protection scheme.

Moving back home from London felt to me like stepping out of a time machine. We're talking about a rubbishy time machine admittedly; one that's been wired up wrong, so you leave it to find that your surroundings are exactly the same but you've suddenly become old and tired and bald and fat.

None of the streets and shops and people have changed, but I have to keep reminding myself that I'm no longer a shy, gangly, awkward schoolkid. For instance, when I'm walking past a crowd of teenagers at a bus stop, I still briefly worry that they'll start jeering at me. It takes a conscious effort to remember that they probably won't, because now I'm twice the size of them, and I also perfectly fit the description of every single creepy, suspicious-looking, gone-to-seed stranger they've been taught never to engage with.

But for Robyn, coming here must have been like landing on a different planet. Our upbringings couldn't have been more different – she's posh enough to have attended the same private school as various minor royals, I went to a local comprehensive that was once named the sixty-third worst in the country; I'd never been to Fortnum & Mason's, she'd never been to Greggs – so there is no universe in which Ashford could have ever fitted into her long-term life plan.

When we moved to Ashford – even though moving here was partly her idea – she didn't know the place at all. She didn't know where anything was. She didn't know how anything operated. She'd lived in London for a decade at this stage, so she was thrown by the fact that all the shops closed at five thirty on the nose. The lack of Oyster cards meant that she had to physically pass a handful of coins to a man before she could ride on a bus, the way people used to in the Middle Ages. And Uber still hasn't got here, so you still actually have to use your phone as a phone and verbally ask another human being if they'd be so inclined to drive a car to your house before you can go anywhere. There was bound to be a bit of an adjustment period.

But, in a way, this was a good thing. Robyn got to see the town with fresh eyes, while all I ever saw were the scars and welts of my own crazy historical prejudices, so in truth she was actually much more open to living here than me. This, in a nutshell, was our entire house-hunting process:

'This place looks nice.'

'It isn't nice. It's on the wrong side of the railway line.'

'What about this place?'

'Ugh, that's across a bridge.'

'This place has got a massive garden.'

'But that's where all the scummy kids from school lived.'

'How about this house? It's on a river, and it comes with its own boat.'

'Yeah, but that's really close to where my ex-girlfriend's mum lives.'

'Jesus, fine. Here? It costs 10p a month and the landlord buys you chocolate every day.'

'They found the body of a little girl thirty feet from the front gate in 1984. Look, open Google Maps, I can show you exactly where she was murdered.'

'No, don't do that. What about this place? It has twelve bedrooms and a golden bathtub that's hooked up to an unlimited stream of free champagne.'

'Nah, a guy used to keep ferrets two doors down from there. I think he went to prison once. We probably shouldn't.'

The directionless spiral of negotiation lasted for ever, until we managed to whittle down our options to a house that somehow fitted all my berserk geographical criteria. We moved in, and Robyn didn't leave the house for two and a half months. First she was so completely pregnant – struck down with swollen ankles and cracked ribs and gestational diabetes – that she couldn't venture out very far. Then, once she had the baby, her emergency Caesarean meant that she couldn't really move at all for about another month. And then the raw physical gruel of looking after a newborn meant that we both spent a few more weeks either holding the baby or passed out in a puddle of vomit and drool. All in all – for the longest amount of time – my wife didn't know a thing about the town she lived in.

Actually, that's an exaggeration. Robyn knew my family. She knew Pete.

Robyn was terrified the first time she ever met Pete. It was relatively early on, long before we'd planned to get married or have kids. Foolishly, I decided that the best location for this meeting should be in Pete's domain. The King of Ashford's glittering palace. His shop.

In retrospect, this was foolish. Work Pete and Home Pete are very different creatures. Home Pete is grumpy and mouthy and prone to making the sort of ridiculous pronouncements about the world that you'd only really expect to hear from a child. Home Pete watches *Sky Sports News* with his hands down his pants. Home Pete burps and farts and texts people photos of human faeces for fun. He's a dick. But at least he's a human dick.

Work Pete is a cyborg. When Pete turns up at work, his mouth physically shrinks by about 60 per cent, until it's just a stern dot hanging from the end of his nose. All Pete ever sees at work is a flickering green-on-black display of ones and zeros. Occasionally his vision will zoom in on a shoplifter or a shirker or a vagrant, and a robotic voice will repeat the phrase 'INTRUDER ALERT' again and again inside his head until he can reset it by going into a corner and blinking six times in quick succession. Work Pete is a glower in a suit. Work Pete is a nightclub bouncer. Work Pete is a Grant Mitchell waxwork that people put next to windows when they go on holiday to scare off burglars.

The first time she met him, Robyn met Work Pete.

I assume that Pete had been standing in front of a vast bank of CCTV feeds in a darkened room, steepling his fingers and murmuring the word 'soon' to himself, because he found us the moment we entered the shop. Introductions were made – which in Robyn's case meant saying 'Hello' and in Pete's case meant saying 'She seems like a good fit, because you're weird too' – and we went up to the store's café to chat.

I say 'chat'. It was more an impressively long monologue about how the café had received the highest possible food hygiene rating on three successive visits, which is more than you could say about any of the shithole restaurants near where we lived, which proves that his shop is the best and Pete is great and London is a stupid place full of filth-covered trash-eaters.

By Pete's standards, it was a perfectly civil encounter. Robyn, meanwhile, barely said a word. She just squeaked three times – her voice occupying the exact midpoint between agreement and terror – and otherwise sat in total silence. It wasn't exactly a roaring success, but on the other hand Pete didn't try and stab anyone in the foot.

*

The second time Robyn met Pete, she met Home Pete. This was a different encounter entirely. Especially since, due to more bad planning on my part, Pete was driving a white van at the time. She was getting to meet UltraPete. She was meeting the Pete who suffixes every sentence with the phrase 'you cunt'. She was meeting the Pete who you never shake hands with, because his hand will still be warm from gently cupping his testicles in front of *Sky Sports News*. She'd already met Dr Jekyll and now, sadly, it was time for her to confront Mr Hyde.

Pete was driving a white van because he was helping us move in together. We were moving in early – just a few months after we'd got together, in fact – because she was being turfed out of her friend's flat and I was fed up with paying over the odds to sleep and work in the windowless basement room of an acoustically unsound church conversion on top of a hill with three total strangers, and it just sort of made sense to take the plunge.

This lightning courtship was out of character for both of us, and I was anxious that Pete would unfairly judge us for it. However, it did mean that he got to drive a white van for the day, so that overrode any apprehension on his part. In fact, I'm pretty sure that I could have been moving in with a convicted and unrepentant child molester who vomited blood and then licked it back up every fifteen minutes and Pete would have been cool with it, so long as it meant he got to drive a van.

The good news was that the move was swift and clean. Neither of us had our own place at that point so there wasn't much furniture, and we weren't moving far. Two quick trips around the corner in Pete's hired van and we were done.

The bad news was that Pete saw the Hat.

I should probably explain the Hat.

About a decade ago, my parents went on holiday to Croatia. I think they enjoyed it. There's a chance that my mum was bitten by a mosquito during the trip, and her arm had swollen up as though she'd been intravenously fed a beach ball, but I'm only assuming that because this happens to Mum almost every single time she ever leaves the country.

All I can say for sure about their holiday is that they came back with a hat for me. The hat was a white baseball cap covered in obnoxious silver dollar signs. Apparently Dad saw it in a shop one day and, even though I've never expressed even a fraction of an interest in this sort of headgear, he bought it for me.

Again, this is what Dad does. There was no explanation. Just a hat and an enigmatic smile. This is what Dad does. He sends me videos of dogs licking the inside of babies' mouths, and he gives me inappropriate hats for reasons I'll never hope to fully understand.

Did he think it would suit me? Did he know that it wouldn't? Did the hat obliquely refer to a forgotten conversation we'd had in the past, to which he'd assigned all manner of cryptic meaning? As a baby, were the first words I ever spoke 'disgusting hat'? Was this part of a private joke about me that he had with my mum? Is that the sort of people they are? The sort of people who make pejorative little cracks about their own son, and his thinning hair, and how he'd still look better than he currently does if he covered up his bald patch with the sort of hideous white baseball cap that fifth-rate rappers wear on the cover of their unreleased debut albums? Is that what they were doing? Because that doesn't actually seem like a very nice thing to do. You know what? Fuck those two.

Anyway, Dad bought me this hat on holiday. Do you know what he bought Pete? Nothing. He bought Pete nothing.

What the hell was he thinking? That's the very first rule of Pete. That's the all-caps warning at the top of his installation guide. That's the first thing he says when you boot him up. You never give anyone more than you give Pete. Could Dad not remember Pete's entire childhood, spent howling and kicking because other people had more than him? Did he not remember Mum in the kitchen, individually counting out the chips onto our plates so that Pete didn't stamp and yell and carve 'PETE CHIP SHIT' into the dining table with his fork? Like an abuse victim, had he deliberately deleted those trauma-inducing memories from his brain? What the hell was he thinking? The man was brazenly tap-dancing through a minefield.

Luckily, Pete is an adult now. He has an important job and numerous responsibilities. He's old enough to realise that adult offspring don't automatically deserve presents whenever their parents go away, and his life is too busy to throw a tantrum just because someone inadvertently failed to buy him a tacky piece of tourist tat. For all his faults, Pete is better than that.

When Pete saw the Hat poking out of a box, my heart still skipped a couple of beats. However silly and inconsequential, the hat was a reminder that I was still the favourite son, and I was worried that this would be enough to push him over the edge. In the end, though, my panic was for nothing. Pete grabbed the box and, without so much as blinking an eye, loaded it into the van. This was progress.

My relief was palpable, especially since I was about to leave Robyn alone in Pete's company for the very first time. There were some breakable items that I wanted to carry around the corner to our new place by hand, so Pete and Robyn got in the van and drove the rest of our stuff there together. This, I figured, would allow them to have a proper conversation without me. Because that's what really forms a friendship, isn't it? If you can have a normal conversation without the presence of a mutual acquaintance, you're good for life. And, deep down, I knew they'd be OK. They seemed to get on for most of the day, and the fact that the Hat thing had passed without incident proved that Pete was on his best behaviour. Really, I had nothing to worry about.

'Interesting about that hat, isn't it?'

That, according to Robyn, was Pete's opening gambit. As soon as the van door closed behind him, and I was far enough out of earshot, that is how my brother chose to frame what was hopefully going to be a lifelong friendship. Not 'Tell me about your family.' Not 'Nice day for it.' Not even 'Look how brilliant I am at driving vans.' No.

'Interesting about that hat, isn't it?'

According to Robyn, this sudden conversational lurch into millinery threw her off guard a little, and her lack of prepared responses left her defenceless in the face of Pete's next onslaught.

'Did he ever tell you how he got that hat? Dad gave it to him. Do you know what he gave me?'

And that was that. Over the course of their journey – just a three-minute journey, covering about a tenth of a mile of the South Circular and a little hill around the corner – Pete had info-dumped every single molecule of insecurity and resentment he ever had about the Hat and all it represented right into her face. Years after my parents gave it to me, years after I'd forgotten about it, he still had a chip on his shoulder.

I arrived at the new place at about the same time they did and, although Pete carried on as if nothing had happened, Robyn kept flashing concerned looks my way. Later, once Pete had gone home, she recounted their conversation and asked if he was always like that. I told her the Knife Story and everything fell into place. *Now* she knew Pete.

Robyn didn't have such a great time of it after Herbie was born. For various reasons her family isn't around, and when she came home from hospital she suddenly found herself stuck in this weird and unfamiliar town with a huge new swarm of relatives that she didn't have six months earlier. Bouts of postnatal depression left her feeling overwhelmed and outnumbered and, at times, quite alone.

I mentioned this to Pete one day. I did it tentatively because it was about feelings and vulnerability, and usually any sort of tender expression tends to bring out the worst in Pete – seriously, I went on holiday once, and he spent five minutes dismissively shouting 'OOH, ARTY' at my photos in the most witheringly aggressive way I've ever heard – so when I told him that she missed her family sometimes, I wasn't surprised when he reacted with a scoff.

'What does she need her family for?' he yelled. 'She's a Heritage now.'

This is the highest compliment my brother is capable of giving.

A MUTINY BREWS

I told Pete and Robyn that I was writing a chapter about them. They reacted with suspicion, pointing towards their shared assumption – their false assumption, I should add – that I derive cruel enjoyment from pitting people against each other. To prove this wasn't the case, I invited them both to read the chapter over lunch and see how above board this all was.

It backfired. What follows is a text conversation between Pete and Robyn, carried out in the immediate aftermath of my suggestion.

Why's your idiot husband wanting
to get both our reactions to something
he wrote about us both?!

You sound angry, Pete.

I'm angry! He's trying to make
us his puppets. Fuck him.
FUCCC-CCKKKK
HHHHHIIIIIIMMMMM!!!!!?

The last question mark was an angry typo.

You realise this is probably going in the book.

STU IS A CUNT.
Tell him to put that in the book.

A CONVERSATION WITH PETE AND ROBYN ABOUT THEIR CHAPTER

Me: Do you feel silly about sending those texts, having read the chapter?

Pete: No! The problem with you, Stu, is that you wind people up. Someone will say something, and you'll make a little note, and then five years later it's in a book. Like the baked-potato thing. The baked-potato thing is the classic example of what you might have done today.

Me: Listen, I've already told the baked-potato story.

Pete: Like, someone tells you something, then you pass it on without context. When you told me to come here, it just made me think, 'Ooh, did I say something about Robyn four years ago that could be twisted around?'

Me: That's just your guilty conscience.

Robyn: No, no, you do wind people up. You have a tone of voice when you're doing it. You start telling people that they're projecting. You say things to your mum like, 'Oh, Pete said blah blah.'

Pete: YEP.

Robyn: 'Mum, Pete said he hated you.'

Pete: IT'S TRUE.

Robyn: 'Pete said you had a go at him the other day. I wonder why.'

Pete: YEAH.

Robyn: There's just this fake innocence.

Pete: 'I've seen Mum every day for the last two weeks, and she says you haven't even spoken to her. Why do you hate her so much?'

Robyn: And the next time I talk to your mum, she'll say, 'Oh, Pete said blah blah blah,' and then they'll have a fight and Stu sits there like, 'My plan has worked.'

Pete: Yeah! You're the enemy!

Robyn: I see you do it, and Pete always gets the brunt of it. I see you, Stu. I ask if you're stirring, and you always say, 'I don't know what you're talking about.'

Me: Listen, can we discuss the hat instead?

Pete: I don't remember this hat conversation. It's such an awful hat. Are you sure the hat conversation wasn't just 'Look at that hat, it's such a fucking disgusting hat'?

Robyn: No, you said, 'The thing about it is, he's always been the favourite son.' We had a conversation about what the hat represented. It was a 'He's always been the favourite son' chat.

Pete: He has.

Robyn: And I thought it was funny, because you were the one helping us move, and Stu was having to carry a TV up a hill on foot because he can't drive.

Pete: Yeah, I know. I'm the better son, but not the favourite son.

Robyn: I didn't know what to say. I didn't know you very well, and you kept shouting, 'ISN'T HE THE FAVOURITE SON? ISN'T HE?' Don't you remember that at all?

Pete: Was I really different the first two times we met?

Robyn: Yeah, the first time in the shop, I was slightly terrified of you.

Pete: I remember. I remember thinking how nervous you were. You were trying too hard.

Robyn: Was I?

Pete: Yeah, you were trying really hard to be funny, and it was funny how hard you were trying to be funny. I can't remember what it was, but you said something so stupid that you just went 'Oh God' afterwards. But it was endearing. It was nice.

Robyn: Yeah, but your reaction to that was just to stare through me without any reaction, as though I was a shoplifter.

Pete: I probably did say that about you being weird. I can see myself saying that. But I only said it because Stu and his other girlfriends never came across as overly compatible. You were really different. He's a bit odd and you're a bit odd, so it kind of works. You're both a bit sort of like, *writery*, and you know, quirky.

Robyn: QUIRKY?

Pete: Yeah, like you both try to be funny.

Robyn: You were terrifying, though. Also, just before we met, I saw a hat that I wanted to buy and Stu said to ask you for a discount, so the whole time I was like, 'When do I ask him?'

Pete: Did I get you a discount?

Robyn: I think so.

Pete: I must have been trying to make an effort, because normally I just tell people to fuck off when they ask for a discount.

Me: Did you like Pete when you met him?

Robyn: I did. Apart from being terrified of him.

Pete: Which Pete did you prefer, Work Pete or Home Pete?

Robyn: Home Pete, only because I tuned out when we were talking at work, because you wouldn't shut up about the café.

Pete: Is this during the phase where I had the app, and I kept looking up the hygiene scores of all the other cafés?

I'm going to interject here, just to point out that another one of Pete's hobbies is brief but total absorption in iPad apps. Five years ago he downloaded an app that told you all the Food Standards Agency hygiene ratings for anywhere that sold food, and he was chronically unable to pass a restaurant or a café or a sandwich shop without looking it up and comparing it to his place of work. He's moved on to the Flightradar24 app now. I spent yesterday afternoon with him, and whenever a plane flew overhead he made everyone guess where it was coming from, where it was going, the airline and the estimated altitude. Then, once we'd guessed, he'd show us a picture of the aeroplane. Fun afternoon.

Robyn: Yeah. I remember thinking that we weren't going to get on, because you only talked about cleanliness. And on the way there, Stu was trying to describe you to me. He said, 'Pete likes football, Pete's really strong.'

Pete: Yeah, I was really strong.

At this point, Pete takes the Hat from me – I had it with me as a visual reminder – and puts it on. It suits him.

Me: I don't know why Dad bought me that.

Pete: It's weird, isn't it? But he does odd things with you that he doesn't do with me.

Me: Like what?

Pete: Well, he's never sent me a video of a baby being licked in the mouth.

Robyn: Well, you don't have a baby. Get a dog and he'll do it, maybe.

Pete: Honestly, Dad's contact with me is like . . . I think you're the first port of call. Let me look at the last message he sent me on Facebook. When was the last time he messaged you?

Me: Last week. He sent me a video of an ice-cream factory. No explanation.

Robyn: You know the thing that intimidated me most when we met? You were wearing a suit, and you were walking really slowly towards us. Really slowly and really confidently, like somebody who owns a casino.

Pete: Right, here we go. The last time I had a conversation with Dad on Facebook was when I was in Australia. January 2014. And that's the only thing I've ever had with him.

Me: You should send him something now.

Pete: When I helped you move, I remember thinking that you lived in the ghetto. There was a car on bricks outside your new place.

Robyn: I am very ghetto.

Pete: I hate London. People who live in London are stupid.

Robyn: Why are they stupid?

Pete: Because what's the point? Why would you want to live in London?

Robyn: How often did you two hang out before we moved back here?

Me: Hardly ever. Birthdays, Christmas, Easter.

Pete: It was always difficult. But I'm glad you're back, especially now you've got Herbie. I'd barely get to see him. London's shit. The thing about London as well, right, is that the area you lived in before wasn't very nice.

Me: It was all right.

Pete: It stank of piss! For the money you paid, how long did it take you to get to central London?

Me: About twenty minutes.

Pete: So it only takes an extra twenty minutes from here, and you've got a whole house, and when you walk outside it doesn't stink of piss. I know it's a matter of opinion, but from a quality-of-life point of view, I don't see what you get there that's so good.

We lived in Forest Hill, by the way, which didn't smell of piss. It smelled of cat food, which is an important distinction to make.

Robyn: You're in amongst everything. If you want to go to a museum, you can just go to a museum.

Pete: But you can just go now. It only takes twenty minutes longer. I'd get it if I was a multimillionaire and lived in a really nice part of London, but not a manky flat in Forest Hill. If you've got the choice of living down here in a nice house, or renting a flat in London for four hundred pounds a month more, you'd pick here.

Robyn: I like the proximity of London. You're able to get to more stuff.

Pete: What stuff do you need?

Robyn: I don't know. Like . . . all the . . . trend stuff? Fashionable food. Like . . . *cubanos.*

Pete: Who?

Robyn: A *cubano*, a special Cuban sandwich.

Pete: Right.

Robyn: I can't think of anything else.

Pete: You can fucking get sandwiches here.

Me: What about the end of the chapter?

Robyn: I thought it was very nice.

Pete: It's true though.

Robyn: Well, thank you. Considering how terrified I was when I met you, and how little I thought we had in common, I'm surprised at how much you feel like family now.

Pete: Well, you are family. You're my sister.

Robyn: Pete's one of my favourite people.

Pete: Aww. And you're the enemy, Stu.

DIARRHOEA AND EMILY

Despite our differences, I reluctantly have to admit that Pete and I are alike in two key ways:

1) We've both called off our own weddings, and

2) We've both (literally) shat ourselves as adults.

I propose we deal with the least embarrassing one of these first.

I shat myself as an adult during a work visit to Nepal in 2010. Ostensibly I was there to explore the country's sexual and reproductive health facilities, in a minivan filled with Scandinavian and Canadian journalists. The trip was extraordinary – inspiring and heartbreaking and dangerous in equal measure – apart from the one morning when my digestive system decided that it wasn't having any of this foreign muck. Which was inopportune, to say the least.

Here's how it went. The charity that organised the trip was taking us to a number of homes around the Kathmandu Valley. Each home contained a new family that had just welcomed a baby under different circumstances. We met a family who gave birth in a hospital, a family who gave birth at home with the aid of a visiting medic, and a family who somehow stuck the whole thing out by themselves. Our presence was a big deal to these families; especially the one who gave birth in hospital, a relatively middle-class brood who'd invited their parents and grandparents along to take part in the big day. As we arrived, we found them all sitting outside their house in rows, as though they were waiting for a school photo to be taken.

This is the moment my stomach rebelled.

As soon as the grandfather, a stiff-backed patriarch, began to welcome us to their home with a formally delivered speech, I was gripped by the sudden urge to expel something foul from my body. I whispered to the organisers that I needed the toilet and, after some urgent negotiation, was directed behind their home, to a three-walled outhouse with a corrugated-iron roof and a hole in the ground.

With seconds to spare, I dropped my trousers and pants, crouched and let nature blast out of my intestines at a trillion miles an hour. It smelled terrible, and I was sweating and moaning and shaking with relief, but at least it was out. I tidied myself up, matted myself down with a napkin stolen at breakfast, and gingerly tiptoed back to see the family.

As soon as I stopped walking, and every member of the family had looked over serenely to acknowledge my return, another wave of mind-blowing diarrhoea hit. This was much more urgent than before, and I turned on my heels and sprinted back to the outhouse, where I spent what felt like fifteen minutes trumping and parping and gasping at my own body's ability to produce such an endless jet of boiling grot. Somewhere in Nepal, there is a family whose memories of their child's first days – the most precious memories they will ever make – will for ever be intertwined with the distant agonised moans and flappy buttock noises of a British journalist who'd been a bit too cavalier with his dinner choices the previous night.

Then I threw up.

Obviously this presented a new problem. When there's only one hole in the room, and you're busy filling it with poo, where should you vomit? I decided that, not to ruin the outhouse any more than I already had, I should try and somehow direct both streams into the toilet at once. This necessitated a frantic dance of panic-stricken twirling and contracting, as I vomited in the hole, then spun around

Stuart Heritage, Best Supporting Brother, 1984.

We kept him in a box, 1984.

Pete's eczema in full effect, 1986-ish.

Snow day, 1987.

On the rocks already, 1987.

Stolen from Pete's Facebook. Sorry Pete.

Pete becomes violently aroused by fire, 2010-ish.

The infamous 'Bali body'shot, 2014.
Sent to me by Pete, alongside the message
'I know it's hard, but try not to wank over this'.

Completing his Iron Man, 2016.

The one useable Shagger-era photo Mike sent me.
(Photo by Mike Hill)

A day out at a theme park. Seoul, 2004.

Pete the best man, teaching me how ties work, 2014.

Herbie meets Uncle Pete, 2015.
One second after this was taken, Pete shouted 'THE HERITAGE BOYS!'

We pretty much keep everyone in a box. France, 2016.

Herbie checks out the bike I bought for Pete, 2016.

A photo I took of Pete when he wasn't looking. The end of the wine tasting adventure, 2016.

The aftermath of the 2013 Nuts Challenge, and the photo that most accurately demonstrates our varying approaches to life.

The world's most hopeless remake of *The Krays*. Bowling alley, 2014. (Photo by Emily Holland)

to continue shitting, then spun around to vomit. Puke, spin, shit, spin, puke. I looked like a cross between a dog getting ready to sit down and an especially disappointing indoor firework, but I did it. Somehow, miraculously, I contained everything.

Now dizzy, dehydrated, mortally embarrassed and sweating copiously, I returned once again to the family, whose serenity was starting to be replaced by a mood somewhere between concern and horror. But at least I was back in the fold. Through the charity's translator, I heard the mother say how proud she was of the staff at the hospi—

But enough about that, because here came Wave Three, gripping me by the throat and arsehole with a ferocity I couldn't have predicted. This time, etiquette be damned. This was an emergency. I ditched the party and pelted at full speed towards the outhouse, where I slipped on a piece of wet grass, careered forwards, smacked my head on the edge of the corrugated-iron roof with a deafening crack, then watched in dismay as it slid off its walls and onto the ground.

So now I'm crapping and vomiting almost simultaneously in the ruined outhouse of the world's politest family, with blood gushing out of my head, four and a half thousand miles from home, sobbing and murmuring for help. Eventually a kindly organiser – basically an angel in human form – pulled me together and cleaned me up and filled me with emergency tablets, mumbling that this exact thing always happens to someone on every trip. Gesturing apologetically, I got back in the minivan and left the family to continue the tour without incident.

Now, you may have spotted that I didn't actually shit myself at any point in that anecdote. That would happen later in the afternoon when, during a discussion with a female journalist, I felt the smallest of farts brewing in my guts. Desperately trying to appear laid-back, I decided to just casually squeak it out in silence. So I did.

Except it wasn't a fart. It was a gallon of leftover diarrhoea that had been percolating in my colon since earlier that morning.

I realised my mistake in a brief window of time that began when a single atom of watery poo left my body, and ended once I'd got it together enough to pull everything shut again. It was a tiny window, maybe the smallest window you have ever seen, but still large enough to allow a boiling mugful of shit to fall out of my bottom. Eyes bulging with horror, I brought the conversation to a close, waddled to the nearest toilet and embarked on a clean-up operation on a scale not seen since *Deepwater Horizon.*

So that's how I shat myself. It was a shameful moment of my life. So shameful, in fact, that you are literally the third person I've ever told about it.

Pete's story is different. An entire carful of people knew that Pete had shat himself, before he'd even got around to wiping.

A couple of years ago, I was on my way to another obstacle race that Pete had forced me into. Since I lived in London at the time, I travelled to the race with my trainer and another client of his that I had never met. Pete travelled up alone. Along the way, Pete apparently realised that he needed the toilet. But he miscalculated the gap between service stations and, unable to hold it in until he found a toilet, let himself go in a Road Chef car park somewhere near Andover. How do I know this? Because he rang me to tell me.

'I'VE JUST SHAT MYSELF!' he yelled into the phone as a greeting, long before I had a chance to tell him that he was on speakerphone. Not that it mattered, in retrospect, because he didn't seem to care that I was in a car with a couple of strangers who now knew the operating capacity of his bowels in intricate details. It was just PRP, he told me. Pre Race Poos. Everyone gets those, don't they?

Pete doesn't introduce himself to everyone by telling them that he's shat himself, but he should. It sets the tone far more effectively than 'Hello'.

*

I remember Pete shitting himself much more vividly than I remember my own tragic bout of trouser-tainting. This is all down to when it happened. Pete shat himself the day before he picked Emily up from the airport.

Before I met my wife, I was due to get married to somebody else. Venues had been booked, save- the-date cards had been sent, outfits had been bought. We'd even chosen what we were going to feed our guests. Everything was progressing nicely, except for the giant knot of doubt that was forming in the pit of my stomach.

As I grow older, I'm coming to realise that I do not cope well with stress. I tend to let things pile up inside me, certain that they'll dissipate of their own accord. But then they don't, and they blow up, and they always take someone out. Always. This is precisely the case with my engagement. Nothing was happening quite as smoothly as I wanted it to and, gradually, each tiny niggle began to coalesce into a deep well of dissatisfaction that I locked away and hoped would pass. But it did not and, five months before the ceremony, I freaked out and called the whole thing off.

It was horrible, and made worse by the knowledge that I was the cause of everyone's unhappiness. My self-loathing, perfectly evident at the best of times, went into overdrive. I'd hurt all sorts of people, and I hated knowing that people knew how badly I'd just depth-charged my own entire future. I still hate that I'm the sort of person capable of doing something so awful. But at least I could claw together a tiny scrap of consolation out of it. As bad as it was, at least I knew that I'd made such an almighty meal of things – ruining everything and turning myself into such a pariah – that nobody who witnessed it would ever be dumb enough to repeat my actions. But wait.

Eighteen months later, Pete repeated my actions. Only, Pete being Pete, he eclipsed my efforts beyond all recognition.

When I broke up with my fiancée, I slept on the sofa of our rented flat for a couple of weeks until I found somewhere else to live, and then

I moved out. But that would have been too simple for Pete. When he called off his engagement, he had to move out of a house that he owned. A house that he'd owned for a grand total of six weeks.

He'd bought the house with his fiancée in October, and by the end of December he wanted out. They'd bought kittens together, too. Two little grey things called Fergie and Busby, now doomed to grow up in a broken home. God knows what happened to those cats. They're probably on crack by now.

None of the family had any idea that this was coming. We spent Christmas Day and Boxing Day in his new house with his fiancée and then, on the 27th, Pete rang me to tell me it was over. At work, unbeknownst to us, he'd met a girl called Emily.

She was about to leave the UK to travel the world for a year. Just before she left, Pete came to the inescapable conclusion that he was actually madly in love with Emily. So he did the decent thing, told his fiancée, called off his wedding and prepared to embark on a brand-new life with the girl of his dreams.

Except, slightly counter to his plans, Emily still went travelling anyway.

This left Pete with only one option: so he moved back in with my parents. It wasn't a perfect set-up by any means – he had to cram his stuff into my tiny old bedroom, and they all had to learn how to live with each other again – but he figured it was worth it, because his main priority was to plan Operation Get Emily.

Although this all came completely out of the blue to us, Pete had apparently been keeping Craig and Mike informed of the situation on a minute-by-minute basis. Luckily, the subject of Emily came up repeatedly when we met to discuss Shagger, during the many, many occasions when they saw my horrified face and did their best to convince me that it was all a horrible phase that Pete had long put behind him. Here's how Craig described the time.

'We were at the gym, and Pete would see Emily walk past – this was before we knew her – and he'd go, "If I didn't have a girlfriend, that'd be the one I went for." And that was that, because he was engaged to be married. And then, like six weeks later, he was like, "Oh, mate."'

Mike jumped in. 'In the end he came up to us and said, "Look, I've really messed up. I've fallen in love, I've fallen in love," and he was all puppydog.'

Craig started talking over Mike, eager to hoover up the best details for himself. 'And then a week later he was like, "I'm going to Australia. I'm going to see her." We were all like, "Pete, are you mad?" I think he enjoyed the whole soap-opera drama of it. When you look back at it, as a story . . .'

'I've told so many people at work about it, ' Mike said. 'About how he chased this girl around the world twice to win her over.'

'He went to the gym twice a day, six days a week for six weeks to get in shape for her,' said Craig. 'He was really trying to impress her.'

By anyone's standards, Operation Get Emily was a stupid idea. Pete was broke from buying a house and then leaving a house in quick succession, but he needed to convince Emily that he was her future. So he sank most of his savings into a return ticket to Australia. He'd fly out there, he thought, pitch himself to her as best he could, and then they'd fly back together to start their new life. It was an insane gesture, and it failed. Pete returned alone, sad and lovesick and poor.

But this is Pete we're talking about. Pete doesn't give up. Within weeks, he'd scared up enough cash to buy a return ticket to Bali, where Emily was planning to visit on the next leg of her trip. This time he could take no chances. He spent hours at the gym, perfecting what came to be known as his Bali Body, just to impress her. He booked hotel rooms and meals, and every single sickening extra – champagne, candles, mounds of petals that spelled out 'I Love You' across their bed – that he could afford. This would be complete shock and awe. He'd either win Emily over, or die trying.

Reader, he won Emily over.

It's a grand, madcap story that – once you remove all the hurt and anguish and confusion caused by the break-up of his first relationship – comes across like an act of pure undiluted romance. Pete junked his life, his home, his money, and those two cats he'd named after his childhood heroes, all to chase a woman he barely knew around the world. It was berserk and impulsive, a Richard Curtis rom-com of a decision, and one that could only possibly be made within the confines of a belief system where love really and truly does conquer all.

But, again, this is Pete we're talking about. His abundance of sudden romance didn't quite stretch itself to a grand airport greeting. When Emily returned to the UK a few weeks later, following the sort of gruelling flight that sucks all the moisture from your body and leaves you feeling like a raisin-eyed corpse, Pete – who, let's not forget, shat himself in a car park about twenty-four hours earlier – went to meet her at the airport. It should have been the glorious climax to a story about all-consuming love. He could have met her with flowers. He could have met her with teddies. He could have met her with the keys to their new home. But no. Because this is Pete we're talking about.

He met her with a rented white van.

Pete never misses a trick. The airport was near an Ikea, and he wanted a couple of wardrobes, and to him it just seemed practical to combine both trips. After a solid day of being cooped up in a cramped plane seat, after a tumultuous period of time when she couldn't even be fully sure that abandoning her travel plans to be with a relative stranger was the right thing to do, after not even telling her own family that she was cutting her trip short and coming home, Pete greeted her by taking her to Ikea. Get in the van. If you're good I'll buy you some meatballs.

I ran away from my wedding thanks purely to doubt, while Pete ran away from his thanks purely to certainty. Mine was quiet and mundane and domestic, his was a full-blown James Bond film. Mine was a tumble into sadness, his a leap of hope.

Our stories are different, but in the most important ways just the same. We both hurt people doing what we did. We both ended up pissing off my mum for a while, to the extent that she started to think she'd brought us up badly. Mostly, though, we both have a lot of good things to show for our decisions. I'd go on to fall in love with a friend, and then marry her, and end up with the world's greatest baby. And Pete has Emily. They're a good fit. I realised this the first time I met her.

I once watched a Ross Kemp documentary about a South American crime gang. Kemp wanted to breach the inner sanctum of the gang and speak to one of its leaders, which entailed a long and humiliating series of initiation tests. First he was handed a cigarette to smoke. Then he was given a hallucinogenic drug to take. Finally, four armed men in ski masks charged in and held him up, screaming incoherently at him while they jabbed machine guns in his face. If Kemp had looked scared, even for a second, the gang leader would have dismissed him out of hand. But he showed bravery in the face of adversity, which meant that he'd proved himself beyond all doubt to be a man, and this created a bond of trust.

I always thought this sort of thing was a put-on, a crappy old relic from much worse times where stoicism in the face of humiliation and unpleasantness was the truest mettle of a man. When ability and sensitivity were secondary to your willingness to be dicked around by an arsehole with a Napoleon complex.

But when I saw how Pete treats new girlfriends, I realised that I was wrong. The initiations he puts these poor women through are harrowing. Before one previous girlfriend met the family for the first time, Pete spent weeks convincing her that Mum (who maybe has one glass of wine at Christmas, tops) was an alcoholic who got uncontrollably violent if a stranger ever made eye contact with her. The truth only came out because Pete couldn't stop hooting with laughter whenever Mum asked a question and this poor girl immediately threw her head down and started addressing all her replies to the carpet. That was her initiation. If she could put up with Pete being this much of a sniggering cock over dinner, then it meant she'd probably be OK with him being a sniggering cock again and again for the rest of their relationship.

Emily's initiation was less elaborate, but no less annoying. The first time I met her, a few months after I'd proposed to Robyn, Pete had come to London so that we could buy our wedding suits, and he'd brought Emily along too. Walking back to the station, Pete and this girl suddenly darted out across a busy road while I – jumpy around traffic since being run over by a car full of screaming women and children twenty years earlier, but that's another story – chose to wait for the lights to change. One I'd crossed the road with the proper amount of due care, Pete seized his chance.

'Call him a pussyhole.'

This was the initiation. A moral conundrum. Either this girl could do one of the rudest things imaginable and mock the survivor of a traffic accident for his perfectly natural reluctance to run across three lanes of moving cars; or she could do the decent thing and defy Pete, and endure a slightly increased level of grumpiness from him for a minimum of at least an hour.

'Pussyhole,' she said.

Again, this incident is memorable not necessarily because Emily called me a pussyhole – although I should point out that it is the sort of behaviour that gets you put in a notebook entitled 'PEOPLE WHO I WILL EVENTUALLY NAME BOOK CHAPTERS AFTER, ALONG WITH THE WORD "DIARRHOEA"' – but because of the day it happened. Emily called me a pussyhole on the day Robyn discovered she was pregnant.

Which is to say that it was the day Robyn phoned me to say she was pregnant. Which is to say it was the day that Robyn phoned *Pete* to say that she was pregnant.

Admittedly she tried calling me first. But I ignored her because I was in the middle of something much more important: trying to work a WHSmith self-service checkout without losing my entire fucking mind. When she called me, I was trying to get this poxy machine to read the barcode on a bottle of Sprite, and failing, and trying to contain what was threatening to become a hugely embarrassingly pissy fit.

So she called Pete, right when I was looking for the coin slot, and I couldn't find the coin slot, and the blood was whooshing about in my ears, and I found myself mentally composing a furious letter to the chairman of WHSmith, berating his decision to install self-service checkouts with such a maddeningly counterintuitive layout.

'What do you want to talk to Stu for?' I heard Pete say, just at the point of frustration where all my nasal hairs were about to ignite and burn my face down like an Indiana Jones baddie.

Pete passed the phone to me.

'What?' I growled, furious that Robyn wasn't able to correctly intuit that I was engaged in the battle of a lifetime with an uppity fucking Gameboy.

Robyn's voice was quiet and dazed.

'I'm . . . um, listen, I'm pregnant,' she stuttered.

Here's how things stood. On the one hand, my girlfriend had told me the biggest news I'd ever heard in my entire life. It wasn't a total surprise because we weren't using birth control, but I wasn't expecting to hear it because I'd recently convinced myself that I was sterile. Still, huge news. Enormous. My heart was swimming as Robyn's words sank in. I was going to be a father.

But on the other hand, I couldn't get this fucking piece of shit checkout machine, this fucking Poundland fucking RoboCop, to accept my 50p coin without spitting it back out at me like some sort of pampered fucking Little Lord Fucking Fauntleroy who'd just been served an improperly garnished lobster. Plus, I didn't want to be all 'Oh darling, you're PREGNANT!' into the phone, because it was early days and I didn't want Pete to know until we were absolutely certain, plus his girlfriend had just called me a pussyhole ten minutes earlier and fuck the fucking pair of them.

And, having weighed all of this up, having wrestled with the fact that Robyn would remember these next words for the rest of her life, here's how I responded:

'OK, that's nice. Let's talk about this more when I get home. Bye.'

Pete and Emily were coming to ours for dinner afterwards, along with Robyn's best friend, which meant that I had to remain taciturn for the entire evening. Nobody could know, because all we had to go on was the result of a supermarket pregnancy test, which seemed premature. So, save for giddy five-second bursts when we'd walk out into the kitchen and mouth, 'OH MY GOD WE'RE HAVING A BABY!' at each other, we had to contain ourselves until everyone left.

Essentially, then, our life as parents began with us concealing the truth to my best man and Robyn's head bridesmaid. Which, to be honest, is still better than how the wedding itself ended.

THE BEST MAN

The first thing I did after marrying Robyn was call her Pete. We'd exchanged rings. We'd said our vows. We'd looked each other in the eye, barely able to contain our emotion, lost together in a moment of pure connection. The registrar called us to the other side of the table, in the middle of this perfect sun-dappled bandstand on a hill that overlooked London in all its distant majesty, so that we could sign our wedding certificate in front of the people we loved most in all the world.

I motioned to my wife.

'Over here, Pete,' I said to her.

'WHAT?' my startled new wife scream-replied at the top of her voice. In many ways this moment set the tone for our entire marriage.

I blame Pete for this. Actually, I blame myself for asking Pete to be my best man.

Pete's main job as best man was to organise my stag night. Which was a difficult task for him, because I didn't actually want a stag night. I couldn't make it clear enough to him that I didn't want a stag night. I hate stag nights. I hate how ugly and boisterous and tribal and male they are. And this is at the best of times, on stag nights that haven't been organised by Pete Heritage.

If anything was ever going to underline the fundamental difference between us, with me coming out looking worse, it was a stag night. These things are right in Pete's wheelhouse, because he gets to be in charge of everything and the life of the party, but they directly play into my tendency to be awkward and angry and miserable when confronted with any form of organised fun. To illustrate this, my top three choices for a stag night, in reverse order, are:

3) Going to a fancy pub with some of my closest friends and having a nice drink.

2) Going to a mediocre pub that's close to my house with some of my closest friends and having a nice drink.

1) Me, by myself, falling asleep in front of the television fully clothed at 7.45 p.m.

And, although I haven't asked him, I'd guess that Pete's top three choices for a stag night in reverse order, are:

3) Tits.

2) Fighting.

1) Fighting and tits, in fancy dress.

So, naturally, I was concerned about what Pete had planned. For weeks I kept quiet about the prospect of a stag night, hoping that he'd forget. But Pete never forgets. So he texted me:

Oi, punk ass motherfucker! Stag do?

So I replied.

Dunno yet. Why?

Because I feel a responsibility as
best man to actually do something
before you call off the wedding again.

Maybe. Nothing big though.

He absorbed my request, then sent me this:

Massive fucking piss up in Prague!!!

Drug fuelled bender in Amsterdam.

Copious amounts of stripper.
Copious!!! (Am I spelling that ok?)

I talked him down from the trip abroad (which actually didn't take much, since we both broadly agreed that anyone who forces an expensive overseas trip on their friends as part of a stag party deserves to die in a fire) and a plan started to form.

To his credit, this is when you want Pete on your side. He organised a modular, completely opt-in, itinerary for the day. There'd be a trip to a theme park, then a pub, then something after that, then a night in a hotel. If people wanted to do the whole caboodle, they could. If they just wanted to drop in for a bit, that was OK too. No pressure, no hard feelings, no fretting about wildly overspending. It was, save for Pete's ensuing barrage of texts about strippers and my defeated lies about how strippers had been banned in all of central London, the perfectly organised stag event.

But then, three days before, Robyn and I had our first prenatal scan in hospital, and things hadn't gone well. The scan detected an abnormal thickness in our baby's neck which, when combined with a couple of other factors, suggested a high likelihood that he'd be born with a physical or cognitive disability. The worst-case scenario would be that he'd go on to develop Edwards' syndrome, a condition with a median expected lifespan of about a week.

If the scan determines a one in four hundred chance of your baby being born with a disorder like this, it's classified as a high-risk pregnancy. Our chance, we were told, was one in twenty-two. The hospital suggested an amniocentesis test to find out for sure, and that we should do it straight away. We were told that the test would involve a painful procedure in which a giant syringe would be plunged through Robyn's abdomen into her placenta. This would give us a definitive answer, but it also carried an increased chance of miscarriage.

Robyn decided to take the test, and it was just as horrible and painful and draining as we expected. Worse still, though, was the thought that this pea-sized fragment of a child – who we hadn't even met or named, but already loved with every last atom we had – might be in serious trouble. That week, while we were waiting to get the test results back, was brutal, full of unease and uncertainty and all-out crying. The only thing either of us wanted to do for that entire week was crawl under a duvet and stay there for ever.

This was the week of my stag night.

Something I've learned over the last few years is that, whenever I've just been given some bad news, my ability to understand train timetables vanishes completely. Completely. As soon as things start going wrong, I end up getting on the wrong train, on the wrong platform, at the wrong time, going in entirely the wrong direction. This happened three times that week; twice of them on the way to Thorpe Park.

This is why I was late for my own stag. And this is why I was too defeated to struggle when Pete handed me my fancy-dress outfit for the day.

I hate fancy dress. Fancy dress is the enemy of fun. If you ever wear fancy dress, you're telling the world two things about yourself. First, you're telling them that this was all planned far in advance, which means you're currently experiencing organised fun. And, even though organised fun is the worst sort of fun, it's the only sort of fun you're capable of experiencing due to your bizarre adversity to spontaneity.

And, second, you're telling them that your personality is so wan and poorly defined that you have to spend your days dressed up like a wacky dimwit to somehow compensate for your superpowered and lifelong dreariness. Fancy dress is the apogee of bellendry, and I will fistfight anybody who chooses to dispute this.

But, on this miserable day, with my head a million miles from where it should be, I was too tired to argue. So Pete handed me some lederhosen, and by God I looked astonishing in them. Like, just flat-out amazing. I pulled them off with style and verve and, in retrospect, I truly believe that I was born to wear nothing but lederhosen for my entire life. Inexplicably – maybe it was vanity, maybe it was seeing all my friends, maybe it was the pleasant sensation of having my genitals cupped by £6.99's worth of pleather – my mood began to lift.

Pete is unexpectedly great at this. His sheer bloody-mindedness is such that he can create an atmosphere out of nothing but thin air. It's a happy flip side to his unwillingness to lose at Ludo as a kid. Back then, he'd scream and rumble with such force that he'd ruin everyone's day. But now he knows how to harness it a little and, if he wants you to have fun, there's a very good chance that you'll end up being forced into having some amount of fun.

Obviously he can't sustain that for an entire day, though, because without careful concentration he can still veer off and become the ur-Pete. This is roughly what happened during the evening segment of the stag night, when he lined up sambuca after sambuca for everyone inside a claustrophobic basement bar heaving with the sort of aggressive coke-snorting London nimrods I've spent my entire life trying to avoid. Just before kicking-out time, right as events were starting to swirl into a colourless smear, Pete revealed that he'd booked the hotel he did purely because it was right next to a strip club.

'Let's all go see some TIDDIES!' he bellowed at the sky, possibly in the hope that the moon would blink into life and go, 'Cor, I love tits. You're a ledge, Pete. Proper bantz,' back at him.

Somehow managing to hail a cab exclusively by howling the word 'TIDDIES' fifteen times in a row, Pete rounded up the most enthusiastic tit-lookers of the group and shot off into the distance. The remnants – among them me, my cousin-in-law and my dad, who'd managed to get comprehensively shitfaced despite spending the entire duration of his time in the pub silently playing a real-time military strategy game on his iPad – got in the next cab and shuffled off into the hotel. I put Dad to bed, by which I mean that I watched Dad topple over sideways onto his bed, and found my own room for the night.

And, again, that was fine. The whole day was opt-in. If you didn't want to go to Thorpe Park, you didn't have to. If you didn't want to go to the pub, you didn't have to. If you didn't want to follow the universe's loudest corporeal sambuca fume into Spearmint Rhino because you didn't like the prospect of watching a young woman's soul wither up and die because an overconfident berk wouldn't stop shouting, 'TIDDIES! TIDDIES! TIDDIES!' an inch from her broken-hearted face, then that was fine too.

The point is that Pete had catered for everyone. The cousins with families who had to be back for tea. The hungover friends who pleaded with me the next morning over breakfast not to tell their wives that they'd been to a strip club. Dad, who was able to connect to the nearest Wi-Fi and continue to beat three ten-year-olds at whichever dismal freemium military game he was into at that point in time. And me. Fun-hating, miserable, distracted me. Pete had somehow brought me out of my fug, and that's really all you can ask for in a best man, isn't it?

The baby had been given the all-clear, my commitment to Robyn had already been set in stone by the baby in her belly, my trust in Pete was at an all-time high, and so, by the morning of the wedding, I was almost supernaturally calm. I was also, if I'm honest, a little bored. Pete had slept on my sofa the previous night and, by the time we'd woken up, been to the gym and eaten breakfast, there wasn't really an awful lot to do. We had an entire morning to kill, and nothing to kill it with.

So, unwilling to get dressed too early in case I got food down myself or fell into a toilet, we both spent the morning sitting around in our underwear. I had just bought a Sonos music player for my living room, and Pete had clocked this pretty quickly. He realised that, if he downloaded the app to his phone, he could repeatedly hijack my carefully curated playlist of soothing pre-wedding songs with a succession of unlistenable WWE entrance themes.

Every couple of minutes, my internal sense of peace would be shattered by some godawful sub-Limp Bizkit slab of noisy adolescent awfulness that had been expressly designed to excite rednecks.

This is how my morning was spent:

'Pete.'

'What? I didn't do anything.'

I'd resume my playlist. Then the song would end and, again, Pete would cue up another shrieking mound of shit that sounded like the internal monologue of an aggressively hormonal fourteen-year-old boy being told off by his mum.

'Pete.'

'What?'

Another nice song, followed by another bellowed *Biker Mice From Mars* theme-tune cover version, designed to mask the intrinsic visual creepiness of a middle-aged man walking fifty feet to a wrestling ring in his pants.

'Pete!'

Then another song, transcribed directly from the brain of someone in the midst of an impromptu murder-suicide.

'Pete.'

Noise. Just noise. Possibly the noise of a cat being thrown down a staircase in a metal dustbin, but played so loudly that I feared for the structural integrity of my building.

'*Pete!*'

This went on for the entire morning. 'Pete,' I'd say. 'Pete. Pete. Pete. Pete. Pete. Pete. Pete. Pete. Pete. Pete.' Over and over again, whenever he deliberately did anything out of boredom to antagonise me, which was constantly. 'Pete.'

When we left my flat, my unruffled facade began to crack. On the way to the wedding at the Horniman Museum in Forest Hill, I stopped off to make sure the flowers had been properly delivered to the bar where we were having the reception. Except it wasn't open yet, so the flowers had been chucked into bin bags and wedged into an alley. Not a big thing by any means, but enough to make my eye twitch a little.

Then we got to the museum, and I realised that I'd completely neglected to prepare for the bit where you're locked in a library by yourself with two officials, and they both grill you about the legitimacy of your wedding by asking what your wife's full name is, even though nobody ever calls your wife by her full name, and she's got six almost identical middle names, and you've only ever got it right once before, but you concentrate and dig deep and just about get away with it.

Then they ask you for your dad's occupation, and you say 'plumber' instead of 'plumbing and heating engineer', and instantly start crapping yourself because you're convinced that they're going to cancel the wedding and imprison you for fraud.

Once that ordeal was over, I finally got to put the last part of the wedding in place. The music. There was no sound system or electricity in the bandstand, which might have posed a problem to a lesser human, but I'd thought ahead and bought a battery-operated Bluetooth speaker and created a Spotify playlist on my phone containing the wedding march and everything else we wanted to hear during the ceremony. I did this because I am a genius who always thinks of everything.

Except I hadn't thought to make sure this worked in advance. Had I done so, I'd have realised that there was no mobile coverage whatsoever on top of this poxy hill, which meant that Spotify wouldn't work, which meant that there wouldn't be any music during the ceremony, and my bride-to-be was a maximum of fifteen minutes away. This would have been solved if I'd have pressed one button and made the playlist available offline. But I didn't do that, because I am an idiot who never thinks of anything.

Now completely in the grip of full-on panic, I sped through my mental Rolodex of backup plans and struck upon the only sensible solution.

Quit.

I'd just quit. There wouldn't be any music at the wedding, I decided. I'd mucked up, and it was too late to change anything, so we'd just have a silent wedding instead. Defeated, I walked over to my guests and started asking if perhaps they wouldn't mind singing a distracted, half-forgotten, unaccompanied version of 'Here Comes the Bride' when they saw Robyn coming.

Then Pete came charging up.

'Pete,' I began. 'Don't worry, I'm pretty sure Uncle Vince knows most of the words to "Here Comes the—"'

'Don't be a prick. Give me the speaker.'

This is why you pick Peter Heritage as your best man. The boy never gives up. My solution – 'Ech, whatever, it'll be fine' – was blasted out of the water by his infuriating can-do, I'll-sleep-when-I'm-dead, victory-at-all-costs attitude. He sprinted away to the first place with acceptable mobile coverage – which turned out to be about a mile away – then downloaded iTunes versions of every song on my playlist, then came sprinting back up the hill, speaker and phone raised above his head in a frantic salute of fuck-you-world victory, put the speaker down at my feet, grinned the biggest grin I'd ever seen and pressed play just as Robyn rounded the corner.

'Pete,' I whispered in gratitude.

So that's why I called my wife Pete the second we got married. I spent that entire morning repeating his name over and over again, in every conceivable way. I'd said it out of boredom, out of annoyance, out of irritation, out of panic, out of fear, out of gratitude and out of love. And, in the end, even though she brings it up at literally every single convenience, I don't think my wife really minded. There are many worse things to be called than Pete.

Like fucking *Tyson*.

TYSON

There's a strong chance that the first voice my son heard was Pete's. If that's true, there's an equally strong chance that the first words my son ever heard – the words that first alerted him to the presence of others, that hinted that there might be an entire world waiting for him outside the warm comfort of the womb – were 'TYSON! I BLOODY LOVE YOU, TYSON!'

My son's name is Herbie.

If you have kids, you'll know that one of the worst parts of being a parent is the range of clothing available to newborn babies. You won't notice until you actually have to buy some, but the bulk of clothing designed for newborn babies is revolting.

One of the first outfits my son received was a grey romper suit with the words 'DADDY IS MY SUPERHERO' printed across it. Under no circumstance would I ever allow my son to wear this romper suit. My refusal was absolute. It came in a multipack along with another one that said 'MUMMY IS SUPER COOL'. That one I was fine with, because my wife really is objectively cool – she's funny and smart, she had a song in the charts once, and my cousins' kids go all bandy-legged whenever they see her because she dyed her hair once – and also, importantly, because that romper suit didn't have the word 'my' in it.

This is a crucial distinction. 'MUMMY IS SUPER COOL' isn't possessive in any way. It's just a blanket declaration of super-coolness. But 'DADDY IS MY SUPERHERO' assumes that my son literally thinks I'm his superhero. It assumes a scenario in which my son – my three-week-old son, small and helpless – first gained the mental capacity to identify me as his father, then came to understand the relatively modern cultural trope of the superhero, then linked these two pieces of information in a moment of joined-up thinking that immediately singled him out as history's cleverest baby, and then sewed this slogan onto an item of his own clothing. Which seemed unlikely, given that at that point in his life he spent eighteen hours a day sleeping and the other six shitting fucking Marmite all over the place.

I wasn't his superhero. I wasn't his anything. At best, I was a blur. Worse, I was the least impressive blur of the two main blurs he saw. I was the blur that couldn't even squirt food out of its tit for him. So – and I'll admit that there's a chance I'm overthinking this – to put him in a romper suit reading 'DADDY IS MY SUPERHERO' is to tell the world an enormous lie. Really, it's telling the world that *I* think *I'm* my son's superhero, which is an act of almost unthinkable hubris given that I spent quite a lot of my time during his first few months watching *Game of Thrones* with him balanced on my lap.

Besides, by sitting out the process of dressing him in clothes that state ideas he cannot possibly have, I've been able to see my son figure me out on his own terms, and that's been incredible. Now, when he wakes up in the morning, he'll come running to see me with his arms outstretched, excitedly yelling the word 'Daddun!' over and over again, and I'll feel as though my heart has burst wide open inside my chest. If I'd let him wear that 'DADDY IS A SUPERHERO' monstrosity, I guarantee there'd be a tiny part of me that'd think, Oh, sure, you're only saying that because I want you to.

Still, as bad as these clothes are, at least no one gave us any uncle Babygros. Uncle baby clothes are everywhere, and they're awful. Just look around. The Internet is clogged ragged with clothes that artificially overstate the value of uncles in relation to newborn babies. I just spent three seconds looking this up on Google, and these are genuinely – *genuinely* – some of the first romper-suit slogans I found:

- IF YOU THINK I'M CUTE, YOU SHOULD SEE MY UNCLE
- I GET MY AWESOME FROM MY UNCLE
- WARNING: I HAVE A HOT UNCLE
- MY UNCLE IS A GOD, YOU MUST BOW BEFORE HIM
- MY UNCLE SAVED LIVES TODAY, WHAT DID YOURS DO?

It's such a bizarre state of affairs. They're all terrifying, mercilessly over-compensatory statements of self-worth that – at least in one case – seem to suggest that your brother is so unstoppably sexy that your own newborn child actually sort of wants to fuck him.

I spent the entirety of my wife's pregnancy begging Pete not to buy any outfits like this. Because they wouldn't get worn. Of course they wouldn't. Nobody in their right mind would let their kids wear clothes like that. And, with Pete, it's important to set boundaries like this and then enforce them as ruthlessly as possible. If you don't, you invariably run the risk of being trampled to death under the weight of all his stupid ideas. So with this in mind I only have my own mental grit to thank for the fact that my son is called Herbie and not Tyson.

God, Pete wanted to call him Tyson so much. Admittedly, this took a while to sink in. There's always something of a grey hinterland with Pete, where you never know exactly how serious he's being. Like William Shatner or David Hasselhoff, Pete's character is so overt that he'll sporadically say something that can only logically be read as self-parody, as a wink to the crowd, deployed to let them know that even he realises how ridiculous he is. So you'll laugh along, only to be informed that, no, actually he really has given this a lot of thought and here's a list of reasons why you really should name your firstborn child after a convicted rapist who punches people for a living.

As the pregnancy wore on, our list of Pete vetoes – Peteoes, if you will – got longer and longer. No, we wouldn't let Pete buy our son a Manchester United kit. No, we wouldn't let Pete gel our son's hair into spikes. No, we wouldn't allow his first toy to be a two-foot replica of Dwayne 'The Rock' Johnson that screamed in agony whenever you so much as touched it. No. No. No, Pete. No.

Tysongate reached its zenith during the last gasps of our wedding reception. Everyone had left. The barmen were mopping up. Taxis were waiting outside. My wife and I were both slightly fed up because we'd been on our feet smiling for thirteen hours when our natural state is usually blank-faced sitting, and also because dozens of her colleagues had crashed the party and driven our venue over its fire-safety limit. Pete, meanwhile, had been drinking solidly since very early in the evening and had now become an aggressively boisterous puddle in the middle of the room.

This, I suspect, was my own fault. I had invited my boss to the wedding reception and, like an unusually large number of people who I describe my brother to, he couldn't quite believe that Pete was a real person. He came to my wedding reception, for the most part, just to meet Pete. Looking back, my mistake was to mention this to Pete. My boss ended up meeting UltraPete. He met Shagger Pete, the tiddies Pete, the Pete that's been triple-distilled to remove all traces of restraint. He met, in short, the Pete who can only communicate with other people by shouting the word 'SAMBUCA!!!!!' as loudly and with as many exclamation marks as possible.

That was all we really heard that night. We'd be whirling around the room in the way that just-married couples do during their receptions, not really drinking or eating or dancing but just relentlessly thanking well-wishers again and again for coming, and from somewhere near the bar we'd hear a battle cry of 'SAAAAAAAAAAM-BUCA!!!' and we'd turn around and see Pete belligerently forcing a relatively high-ranking member of the British media to reluctantly do shots with him.

This is why Pete was in that particular state by the end of the night, and that's why he wouldn't let my wife upstairs to get a taxi home. He was too busy hunkering down on his hands and knees in this almost completely deserted bar, yelling into her five-months-pregnant stomach through cupped hands, in the same way an international aid worker would yell at undiscovered survivors in the aftermath of an earthquake. 'TYSON! I BLOODY LOVE YOU, TYSON!'

I'm not entirely sure what the intention was here. There's a tiny part of me that believes this was a deliberately all-guns-blazing last stand, schemed up to sway us towards the Church of Tyson; that upon hearing the word 'Tyson' yelled through a mist of spittle and fumes, my unborn son would kick or jump, or maybe even poke his head out between my wife's legs and go, 'Uncle Pete! Shots! Weyyyy!' and then for ever more he'd have to be known as Tyson.

But, deep down, I know the truth. Pete was doing it because this was his way of showing us that he really, really wanted to be the best uncle possible. And I have no doubt that one day he'll get there. He just struggles with the day-to-day stuff for now.

One quality Pete shares with my mum is the ability to immediately form an opinion about someone, and then cling on to that opinion against all odds until the very end of time itself. It's quite an impressive ability, almost entirely fuelled by stubbornness, but it does tend to ignore the fact that people are capable of change.

I was an almost supernaturally ham-handed child, for example, and this reputation stuck with my family well into adulthood. I'm now perpetually doomed to be known as the effete intellectual of my family; the one who can read a book but couldn't use a hammer if it smacked him between the arsecheeks. And this is unfair. I mow lawns now. I assemble flat-pack furniture by myself. I've semi-successfully managed to grow a series of nearly-masculine almost-beards. But the reputation persists.

And I'm fine with this, really I am, but it seems a bit steep to use the same approach to judge a newborn baby.

Herbie was born into a state of chaos. Forty days before he arrived, we moved to a different town. Thirty-seven days before he arrived, my childhood home caught fire and rendered my parents homeless. Thirty-one days before he arrived, the whole family celebrated a small, cramped ad-hoc Christmas Day in the madness of our barely furnished house, storing all the presents near the back door because they stank of smoke. A week before he arrived, my parents moved out of the Holiday Inn in which they'd improvised a home – filling a jug of milk at breakfast each day, and putting it outside on the windowsill to keep it fresh – and into a temporary rented house that they both hated.

And then, eventually, he arrived. The birth veered in and out of nightmare, as labour stalled and Robyn went into sepsis and an emergency Caesarean had to be performed among a din of alarms at 4 a.m. Then, when it was time for her to say hello to him, she fainted from blood loss. Finally, a midwife placed him into her arms, and that's where he stayed for weeks. Herbie craved physical contact, and he'd scream himself hoarse whenever he was left alone. This clinginess, we were told, was to be expected after such a traumatic birth.

For the entirety of his first fortnight on earth, one of us was constantly holding him. We'd pass him backwards and forwards throughout the night, taking two-hour shifts to sleep while the other cradled him to keep him soothed.

Things slowly improved in time, but for a while Herbie was incredibly attached to us, and only us. If my dad held him, he cried. If my mum held him, he cried. If Pete held him, he cried. And this helped them forge the impression that Herbie not only hated them, but would also continue to hate them until the sun exploded and swallowed up the planet.

It does seem a little unfair to pin a lifelong reputation on a baby's earliest behaviour, especially since Herbie continues to change every single day. He's fourteen months old as I write this, and every day we wake up to a slightly different boy. He'll be a bit more coordinated, or he'll make a new noise, or he'll have a new tooth, or his face will have taken another lunge towards adulthood. This morning, he decided that the top of my head is hilarious. Which, to be honest, it is – viewed from above, I have a hairline like a decimated forest – but it's the first time he's ever laughed quite so hard at it.

In the end, Mum won Herbie over with what amounted to exposure therapy. We visited all the time, again and again, until Herbie's screams were first quelled into suspicion and then eventually blossomed into all-out adoration. They're inseparable now. They gad about together constantly, dancing around in her living room or chasing each other up and down her garden. Herbie even goes nuts for my dad now, which is heartening since for the longest time – possibly because, to very small children, Dad can sometimes look a bit like a seaside *Nosferatu* caricature – he was scared witless of him.

Pete, meanwhile, is a tougher nut to crack. He's busier than my parents, which means that we can't aggressively impose ourselves on him quite as much as we've done with the others. There is also the fact that Pete is Pete, and he's Pete to whoever he meets, and he's unable to modulate this unadulterated Peteness with anyone, even tiny babies.

So, when they meet, Pete tends to shove his giant – yet bizarrely tiny-mouthed – face an inch away from Herbie's and shout-grunt something like 'ALL RIGHT, HERBIE?' at him.

'No, Pete,' we'll explain. 'That's not how you act with babies. They react better to sing-song voices. Speak more slowly; make your voice go higher. Sound as if you're actually happy to see him.'

So that's what Pete will do. Except, and I can't work out whether this is because he's over-committing or under-committing, it'll always come off as violently insincere. Imagine how you'd sound if you'd just somehow accidentally set yourself on fire in slow motion. That's what Pete sounds like when he's really trying to talk to a baby.

'ALLLL-riiiiight, HERbie, ARE youuuuuuu havING a nice TIIIIIIME on thissss fine MORNinGUH?'

'Pete, that's terrifying. Try smiling when you say it, so he knows you're his friend.'

Again, this never works. Pete is bizarrely unable to smile sincerely at a child. Instead he warps his face into a demonic gurn, all teeth and tongue and squint, and repeats the phrase, only louder and longer and vastly more atonal. It's terrifying to watch as an adult, so God knows what it must be like for a baby, suddenly confronted with this leering frightmask screaming in tongues a centimetre away from your face.

'Nah. See? Hates me,' Pete will mumble as he hands our rigid, bawling and possibly urinating child back to us, and that'll be that.

I think this might just be a period of downtime in Pete and Herbie's relationship. And that's perfectly natural. After all, the first time we left Pete and Herbie alone together, it didn't exactly go swimmingly.

When Herbie was about five months old, and Robyn and I hadn't spent a second of babyless time together since the moment he was born, we asked Pete to babysit so we could go out to the cinema. It turned out to be an emotionally charged afternoon for everyone involved.

We were both still giddy about being let out of the house alone, but our attempts not to acknowledge the phantom limb that was our son ended in catastrophe when we saw a baby onscreen and both started bawling our eyes out.

Once the film finished, we concertinaed our plans for a nice dinner into an anxious KFC inhalation, and we raced home to see Herbie, who we'd both missed beyond words.

Before we left, I'd given Pete the standard newborn training rundown:

'This is a baby. Babies cry for three reasons. They cry because they're hungry, they cry because they're sleepy or they cry because they've shat themselves. If they're hungry, this is what you feed them.

If they're sleepy, this is how you get them to sleep. If they've shat themselves, this is how you clean them up. Got it?'

'Got it.'

'Good luck.'

However, there was a fourth scenario we hadn't counted on. Apparently babies – especially needy babies whose only constant in life has been the presence of at least one parent – also cry if they don't know where their mum and dad have gone.

Herbie started crying about half an hour after we left. He was still crying when we returned.

'Pete hasn't texted,' I told my wife as we speed-walked along our road hand in hand. 'They're probably having a great time.'

'We should do this more often!' my wife trilled.

Then we got home. My memory of what happened next isn't completely intact, but I seem to remember the front door being blasted off its hinges just as we came through the front gate, and the pair of us being swept down the street on a tsunami of tears and piss and snot. Also, I think the house might have been vibrating. And there's a good chance that a vast black cloud had formed above the roof of our house, like when the Gatekeeper met the Keymaster in *Ghostbusters*, but I'm not ready to commit to that part as fact yet.

What did definitely happen, though, was the screaming. Screaming like I'd never heard before. While we were out, Herbie had started screaming, and he'd continued screaming until his voice was shot, and then he'd kept on screaming long after that. It was a pained, raw scream of total exhaustion. His face was clenched tight and bright purple.

So was Pete's.

Pete was drenched in sweat, and every vein in his body seemed to have made a lunatic dash for the surface. His face was purple, and so were his eyeballs. If he hadn't already been crying, it wouldn't have taken an awful lot to set him off. He was bruised and battered and spent. He was a waif, a complete wreck of a man. I'd never seen him like this, not even briefly, in my entire life.

I ran over and picked Herbie up. Herbie immediately fell asleep in my arms. The ordeal was over.

'See? Hates me,' Pete croaked, shaking and broken.

This encounter coloured their relationship for a while. And rightly so, probably. The first year of parenthood is basically frantic trial and error. You spend it exhausting every possible option to every possible scenario until you find one that keeps your baby happy, and then that becomes the norm for the rest of your life. A new baby is – I assume – like a second-hand car. They're all riddled with highly individual quirks that need highly original solutions. Drive the car for long enough and you'll know that the clutch sticks and that the handbrake needs a slight jerk to the right to work. That'll become second nature to you over time, but the guy you sell it to will think he's been sold a piece of shit.

That's what happened with Pete. We'd had months to form our lives around the idiosyncratic whims of our son, to the point at which we didn't even notice ourselves doing it. But Pete, who's slightly less malleable by nature anyway, came into it blind. He thought he'd been sold a piece of shit.

Also, it probably doesn't help that Pete has more or less spent his entire life forcing his will upon other people. It's what made him such a great department-store manager – it was his own little empire, he got to be its totalitarian dictator, and he made his underlings all take an oath of fealty to make sure that every little detail was exactly the way he wanted it – but it fails miserably when there's a crying baby involved. You can't reason with a crying baby. You can't threaten them. You think you can bribe them, but what you're really doing is distracting them a little. The only thing you can do is love them, and hope that gets through. Other than that, you're completely, totally, frustratingly powerless.

*

Not that it matters, of course. Pete might not be cut out for parenting just yet anyway. He's turned into a borderline obsessive clean freak of late, and that doesn't necessarily go hand in hand with having a baby. Our house, make no mistake, is a full-scale disaster zone. Toys are cluttered together all over the floor. Washing-up remains constantly undone, for ever on the to-do list underneath the constant machine-gun fire of more pressing emergencies. Clothes, washed and unwashed, have piled up together in vast drifts in the corner of every room. Until very recently we'd turned our coffee table up on its end and wedged it against the TV like a makeshift wartime barricade, so that Herbie wouldn't crawl over and yank it to the floor. We've resigned ourselves to the fact that we shouldn't buy a nice sofa, a sofa that isn't smeared and stained with foodstuff and bodily matter, for at least a decade. By rights, our house should either be taped up or burnt down.

Pete's place, though, is impeccable. His kitchen is brand new, custom designed and perfectly white. His side tables are littered with grabbable hazards. He even has a glass-topped dining table, for crying out loud. That'd be unthinkable for us. If we weren't worrying about Herbie smashing it and hurting himself, the thought alone of messy fingerprints would be enough to have us running for the hills.

You can tell he isn't ready. Not yet. The yelps of panic he emits whenever he sees Herbie tottering towards his TV prove that. The way he doesn't instinctively tear around any room that Herbie enters, grabbing up all the sharp, breakable and fluid-covered items before Herbie sees them proves that. The way that he still blames Herbie, for some unknown reason, for the loss of a three-inch stretch of under-counter LED kitchen lighting that went missing on Christmas Day – even though Herbie lacks both the dexterity and the imperative to steal a minuscule piece of mood lighting for his own gain, and even though the two chihuahuas who were in the house at the time are easily stupid enough to have eaten it – proves that.

But it's OK. The older Herbie gets, the better Pete becomes equipped to cope with him. You can tell that they're growing into each other. Hand on heart, every time we've seen Pete since Herbie was born, he has almost immediately asked, 'Can I swing him by his ankles yet?' The answer so far has always been no, but it's only a matter of time.

Just recently, I was changing Herbie's nappy and Pete came in, because he wanted to see if Herbie's testicles were still as enormous as they were on the day he was born. But he noticed Herbie scratching at a small patch of eczema on his belly. Without any prompting whatsoever, Pete quietened his voice by about forty decibels and, in a completely natural, soft, sing-song voice, started talking to him. 'Don't scratch,' he cooed. 'Don't scratch the eczema. That's what I did, and it just makes it worse. No more scratching, Herbie.'

It was as warm and genuine a moment as I've ever seen between them. Pete must have seen me watching, because he stiffened a little and puffed out his chest in faux-defiance.

'King of eczema, aren't I?'

WEDNESDAY NIGHT DINNER CLUB

After moving back to Ashford, I saw more of Pete than at any time since childhood. On one hand, this was great. He kept on top of logistics after the fire. He picked us up from hospital when Herbie was born. When the pressures of early parenthood – the stress, the exhaustion, the sensation of suddenly being walled in – started getting to Robyn, he took her out to the seaside for the afternoon. When Pete wants to be nice, he's one of the most thoughtful people you will ever meet.

The problem is that Pete doesn't always want to be nice. Whether he does or not is a total dice roll. There are two versions of Pete that I dread encountering most.

The first is your typical bad-mood Pete. This is the Pete who wheels around convinced that everyone is out to get him, rattling everyone's locks until he can find someone to fight. This Pete is selfish and illogical and tedious to deal with, especially when you're as stressed and high-frequency and tooth-grindy as I often am.

But the second Pete is even worse. This is Pete in a belligerently good mood, the Pete who insults people for bants and then gets outraged when they're offended. This version of Pete is the one who made Christmas 2014 slightly more difficult than it needed to be. This was the Christmas we hosted at short notice after the fire.

During lunch, I brought out the Christmas pudding, doused it with booze and gave it to my mum to set alight. Only the lighter didn't work, which prompted Pete to bellow, 'OI MUM, I THOUGHT YOU WERE GOOD AT BURNING THINGS DOWN HA HA HA!' to utter disbelieving silence from everyone at the table. Normal people know where the line is and they're smart enough to steer well clear. Pete does not see the line. This is why we fight.

And when we fight, it always follows exactly the same pattern. He'll bluster in through the front door, bullish and annoyed at nothing, and start demanding things that I'm too tired to give him. I'll respond frostily and then we'll have a period of not talking to each other.

This last part, I suspect, is mainly down to me. I am exceptional at shutting people out of my life. If somebody crosses me, or insults me, or asks too much of me, or makes my life even a fraction of a per cent more complicated than it needs to be, that's it. The shutters come down, communication seizes up and I move on without them. I am great at this. I am a world-class shutter-outer, with one notable exception.

I've lost count of the times that I'd have shut Pete out if he wasn't my brother. I suspect that, from both of our perspectives, our lives are just a long list of each other's shit that we have to put up with, any single item of which would warrant a casting out if it came from anybody else. If he wasn't my brother, I'd have surgically removed Pete from my orbit at childhood, and he'd probably do the same. But oh no, we still have to see each other for birthdays and Christmas, and there's no getting away from that, which means that a few times a year tempers will flare and fists will clench and afterwards we'll ignore each other for a few weeks.

We're going through one of those moments right now, in fact. In a last-gasp push to get this book finished and published on time, I've gone to France for a week to work without distraction. At least, that was the intention. What actually happened is that things got out of hand and now my family has come with me. My entire family. Robyn, Herbie, Pete, Emily, Mum and Dad are all here in the same house, along with Robyn's best friend Ellie. With the possible exception of Craig, Mike and the dead-handed owl guy, pretty much the entire cast of characters from this book are all currently living under the same roof at the same time. And it's dreadful. I'm having a miserable time. Pete isn't helping.

This morning, Pete, Emily and Robyn went to the supermarket down the road to pick up supplies. Something happened along the way – I don't know what yet – and they didn't return for three hours. When they came back, Herbie was in the living room, asleep on my dad's chest.

Emily was first through the door. 'Well, Pete made that three times more stressful than it needed to be,' she growled by way of a hello.

She was followed by Robyn, carrying the shell-shocked expression of someone who had Been Through Something.

Then came Pete, who must have sensed that he was being talked about.

'Don't you fucking shout at me,' he yelled at me for no reason at the top of his voice two steps through the door, before I'd even said a word, his face a purple picture of dumb bovine rage.

'Pete, shut the fuck up,' I mouthed back, motioning to Herbie, who was miraculously still asleep. In retrospect, I could have worded this more politely, because it gave Pete the opening he'd been looking for.

'DON'T FUCKING TELL ME TO SHUT THE FUCK UP!' he roared, his brain a fat knot of inarticulate fury. 'I JUST SPENT THREE FUCKING HOURS DOING YOUR FUCKING SHOPPING!'

Still worried about Herbie waking up, and still clearly not having learned my lesson about swearing at Pete when he's angry, I mouthed, 'Shut the fuck up,' at him again.

'Language,' my mum chided.

'But he's a cunt,' he screamed back at her. 'A CUNT!'

It's been about five hours, and that was the last time we spoke. This sort of thing has happened over and over again throughout our lives, four or five times a year at least, and I know exactly how it'll play out. His anger will soften to a simmer but I – chilly motherfucker that I am – will want him out of my life completely. I won't talk to him, I won't look at him. He'll simply cease to be part of my existence. Then, gradually, we'll tentatively feel our way back to normality. These are unusual circumstances, so I suspect we'll be forced together for an openly hostile dinner later, but an impasse like this can often last for months.

We're both aware of this behaviour to varying degrees, and that's why we struck upon the Wednesday Night Dinner Club when we moved back here to Kent. In theory, it was a masterstroke. Once a week, we'd take turns cooking dinner after work. He'd come to mine with Emily – or I'd take Robyn and Herbie to his – and we'd eat together and watch a film. It was such a great idea; providing the sort of brotherly connection that we'd lacked while I'd been away.

It also did two important things to minimise our flare-ups. First, the standing appointments gave us structure. No matter what ridiculous fights we got into, we knew that we'd have to see each other again the following week, which might have helped to regulate our behaviour towards each other. The second thing was that we had the fail-safe of Robyn and Emily to act as buffers.

Robyn and Emily have seen enough of our fights to know when one is brewing, and they've developed a handy little peacemaker-communication network as a result. When things get really bad, as they have done a couple of times over the last twelve months, they'll meet up for lunch and check in on our behalf and engineer meetings we otherwise wouldn't have had. They're like a marriage-guidance service for uppity dickhead siblings.

*

Although it was started with the best of intentions, the Wednesday Night Dinner Club began to fall apart after about nine months. Very slowly – so slowly that we barely even noticed – all manner of tiny events cumulatively conspired to prevent it. Pete's new job required a commute to London, so he got home later in the evening than he used to. Plus, once he got back from work, he'd inevitably have to spend a few hours running or swimming or riding a bike as part of his never-ending Ironman training schedule and, since we tended not to serve meals exclusively consisting of raw egg and liquidised chicken, we started to drop down his list of priorities.

And he began to drop down our list, too. As Herbie got older, Wednesday Night Dinners got trickier for us too.

When he was a newborn, the Wednesday Night Dinner Club fitted Herbie perfectly. He didn't move. He didn't have to go anywhere. We could just strap him in a sling and get on with our normal lives. If you're determined and not particularly phased by the prospect of getting poo under your fingernails, a newborn baby will barely impact upon your social life.

But Herbie as a toddler is a completely different proposition. By now his napping schedule has hardened into scripture. He knows when he's due food, and he knows when he's due sleep, and if you don't give him these things when he's expecting them, he'll turn ratty and temperamental and nobody will have any fun.

Clearly, this makes having a sophisticated post-work dinner with other people almost impossible. Especially when you're at someone else's house. Especially when that someone else is incredibly touchy about the prospect of getting little tiny handprints all over the screen of his unnecessarily enormous television set, because all his stupid male insecurities are wrapped up in his possessions.

Is that the reason that the Wednesday Night Dinner Club died? It could be. Or it could be that, after a long day at work, Pete and I can be equally guilty of grumpiness; him retreating behind his iPad to play a game with his hands down his pants, me naffing off to the kitchen to be away from everyone.

I'm convinced that there's another, bigger reason why the Wednesday Night Dinner Club died. A reason that sucked the fun out of proceedings week after week after week. And that reason was Pete's choice of films. Pete wouldn't know a good film if it kicked him in the arse.

If I had my way, each and every Wednesday Night Dinner Club would conclude with a screening of *There Will Be Blood*, in total darkness and total silence except for the moments when I could justifiably yell, 'This is a film. THIS IS A FILM!' at everyone. This would happen every week, and nobody would ever complain about it because *There Will Be Blood* is the best film ever made and any fool can see that and I have amazing taste in films.

However, sometimes I have to let other people have their way. In Robyn and Emily's case, this means watching a dreary horror film where nothing happens for an hour and then one person screams and it all turns out to be because a little girl from the next village hanged herself once.

In Pete's case, this means watching some of the worst films ever made. My God, Pete likes shit films. Pete likes low-budget films called things like *DEATHKILL* or *HOOLIGAN VICTORY* or *TOXIN 2: THE PUPPETMASTER* that used to go straight to DVD but now clog up Netflix categories called things like 'Critically Derided Action Bollocks' or 'Angry Twats With Guns' or 'Adolescent Male Murder-Suicide Fantasies'. If a film was shot on the cheap in Bratislava, he'll watch it. If it's got a gone-to-seed gangsta rapper in a lead role, he'll watch it twice. If it has Vinnie Jones in it – anywhere at all – he'll watch it on a loop for a day and then think about it when he masturbates.

But if it has Danny Dyer in it, then God help us all.

Pete loves Danny Dyer. In fact, that seems like the world's most catastrophic understatement. Pete adores Danny Dyer. He models himself on Danny Dyer. I think that, deep down, he wishes he was Danny Dyer.

Pete's favourite film of all time is *The Business*, a film in which Danny Dyer goes to Spain and opens a bar and shoots some people and calls everyone the C-word a lot. That's Pete's favourite film. He's called it a classic. He's called it legendary. No joke. He wasn't being ironic. This is what I have to put up with.

(He's brought *The Business* with him to France, too. He got upset when I said I didn't want to watch it with him. This is what I have to put up with.)

There's a very good chance that the rest of Pete's top ten are all Danny Dyer films too. Any of those films he made between 2000 and 2012, when his career was bottoming out, called things like *Borstal Boy* and *Dead Man Running* and *Pimp*, churned out to ever-diminishing returns. Those are the films that Pete loves best in all the world.

The only way that Pete could enjoy Danny Dyer any more than he currently does would be if Danny Dyer miraculously got a role in *Star Wars*, playing a character called Farkov Yuslagg, who introduces himself by walking right up to camera and growling, 'Lez 'ave it then, Kylo Ren, ya muggy cahnt.'

Now, I like Danny Dyer too. I think his role in *EastEnders* is a masterpiece of critical reframing. It somehow gathered together all the unsavoury aspects of Danny Dyer's personality – all the things that made him such a national joke for so long – and repackaged them in a way that suddenly gave him mass appeal. On *EastEnders,* Danny Dyer finally makes sense.

Pete does not share this opinion. Pete thinks that *EastEnders* is the worst thing that has ever happened to Danny Dyer. As far as Pete is concerned, that's not even Danny Dyer onscreen. The guy in *EastEnders* spends his life smiling and being kind and loving his family. That isn't Danny Dyer. If the real Danny Dyer was handed the keys to the Queen Vic, he'd immediately turn it into a 1980s-themed fun pub, drink twenty pints of Foster's, stab Phil Mitchell in the side of the head with a pickaxe, jump up onto the bar, drop his trousers and shout, 'I'M PWOPER MASHED OFF ME TITS, YA MUGGY CAHNT!' while everyone went 'Weeeey!' and danced to 'Gold' by Spandau Ballet.

Every day that Danny Dyer does not do that in *EastEnders* is like a knife through Pete's heart.

I asked Pete about his favourite non-Dyer films recently. This, verbatim, is the conversation we had:

Pete: I like *Interstellar*. Chris Nolan's pretty much the best director in the world. Anything Chris Nolan does is bang-on good.

Me: Have you seen *Memento*?

Pete: No, what's that?

Me: It's his film about an amnesiac who tattoos messages on his body.

Pete: Why doesn't he just make a note?

Me: He does, on his body.

Pete: Yeah, but why doesn't he use a pad?

Me: He might lose the pad.

Pete: His phone, then. Why doesn't he just get his phone out?

This is what I have to put up with.

WRESTLING WITH PETER HERITAGE

I'm not hugely into self-improvement by any means, but that hasn't stopped me from trying to keep more of an open mind about the world lately.

Like a lot of people, I suspect that I'm a little too quick to judge anything I ever come into contact with. And, like a lot of people, I suspect it isn't doing me much good. If I'm not careful, my instinctive reaction to any new circumstance will be 'Well, this is shit', because jumping to a kneejerk conclusion is much easier than taking the time to honestly consider its merits.

I know this tendency gets me into trouble – to this day, every girl I've ever been out with has at least once burst into tears and asked me why I hate everything – but the thing is, it's just so much fun.

Heritageness, my wife calls it. Heritageness is happy anger. It's how I invigorate myself. Confronted with a minor annoyance – a bad TV show, a faulty printer, an audience which claps at a comedian's jokes instead of laughing at them – I'll launch into a gleefully pissed-off rant about it, and by the end of it I'll briefly feel slightly better about myself.

Honestly, though, I'm getting a little bit tired of Heritageness. Especially now I have Herbie. Herbie's innocence is glorious. Everything he sees for the first time astonishes him. It *astonishes* him.

His eyes widen and his chest expands and he becomes so overwhelmed with delight that I'm worried he might burst. We went to a farm recently, and every time he saw an animal that he'd only ever seen in books before, he'd grab on to me and look up at me with an expression that screamed, 'You're seeing this too, right?'

Left to my own devices, I turn into the kid who gets off on telling his friends that Santa doesn't exist. And that's not the sort of parent I want to be. So lately, I've been trying to sit on the Heritageness a little. I want to be more like Herbie, and open myself up to new experiences that I can judge on their own merits. I want to start feeling astonished again.

Pete is a fountain of new experiences. Because Pete likes all sort of dumb shit.

To me (a man who has never really managed to maintain a lasting interest in anything), all of Pete's hobbies seem incredibly tedious. Running, *Sky Sports News*, iPad games about farm maintenance. I haven't ever been able to see the point in a single one of them.

And this is as much my fault for judging him as it is his for having crap ideas. So, after the Wednesday Night Dinner Club ended, I attempted to rectify this. To gain a new insight into Pete, to better understand why he is how he is, I decided to accompany him for an activity of his own choosing. Just us. No wives, no girlfriends, no children, no parents. Just me and Pete, doing whatever he wanted, however he wanted to do it.

Well, maybe not anything. Clearly there had to be some ground rules first. I wouldn't be able to shadow him at work, even though I suspect that's his most natural environment, because all he does these days is facilitate the distribution of gift cards and, faced with the prospect of watching a man write emails all day, I have a feeling that I'd have flung myself out of an open window by lunchtime.

Also, no exercise. Even though exercise accounts for about 80 per cent of his leisure time, I made it clear that Pete could not involve me in anything even vaguely related to physical exertion. This was for the simple fact that Pete was fit and I was not, and doubling over and vomiting into a ditch fifteen minutes into an all-terrain marathon of his creation didn't strike me as much fun, not least because he'd inevitably call me a pussy every day for the rest of my life.

Realistically, this only left spectator sports. Pete loves being part of an audience and losing himself in a moment of shared experience. I, on the other hand, do not – a football match that's boring on TV will always be much more boring in the flesh because you can't wander off and make a sandwich – plus I'm so buttoned up that I even have trouble clapping at concerts, because I'm afraid the singer will draw everything to a halt in order to single me out for my ridiculous display of emotional ostentation.

If we were going to participate in a spectator sport, I knew that it only really left him with two options: football or wrestling.

He chose both.

We agreed on the itinerary for our day: at 2 p.m., I'd walk to his house and we'd watch England play football on his wall-sized television. Then, once the full-time whistle blew, we'd hop in his car, drive to Bournemouth and watch an evening of imported American wrestling together. To me, this suggestion was perfect. I'd get to see him in his three favourite environments – watching TV, driving a car and shouting at people in their pants.

Watching TV

I arrived at Pete's fifteen seconds into the 2016 European Championship match between England and Wales, and handed him the Scotch egg and bunch of grapes he'd ordered me to buy for him. Instead of saying thank you, he performed a short song that he'd composed a microsecond earlier, entitled 'Grapes Grapes I Love Grapes'.

'Would you even be watching this match if you weren't here?' he asked me suspiciously.

'Of course I would,' I lied. Because of course I wouldn't. It was two o'clock on a Thursday afternoon. If I wasn't with Pete I'd be working, or visiting my mum, or settling Herbie down for his afternoon nap. Or, if by some genuine miracle all these commitments had somehow fallen by the wayside, I'd have maybe spent the time doing something I'd get more pleasure out of, like cleaning out my toenails with a stick.

I don't understand football. God, I've tried. Even though Ashford is geographically about as far from a Premier League team as you can get, football has always been the grease that oiled its social machinations. There was an ice-cream man in town, for example, who'd assign his customers a sauce based purely on the team they supported. I only know that Arsenal play in red because I like strawberries.

At school, every conversation was about football, which meant that I had to learn the basic vocabulary if I wanted to fit in. I even bought a Blackburn Rovers kit, even though I couldn't have given a trillionth of a fraction of a shit about anything that Blackburn Rovers ever did. And for the most part, it worked. I was a football sociopath.

But Pete got into football young – during the 1992 European Championships, when he was nine – and deep. He regularly drives up to Manchester to watch football matches, he plays football videogames, he listens to football podcasts and, for an incredibly long time, he barely seemed to wear anything that wasn't a replica football shirt. For Pete, everything begins and ends with football. He has opinions about football. He understands formations. His total, laser-focused attention can be pointed at a football match and it will remain there until the whistle blows at the end.

I have huge trouble with this. To me, a football match seems abysmally long. And it's worse in the flesh. At least on TV you have commentary and replays and close-ups to hold your attention. Go to watch a match at a stadium – something I've thankfully managed to avoid since 2004 – and you just stand around in the cold, watching a distant murmuration of millionaires bump into each other in the middle of a field. It's rubbish.

'What are they?' Pete asked, pointing at my shoes.

'You've seen these before, Pete,' I told him. 'I bought them a couple of years—'

'I meant, what are they doing on if you're inside my house?'

I begrudgingly took my shoes off and settled in for a full afternoon of this shit.

Still, at least I could use the match as a learning experience. At one point during the first half, a player I didn't recognise did something imperceptible, and Pete responded to it – to this moment of absolute nothing – by mumbling, 'Good. That was good,' to himself.

'Was it good?' I asked, eager to learn.

'Course it fucking was,' he replied, before adding a huffy, 'Are you even watching this?'

'Yes, but I want to know why it was good.'

There was a pause, while Pete thought about how to inform me of the intricacies of the beautiful game as simply as he could. Eventually, his answer came.

'It was good because it was fucking GOOD,' he shouted. 'He brought it down well and passed it well.' Then he added a quick all-caps 'FUCK' to better communicate his annoyance with me.

A minute or two later, Wales got a free kick.

'Nah, he's not going to shoot,' Pete said. 'He's too far out. He's not going to shoot. He's wasting his time.' He leant towards the TV and directly addressed the player. 'You're wasting your time.'

The player shot, and scored. England were 1–0 down.

Pete didn't respond. Which I thought was actually quite grown up of him. Because, after all, it was only a game. When it's all over, win or lose, the result of any sporting event is just a construct created by society in order to— Oh wait, no, hang on, Pete's responding.

'FUUUUUUUUUUUUUUUUUUUUUCK!'

I turned around to look at my brother, who was angrily punching the cushions of his sofa with all his might.

'FUCK! FUCK! FUCK! FUCK! FUCK! YOU *CUNT*!'

All the windows in Pete's house were open. Outside, I could see one of his elderly neighbours obliviously mowing his front lawn.

Half-time came shortly afterwards and, in a moment of abject stupidity, I tried to jolly things up by telling Pete what I had for my tea the night before.

'Have you ever had courgetti, Pete? It's like spaghetti, but it's made of courgettes.'

'I had spaghetti last night. Proper spaghetti. Made of spaghetti. It's what men eat. Did you buy this courgetti?'

'No, I made it. We got a spiraliser.'

'A poncinator, more like.'

Pete cheered up a little after that, amused by his own dazzling wordplay. Then, in the first breaths of the second half, England equalised and he cheered up even more.

I had completely checked out of the game by this point. I couldn't tell if it was a good game or a bad game. As far as I could tell, I was just watching a screensaver. But Pete? Pete was utterly re-energised.

'We're gonna score again, right at the end,' he kept saying over and over again. As the half wore on, he became so completely convinced that England would score the winner in stoppage time that he grabbed his iPad and put a bet on it.

Stoppage time came, and Pete was proved right. England scored the winner. Pete reacted in exactly the same way as he did when England conceded a goal.

'FUUUUUUUUUUUUUUUCK!' he yelled, before standing up, punching his sofa six times in quick succession, grabbing two sofa cushions, hurling them on the ground, swearing some more and shouting arbitrary-seeming surnames at the television.

The full-time whistle blew. England had won. I wasn't sure if it was better for Pete to drive me to Bournemouth victorious or defeated. It probably didn't matter. He was likely to be just as aggressive either way. Still, I wasn't going to judge his violently florid outbursts during the football. I'm pretty much the same whenever I watch *Pointless*.

Driving a Car

Because our tight timetable meant that Pete had to forgo his ritual of watching the televised post-match analysis, in which three men who look like the disapproving father of your first girlfriend shake their heads at each other for half an hour, we spent the first portion of our journey to Bournemouth listening to a football call-in show on his car radio.

This was new. I'd never really listened to a football call-in show before, because I don't like football or listen to the radio or drive a van. But it makes sense that Pete is a fan. Because a football call-in show, it turns out, consists of nothing but people explaining why they're right about stuff.

'Listen, right,' they'll say, 'Jamie Vardy is the most in-form footballer of a generation and that's just a fact.' Or, 'Anyone can see that the flat-back four formation is useless against a team like Slovakia,' or, 'Obviously we should have exploited the weak left wing, a clown could tell you that,' to which my brother will shout the word 'BOLLOCKS' directly at the radio again and again.

It's sort of sweet, in a way. It's as though everyone's playing dress-up football manager together. I'm no expert – this much should be abundantly clear by now – but it seems to me as though football management is a very difficult, very specific job that requires a multitude of skills. You need to be a trainer, a strategist, a spy, an ego-fluffer, a father figure. It's a rare mix of talents and it's why, at last count, the manager of the England football team earns £3 million a year. And yet, after every game, dozens of bonk-headed numpties from Dagenham phone a stranger on the radio just to announce with terrifying dead-eyed conviction that they would have done better if they were in charge.

This is how Pete spends his whole life. Whenever something happens, Pete route-ones the first opinion he can think of, lets it congeal in his brain, and then that's his go-to response for the rest of his life. He treats every new situation like a football call-in radio show. The world is his talkSPORT, and we are all his Stan Collymore.

Once the call-in show ended, Pete proceeded to embark on his preferred method of in-car entertainment; listening to the first five seconds of every single song he owns.

Statistically, you're quite unlikely to ever share a car with Pete, so allow me to talk you through the very singular hell of his listening habits:

Step one: A song will start.

Step two: Pete will turn up the volume.

Step three: Pete will turn to you and shout, 'What's this?'

Step four: Because you will have only heard one guitar strum so far, you will tell Pete that you don't know.

Step five: Pete will shout, 'Come on, you must know!' Then he'll shout, 'Listen!' Then he'll shout, 'What's this?' again. Then he'll keep shouting, 'What's this?' until the noise coming out of his mouth begins to lose all meaning. 'What's this? What's this? Wossthis? Wozthis? Wozis? Ozis? OZIS? OZIS?' Three seconds will have passed.

Step six: Something will click in your brain. 'Oh!' you'll say. 'It's David Bowie!'

Step seven: Pete will nod his head.

Step eight: Even though the intro hasn't finished yet, Pete will skip to the next song and the process will start all over again. These steps will repeat themselves for the duration of the entire journey, no matter how long the journey is. Infuriating.

It's bad enough when Pete is listening to songs you vaguely know, but in recent months he's started to do it with wrestlers' entrance themes too. And that barely even counts as music.

Imagine the hell I was in. It was like being in *Groundhog Day*, if *Groundhog Day* was a film about Bill Murray experiencing an infinite number of identical five-second time loops during which he sat in a car and listened to brief snatches of tinny rock music while an angry boy sitting next to him shouted 'OZIS? OZIS?' over and over again.

It was a relief, then, when we were interrupted by a Jaguar cutting us up on the motorway. Bearing in mind that Pete had just experienced all the emotional peaks and troughs of an international football match, and then spent upwards of an hour listening to bursts of music specifically designed to hype teenage boys into a state of aggressive excitement, this probably wasn't a great idea.

'Let me teach you something about driving,' Pete said. 'Rule number one – how to deal with wankers who cut you up.'

Pete floored the accelerator and, as he passed the Jaguar, started to angrily bellow every single swearword he could think of at the driver.

'That's done it,' Pete told me with total confidence. 'That's scared him.'

But it hadn't scared him enough, because then the Jaguar decided to take another shot at passing us. The driver slowed down as he overtook us, and tried to give Pete a death stare. Pete responded by roaring as though he was trying to summon up the very fires of hell. He roared as I've never heard him roar before; all red eyes and spittle, hurling every foul piece of abuse under the sun at nobody in particular. Honestly, he was so angry that I wouldn't have been surprised if flames had shot out of his mouth.

And it worked, too. This full-blast demonstration of pure malevolence spooked the Jaguar so much that it almost crashed into the central reservation, which pleased Pete enormously.

'What a twat,' he laughed. 'Cut me up, you fucking twat.' Then he turned to me, as if to impart some great piece of wise old knowledge.

'Rule number one.'

Shouting at People in their Pants

Pete and I were introduced to wrestling at exactly the same time, when our Uncle Vince gave us a taped-off-the-telly VHS of the Royal

Rumble in 1992. To me, the tape was an hour of fat old men in their pants trying to push other fat old men in their pants over a rope, accompanied by a commentary track that sounded like a busload of monkeys accidentally being driven through a haywire cattle-prod factory. But Pete fell in love. As soon as the Royal Rumble had ended and Ric Flair, hair like a granny and whooping like an owl, finished screaming his victory speech at 'Mean' Gene Okerlund, something had changed for ever inside Pete.

He immediately rewound it and watched it again, then watched it again, and again, then pestered Uncle Vince to record SummerSlam for him, and Wrestlemania, and the next Royal Rumble, and on and on, with each new tape gradually worn transparent from overuse.

If I know anything about wrestling at all, it's only because Pete monopolised our television with it, or was constantly playing WWF games on the computer, or listening to 1992's dismal WWF Superstars' single 'Slam Jam' (UK chart peak: number four) on a disgusting never-ending loop in his room. Whenever I've moved away from Pete, I've been able to go for months at a time without remembering that wrestling even exists.

Not Pete, though. Pete still loves wrestling with an enthusiasm that borders on the demented. He watches wrestling on television every week. When he commutes to work, he listens to wrestling podcasts. If the WWE (the artist formerly known as the WWF) comes to London, he'll drop everything to buy tickets. When there's a big pay-per-view match on, he'll stay up all night and invite his friends over to watch it live, and make up all sorts of elaborate betting games with their own impenetrable sets of rules to keep things interesting. He even pays a monthly subscription to something called the WWE Network, a sort of Netflix for wrestling that – last time I checked – is 90 per cent comprised of piss-weak sub-Kardashian reality shows about what female wrestlers want to eat for their tea. He's obsessed. Whenever he got a new girlfriend, he'd essentially pin her to his sofa *Clockwork Orange*-style and subject them to such an unceasing torrent of wrestling that they'd end up riddled with industrial quantities of Stockholm syndrome. It was the only way he could be with them.

The show in Bournemouth was a non-televised WWE NXT event, a touring revue of up-and-comers who would one day make it into the big leagues. Knowing that I knew nothing about wrestling, he invited me to his for a barbecue two weeks before the show, so that he could show me a couple of NXT episodes, and explain who the main players were, and also make me build his barbecue for him and cook all his food on it as well.

It was interesting – not least because it turns out that the newest generation of professional wrestlers are all so uniformly bearded and tattooed that they look about thirty seconds away from making you a really nice coffee – but it was meaningless. The names and faces all blended into one, and it quickly became apparent that I wasn't going to get fully onboard with any of this until I saw it live.

As we approached Bournemouth International Centre, my heart sank. All I could see were very stereotypical diehard wrestling fans. They were in their late teens and early twenties and dressed completely in black, with indoor physiques and fringes brushed all the way down to better hide their faces from the world. I was worried that I'd be out of my depth here; that I'd be the old weirdo, the sore thumb who didn't know the rules and ruined the evening for everyone.

Once we got in, though, my fears were all confounded. Professional wrestling isn't anywhere as niche as I expected. The stereotypical wrestling fans I'd seen outside were there, but so were other adults and packs of girls and hundreds of children accompanied by long-suffering mums and people from every single walk of life. People actually like wrestling. Normal people. Non-obsessives. They were here because they wanted a fun night out. And, although I could have never predicted this in a million years, I had a blast.

Away from the hooting and hollering and general redneckery of any professional wrestling I'd ever seen on TV, that night's show was a revelation. It's all bollocks, obviously, staged and rehearsed to high heaven. But in a way, that just made what they did all the more impressive. These performers needed to have the brute physical strength to pick each other up and hurl each other around, but they also needed the agility to fling themselves around the ring, and the timing to sell every fake punch, and the memory to act out the prearranged play-by-play of the match. If that wasn't enough, they also had to respond to the wildcard that was the live audience, who'd spontaneously direct their energy into sudden boos and weird chants, shaping the outcome of the fights as they went. It was dizzying to watch, and insanely easy to get swept up in. It was pantomime. It was the Three Stooges doing *Swan Lake* on steroids.

Wrestling had changed since I'd been away. I checked out for good during a period of time known as the Attitude era, when the primary-coloured superhero shenanigans of what went before began to curdle into a sludgy morass of blood and sexual aggression, complete with suicide attempts and staged necrophilia. But this was different. This was a lot brighter. There were female wrestlers now, designed to appeal to women and not just sex-crazed teenage virgins. There were performers from all over the world who were no longer presented exclusively as offensive national stereotypes. At the end of the show, a wrestler jumped up onstage and sincerely thanked everyone for coming. It all seemed so modern and inclusive and progressive that I'm amazed to admit I actually found myself joining in with the crowd. You must never tell anybody this, but I think I've become a convert.

But as much fun as I was having, Pete was having far more. All his rattiness and weird aggression evaporated as soon as he sat down. He was booing and chanting and laughing along with every fight, taking care to explain situations and moves and histories to me, just as the little boy next to me kept doing to his mum. After the whirlwind of Heritageness we'd been through for the whole day, here we both were, completely unbuttoned and enjoying something together for what it was, with no defensive layers to bust through. Football couldn't do it, and nor could his car, but somehow wrestling managed to bring us together in a way I hadn't thought possible.

On the way back to the car, I stopped at the merch stand and bought a couple of T-shirts. I wanted us both to have a permanent memento of the day, and I found just the right one. Pete's favourite wrestler is arguably a woman named Bayley. Unlike the rest of her peers, Bayley is an unwavering force of positivity. Where other wrestlers walk to the ring grunting and growling and slapping their chests, Bayley dances out to what sounds like a Katy Perry song, grabbing her fans in a series of giant gleeful bear hugs as she goes. I bought us both a Bayley T-shirt. Across the front, in giant yellow letters, are emblazoned three words:

'I'M A HUGGER.'

We got back late that night. Having bonded, and having experienced Pete's second rule of driving – how to safely eat a burger at the wheel of a car – Pete and I began to talk. Usually we avoid any sort of vaguely personal topic, because we're brothers and that's weird, but we were too tired to put up any sort of front, so we suddenly found ourselves opening up. We talked about old friends and lost friends and times gone by, and then Pete started telling me about all the times he'd ever been punched.

This seemed odd. Pete remains the only person I have ever punched in anger, and he's been the only person ever to have punched me in anger. Remove inanimate objects from the equation and we're just not very punchy people. And yet here was Pete, listing all the places where he'd ever been smacked in the face by someone else.

'Who hit you?' I asked.

'Oh, just people. Angry boyfriends, mainly.'

'What?'

'Listen, you could write a whole other book about things you don't know about me,' he laughed.

MY TURN

The wrestling trip was one of the best things I've ever done with Pete. I couldn't have cared less about the sight of oiled-up, nearly-nude fat blokes smacking each other on the head, but that was the joy of it. I went into it with an open mind and made a conscious effort not to sneer or judge, but to appraise it on its own merits.

It had been such a good night, in fact, that I wanted to repay Pete somehow. By taking me to see something he truly enjoyed, and allowing me to be a part of it, Pete had made himself vulnerable to criticism. By his own admission, he doesn't let an awful lot of people in, so it was quite a big thing for him to ask me along. I've known the guy for thirty-three years, but this wrestling trip made me feel closer to him than ever.

'Pete, it was so great that you let me be part of something you enjoy,' I babbled as we drove back from Bournemouth. 'I need to return the favour.'

'I'm up for that,' Pete replied. 'What sort of thing do you like?'

My mind went blank. Because the horrible truth of it is that I don't really like anything. I don't have time to like anything. I mean, I like falling asleep halfway through *Game of Thrones*, but that's more of an involuntary reaction than an actively sought-out pursuit. My favourite thing that sprang to mind is having afternoon naps with

Herbie, but it'd be strange to invite Pete over to crawl into bed with us. Also, he looks as though he probably snores.

Besides, all these pursuits seem a little sleep-heavy, and Pete hates sleep. He's one of those weirdos who considers sleep unproductive. Given the choice, he'd rather be awake around the clock, lifting weights and figuring out how to appropriately vanquish his enemies. He's like that Bon Jovi song 'I'll Sleep When I'm Dead'. I'm like that Bon Jovi song 'Fuck Off I'm Knackered'.

What else do I like? What else have I ever liked? Not a great deal, really, if I'm honest. Anything I enjoyed growing up tended to be solitary in nature. Writing. Reading. Drawing. Staring off into space and listening to difficult 1970s French jazz-pop albums. They were all things that involved pushing the world away for a little while, and it's hard to invite someone to join you in an activity this antisocial. My mind was empty. But there had to be something I enjoyed. There had to be. Think, Stu. *Think*.

Just as I was about to tip head first into a vat of existential angst, Pete piped up.

'You'd better not like wine-tasting tours. I fucking *hate* wine-tasting tours.'

WINE TASTING WITH PETER HERITAGE

I decided to tell Pete that wine-tasting tours were absolutely my very favourite thing to do. Pete groaned. It was more than a groan, in honesty. He sounded like a sackful of bagpipes being crammed into a bucket. He sounded as though he was being injured.

'No,' he protested. 'You're just saying that because I said I didn't like them. I went on a wine tour with Emily in Australia and it was so fucking boring, Stu. I just couldn't see the point of it. I hate fucking wine tours.'

'Well, tough. You asked what I liked, and I like wine tours. I love them. I think they're brilliant.'

More groaning.

This wasn't just a peerless way to annoy Pete. It was convenient, too. One of the best things about this part of the world is that, in terms of climate and soil conditions, it's right up there with the Champagne region when it comes to wine production. The villages and hamlets around Ashford are full of charming little vineyards, all churning out dozens of award-winning wines. There is no other reason why anyone would ever come but, if you like wine, you should really think about visiting Ashford. I found a small independent vineyard, checked the website and saw that they did tours of the place every Saturday at 10 a.m. This, I decided, is what we'd do.

Our outing, however, was still going to be a somewhat watery photocopy of my day with Pete. By going wrestling, I felt as though I got right to the essence of my brother. We did whatever he wanted. We ate whatever he wanted to eat. We drove there in his car. I needed to give our trip an extra push, something that'd get to the very heart of what it was to be me.

'Oh, and we're doing it all on public transport too.'

Pete's groans suddenly took on an abstract, avant-garde timbre. If earlier he'd sounded like a sackful of bagpipes being crammed into a bucket, now he sounded like a sackful of bagpipes being crammed into a bucket of burning cats, before an audience of weeping circus clowns, in space.

'Noooooo, Stu. Whyyyyyyyy? Whyyyyyyyy are you making me do this? Stuuuuuuuuu. I'll drive. I'll drive and you can just write that we caught the bus.'

Nope. This was non-negotiable. He'd already fucked me over on the bike sticker, and I wasn't letting him get his own way with this too. We'd go and taste some wines together, by bus and train. And we'd be doing it because it was one of my very favourite things to do, and not just because I wanted to wind Pete up.

In 1969, the Swiss psychiatrist Elisabeth Kübler-Ross published a book based on her experiences with the terminally ill. *On Death and Dying* became internationally known for its theory of the five stages of grief: denial, anger, bargaining, depression and acceptance. The Kübler-Ross model has sometimes been criticised by other psychiatrists for not taking personal surroundings into consideration – in a positive and nurturing environment, they claim, some of these stages will be absent from the grieving process – but it is nevertheless the benchmark when it comes to understanding the experience of grief.

Once I told Pete that we were getting a bus to a vineyard, he went through each and every one of Elisabeth Kübler-Ross's stages in rapid succession, grieving the day off he'd just lost. Arguably, this is because I did not provide a positive and nurturing environment for him.

It was all there. Denial, in his initial refusal to play along with my plan. Anger, in his raging against the perceived injustice of having to leave his car at home. Bargaining and bargaining and bargaining ('I'll drive and help you lie about it!' 'If this day is supposed to be about how you get around, then I can drive you because you're always fucking cadging lifts off people anyway'). Depression. Actually, it wasn't all there, because Pete doesn't do acceptance, but four out of five isn't bad.

He went on and on about it. He called my mum and complained about it to her. He complained about it to Robyn. Whenever I brought it up he narrowed his eyes, went quiet and took on a distant gaze, as if he was internally retreating to a better place that only he could see; a place full of Roy Keane and whey protein. The thought of buses repulsed him. They were full of grannies and drug addicts, he said. They were embarrassing to be seen on. He hadn't been on a bus for sixteen years, he calculated, and he resented having to go on one for me.

His bargaining almost worked, by the way. To get to the vineyard, I worked out that we needed to walk twenty minutes to the train station, go two stops on the train, walk to the bus stop, go four stops on the bus, get off and then walk for forty minutes down a muddy public footpath. It was an almost two-hour journey. If I'd let Pete drive, we'd have been there in less than twenty minutes.

And it had been raining. A lot.

Pete's arguments rang around in my head. Surely, if someone offered me a lift, I'd take it over a glum trudge through shin-deep mud. The day before we left, with my resolve at its weakest, I texted Pete:

Fuck it, shall we drive tomorrow?

All Pete had to do here was say yes. He'd say yes and I'd agree and we'd both save ourselves a lot of strife. But that's not what he did. Instead he texted:

Ha ha! Your call.

This planted *another* seed of doubt in my mind. Should I be letting him drive me there? I knew that my original plan was going to be boring and uncomfortable, but that was because I wanted Pete to be bored and uncomfortable. I couldn't spare him that part of my world. But, still, a twenty-minute car ride did sound better than two hours on public transport. Eventually, after flip-flopping for hours, I made up my mind:

No, sod it. Public transport.
Our train leaves at 8am.

Cunt.

The night before our trip, it pelted down with rain. It rained with such ferocity that it actually woke me up. I checked Google Maps to see if there was a shorter way to the vineyard from the bus stop. There wasn't. At ten to seven, again doubting the wisdom of my plan, I sent Pete another text.

Seriously, we have to walk down
a footpath through the woods.
It's going to be really muddy.
Drive?

Your call, but I need to know
now otherwise I'll be late.

If you're OK with mud, we'll get the train.

Fuck you.

Is that a no?

Your fucking call.
Grow a pair and make a decision!

Train. Wear old shoes.

I hate you.

Pete likes all his seconds and minutes to be accounted for, and anything that steals those from him is automatically the enemy. Pete's ideal restaurant would be a place where his starter is waiting for him when he gets there, the main course arrives ten mouthfuls later and he's paid and left before he's finished chewing. The boy even resents sleep for robbing him of productivity, a notion so thoroughly alien to most normal people that there's a fighting chance he could be arrested for simply saying it out loud in public.

To Pete, public transport – a system of transit whereby you have to obey somebody else's schedule no matter what happens to be going on in your own life – is anathema. What if you take a train to an appointment and you get there fifteen minutes early? You can't just usefully kill fifteen spare minutes, especially if you haven't brought your gym kit with you. To Pete, public transport is for losers. It's for people too stupid or too poor to learn to drive. It's for me, essentially.

Me? I live for wasted time. To me, a train journey is a place to wind down. After a day spent working and parenting and cooking and taking care of things around the house, a train journey represents precious time alone. Time when I can read a book, or listen to a podcast, or have a nap, or contentedly gaze out of the window at nothing for a few hours. I went to a stag weekend in Leeds a year or two ago. I found out when everyone else was getting there, and then deliberately booked tickets on a different train just so I'd have a few hours to myself for once. Because, sure, male bonding is fun, but it's nothing compared to waking up in a puddle of your own dribble next to a stranger, with no idea what just happened in the last three episodes of *Serial*.

Obviously my love of public transport has its caveats. I don't love public transport during peak hours, when you essentially have to mortgage your house in order to spend forty-five minutes pressed into a crowded footwell while a flustered cyclist keeps absent-mindedly performing an incremental vasectomy on you with his handlebar. Nor do I love any form of public transport during the summer, because that uniformly leaves me in a state of such damp-knickered chub-rub that it feels as though someone has taken a potato peeler to my perineum before turning a vinegar hose on it. And, fine, while I'm here I'll admit that I'm irrationally scared of buses. But apart from that, all public transport is terrific.

Pete wasn't kidding about hating vineyards, by the way. His first-ever argument with Emily, he told me, was about vineyards. When he went out to Australia on his ridiculous quest to win her over, Emily took him on a full day of wine tasting; a day with an itinerary and coach transfers and many, many identical vineyards. Before long, thanks to a combination of boredom and the swirl of drunk Australians around him – 'There is nothing worse than a bunch of drunk Australians,' he insisted – Pete got surly. And when Pete gets surly, the best thing to do is tiptoe around him.

Spend enough time with Pete and you'll be able to spot this coming; his shoulders will droop, his gaze will lengthen and he'll fall silent. This is because he's saving up all his energy for the planet-shaking three-second tantrum that'll inevitably erupt the next time someone says something he vaguely disagrees with.

But if you're new to his ways, this might have struck you as, say, the behaviour of someone enthralled by the acres and acres of Australian vines around him. This must be what Emily did, because their trip ended in a giant argument.

But, still, regardless of his past experiences, I was sure that I could change his mind. After all, this was a local vineyard. We'd be supporting the local economy, plus I'd get to see all the beautiful Kent countryside that he kept wanging on about. Win-win, surely.

Nope.

The day of the trip came, and we met at the station at 7.45 a.m. Pete, annoyed that I'd made him reschedule a pre-Ironman swimming session for this, made me buy him a *croque-monsieur* at the platform café. The train came, we had a nice chat, and fifteen minutes later we'd completed our first leg of the journey. 'That wasn't actually too bad,' Pete reluctantly admitted.

Better yet, just as we left the station, our bus pulled up. The timing was perfect and, although the tickets were so expensive that I used almost all the money I had with me to pay for them, I could tell that Pete was softening. 'Let's go up on the top deck!' he yelled, like a kid.

The only passengers on the top deck were two people shouting foreign languages into their phones and an old man who kept swearing to himself. I tried to keep Pete engaged and distracted but I could see that his shoulders were drooping. His gaze was lengthening. Things were going south, but worse was to come.

We got off the bus and it very quickly became apparent that there wasn't going to be any pavement for us to walk along. 'If I get hit by a fucking car . . .' Pete yelled, before allowing the threat to trail away to nothing. At this point, I noticed that his definition of 'old shoes' was a pair of flimsy white plimsolls that he'd bought two years earlier, but I kept quiet because perhaps the footpath wouldn't be that muddy.

The first part was fine. It was just a gravelly track past a couple of farms. Perhaps because it was better than he'd expected, it helped Pete to open up. In a very Peteish way, admittedly.

'I hope today isn't all friendly and interactive,' he huffed. 'I don't want the guy to expect me to ask any questions. I just want to stand at the back and shut up. That's it.'

I told him that I'd appreciate it if he asked at least a couple of questions, to stop the whole thing from being too cripplingly awkward, but he'd already moved on.

'You could have just come over to mine and watched *Sky Sports News* with me instead. That would have been nice, and we wouldn't have had to catch any fucking buses.'

This would never have happened in a billion years, because I cannot understand *Sky Sports News*. I've tried so hard, because it's legitimately Pete's favourite television channel, but I cannot. It's like Ceefax, but read out by a bloke. It's CNN, but about pointlessly trivial stuff like whether or not the Stoke City goalkeeper has a sore neck or not. It's as if someone made a Teddy Ruxpin doll based on the dullest percentile of drinkers in every pub in the country, and then filmed it around the clock as a bizarre punishment for the world. But I didn't dare tell this to Pete because his shoulders were already drooping, so instead I started asking him about his wine preferences.

'Do you like red wine, Pete?'

'I fucking hate red wine,' he barked.

'That's OK,' I countered cheerily. 'The climate of the UK lends itself more to white wine anyway, and I think the soil composition in this part of the country is roughly analogous to that of the Champagne region of France.'

Rookie error. I'd shown a trace amount of enthusiasm for a vaguely effete subject, and I knew how Pete would react.

'Ooh,' he warbled back in a funny voice. '"The soil composition in this part of the country." Ha ha ha. You ponce.'

I tried changing the subject.

'Do you know what film I saw last night?' I asked.

'I don't know. Was it *How to be a Fucking Cunt* by Stuart Heritage? HA HA HA HA HA!'

Pete was thrilled with this joke.

Then the gravel gave way to a tractor track: two deep, waterlogged trenches separated by a thick slick of wet mud. And then it started to rain.

We reached the vineyard about half an hour later, caked in mud from the knees down, a full hour before our tour was set to start. We were there so early, in fact, that the vineyard wasn't even open. Pete's mood remained at rock bottom. If he'd driven us, he said, not only would we have been dry and warm and clean, but we'd still be at home. Even though I assured him that this wasn't wasted time, because it was precious time that we got to hang out with each other, Pete was almost pulsating with anger.

Outside the entrance to the vineyard were a few small potted vines that you could take home and grow in your garden. Although he hates wine, Pete eats a lot of grapes, so I suggested that he should buy one for himself and carry it home.

'Why?' he barked. 'I live five minutes away from a Waitrose. I can just buy all my grapes there. You should put that in your fucking book, that I only live five minutes away from a Waitrose. That way people will know I live in a nice area. Meanwhile you live five minutes from a fucking LIDL! HA! HA! HA! HA! PONCE.'

Thankfully, the vineyard opened up soon after, and a woman invited us into the shop for a cup of tea. Less thankfully, the other people on the tour followed suit. And, God, they were chatty.

There was a young man in jeans and a body warmer who drove a 4x4 and kept running outside to shout the word 'scaleability' into his phone. There was a rich old white-haired man accompanied by a woman – I couldn't work out if she was his wife or daughter – who plainly hated his guts. There was a huge group of women, accompanied by one man, who all seemed like best friends even though they kept asking each other such rudimentary personal questions that they must have only just met. And then there was us, sitting at the back, far away from everyone, silently.

Well, almost silently. As they started to arrive, Pete whispered, 'I am dying inside,' but that was about it. Once everyone had arrived, a nice man called Nigel handed us each an umbrella and we set off into the vineyard itself.

And, actually, I found it quite interesting. Before the tour began, Nigel told us the history of the area. My area. He told us that the name Weald of Kent was derived from the old English word 'wold', meaning forest, and that the local village names all had suffixes – like -den and -hurst – that suggested they were originally just clearings in the wood. He told us that the woodland, when combined with the chemical make-up of the soil, helped to make the area one of the country's leading ironworks for centuries.

This was all fascinating to me. It was all about where I'm from, and all the generations of industry that shaped it. And I realised that I was part of it, and it was part of me, and that wouldn't change no matter how hard I tried to run from it. It sounds corny but, standing there, in a field that had been in use since the Iron Age, next to my brother, felt like a moment of real connection. I felt as though I was part of something bigger than myself. Even Pete grunted with interest a couple of times. Maybe dragging him out all this way against his will was going to be worth it.

Nope.

Pete had immediately taken against one of the group: a woman who was keen to ask questions about the vineyard, but only if the answers would confirm things she already knew. The law of averages states that there will always be one of these in every group like this, and while everyone will find them mind-numbingly tiresome, they'll keep their frustrations to themselves in order to maintain cohesion. What the law of averages doesn't tell you, though, is that a Pete in the group will throw the entire natural order of things completely off-balance.

His protestations started off small enough, with him just getting his phone out whenever this poor woman opened her mouth. But when he deemed that to be too subtle, he started adding audible tuts into the mix. It still didn't work, and the woman still ground everything to a halt every few paces with an 'Isn't it right that . . . ?' or 'Is this because . . . ?' so Pete had to go drastic. After about an hour of looking at vines (which Pete took against because they looked exactly the same as the ones he'd seen in Australia) and the inside of the bottling plant (which he confessed to not minding, because there was a big stack of bottles and he was impressed at their loadbearing capabilities), the woman infuriated him so much that, whenever she spoke, he gave her a hard stare and shook his head. It didn't put her off – which is weird because it looked exactly like the sort of thing that a member of the Mafia would do three days before your body washed up in bits on the shore of a lake – but it certainly made things about fifty times more excruciating for me.

There was a tasting session once the tour concluded, with a chance to sample the vineyard's eight different wines and six different ciders. I was looking forward to this bit most of all, because I thought it would help to educate Pete's palate a little.

Pete has never liked wine, and I suspected that this was down to his inverted snobbery. Beer is easy – you ask for a beer, someone gives you a beer and you drink the beer – but wine is a bit more complex. The dizzying number of grapes and blends and vineyards and years and labels and costs can be intimidating. My guess was that Pete had decided that wine wasn't worth the hassle, and a switch went off in his brain one day and all wine was for ever judged to be stupid. Plus, you know, the glasses were poncey and only ponces drink wine and blah blah blah.

But this? This was the perfect opportunity for Pete to learn about wine from an expert. As they poured their sample glasses, the staff gave a little explanation of what the wine was, and how it was made, and the best way to enjoy it. Maybe, I thought, with a little bit of background information, Pete might be able to get over his prejudices and start to enjoy wine on its own merits.

NOPE.

Pete tried one sip of wine – the driest of the lot – and then disappeared. I was stuck at the front with the rest of the tour group, involuntarily mired in a nightmarish conversation with the middle-aged man who came with the seven women, about which wine would have the best chance of success if one of them came to his for the evening if you know what he means, and Pete just vanished. I looked around and saw him miles away, pinned to the furthest wall in the room as though the Blair Witch had just got him. He looked sullen and drawn, and he was helping himself to fistful after fistful of the bread left out to accompany the various jam samples around the room.

A woman who worked at the vineyard held up a bottle and motioned to Pete. 'Does your friend, er . . . ?' she asked me. I silently shook my head at her. I didn't have the energy to convince him. Pete had defeated me again. I decided that enough was enough, and told Pete I was putting him out of his misery.

'What would you give today, out of ten?' I asked as we left.

He thought for a while.

'Two,' he replied, adding, 'Point five,' when he saw how crestfallen I was.

That score was about to drop considerably.

'I'm not walking through the fucking mud again,' Pete said, even though it was the only way back to the bus stop to take us home. 'I don't care if it's the only way back to the bus stop to take us home. Find another way.'

To my eternal credit, that's what I did. If we turned left at the entrance instead of turning right, I determined, we could follow the road out and around, then get back on the main road, walk for a bit and find another bus stop. It'd take a little longer, but I wouldn't have to put up with Pete whining about mud any more, so it was worth it.

But this was the deep countryside. None of the roads had pavements.

'Well, this is fucking roadkill,' he yelled, punching roadside plants with all his might as traffic fired past a couple of feet from us. His tone suggested that he was being perfectly serious, and that I should tread lightly.

'How much has this trip cost you anyway?' he spat.

I figured it out – £4 each for the train, £6 each for the bus. Twenty quid, there and back.

'Do you know how much it cost us to go to the wrestling? Thirty pounds! And that was all the way to fucking Bournemouth.'

I began to tell Pete that he probably had a point, but he was too busy getting stuff off his chest to hear me.

'I look like a fucking asylum seeker, walking down the road like this. What if someone I know sees me like this? They're going to wonder what went wrong. I could have run to this place in the time it took us to get a bus here. Why have we been walking for so long? I thought you said there was a bus stop nearby.'

I told Pete that there *was* a bus stop nearby, but we had to find another one because he threw such a pissy tantrum about walking through the mud.

'Don't fucking blame me for this!' he shouted, genuinely angry. Every big, serious argument we've ever had has started like this; with him raging against something and me pointing out that he's partly to blame. All the times we've ever had full-blown arguments, arguments that have rolled on for months of icy quasi-estrangement, have all stemmed from moments like this. So, for the sake of our relationship, I kept quiet and marched the two miles to the bus stop in the next village.

'How long until the bus gets here, then?' Pete asked as we took refuge in the graffiti-covered bus stop.

'Forty minutes,' I replied confidently.

'Fucking WHAT?' Pete yelled, having immediately figured out that he could have driven home and back in the time it would have taken us to wait. 'What are we supposed to do until then?'

'I dunno,' I replied unhelpfully. 'We could get something to eat, or walk around, or just sit and enjoy the view.'

Pete groaned. And it was there, in one of those stomach-lurching moments of sickness you get when you accidentally press 'reply all' after slagging off a colleague in an email, that I realised I'd misread the timetable. I took a careful intake of breath, fearful that it might be my last.

'Pete . . .'

'WHAT?'

'The bus isn't coming in forty minutes.'

'GOOD.'

'It's coming in *one hour* and forty minutes.'

It took Elisabeth Kübler-Ross an entire book to explain her grief-cycle theory, and even then she had to leave out many subtleties that can cause the effects of grief to vary from one person to another. What Kübler-Ross needed was Pete. She could have just wheeled Pete onstage in front of hundreds of rapt psychology students, told him that he had to wait an hour and a half for a bus and – bam – Pete would whistle through a perfect, perfectly encapsulated quickfire round of each and every stage of grief in such a textbook way that she could have packed up and left on the spot.

I know this because this is how Pete reacted when I told him the news:

'Fuck off, no, it isn't. Why the fuck didn't you check the bus timetable before you left this morning, you wanker? I'm not fucking waiting here for an hour and a half in the middle of nowhere in this bloody bus stop because some prick couldn't read a bus timetable. I know, I'll call Emily and get her to pick us up. Oh Jesus, I can't do that because I left the car in the train station car park. Oh God, what are we going to do?'

Denial, anger, bargaining and depression, all in the space of twenty seconds. Pete hates wasting time, even when it comes to evidence-based psychological behavioural cycles.

You'll notice that I missed acceptance off that list. In lieu of acceptance, Pete does threats. He turned to me in the bus stop and growled.

'Call me a fucking taxi.'

The total cost of our day out – the twenty-six-mile round trip that took six hours to complete, including the taxi ride back to the station – was £31.90, £2 more than it cost Pete to drive 310 miles to the wrestling and back. Add in the wine that I felt duty-bound to purchase, and all the snacks that Pete kept demanding throughout the day, and it's a wonder that I've got enough money left to feed my kid.

But I still maintain that it was worth it. Thanks to the vineyard, I know more about the history of where I grew up. Thanks to the wine tasting, I know that Pete really likes little baskets of complimentary bread. And thanks to our journey there and back, I know that some people are born to drive and some people are born to be driven.

And I got to spend a good chunk of time with Pete. With all the other stuff that's been going on lately, that barely happens any more.

MUM

We were inundated with visitors after the fire. All these long-lost figures from my childhood, turning up to meet Herbie for the first time and make sure everyone had everything they needed. The weird thing is, though, they'd all behave the same way. They'd drink some tea, they'd talk about the fire, they'd coo at the baby. And then – and this always happened, absolutely without fail – about three-quarters of the way through their visit, they'd lean in and ask if my mum was OK.

'I think so,' I'd lie. 'I mean, the fire shook her up a bit, but she's coping.'

'Are you sure?' they'd double-check. 'She doesn't look herself. She's so thin.'

I knew she looked thin. Over the course of about a year – slowly at first, and then more noticeably – Mum had started to lose weight. She looked thin at my wedding, but I'd put that down to her wanting to fit into her outfit. By Christmas, though, it was inescapable. She was gaunt. Standing in what used to be our living room on the day of the fire, Mum was writing down some details to pass on to the insurance company and I noticed that her handwriting had suddenly taken on an unmistakably spidery appearance. It was little-old-lady handwriting. Which was odd, because she wasn't particularly old. She was sixty-three.

We were brought by my mum. In the 1980s, as the Thatcher government presided over the highest unemployment figures since the Second World War, my dad struggled to find work. With a wife and two kids to support, and the construction industry cratering at home, he found himself asking a friend of a friend if he knew of any work. This contact suggested Saudi Arabia, then a newly rich country lacking the skilled workforce it required to build a modern infrastructure. With no other options, Dad packed up, left home and became a migrant worker. It was *Auf Wiedersehen, Pet* in real life. Dad rode out the recession by working abroad, and we got by on the wages he sent home.

This seemed perfectly fine when I was a kid. But if I were in his position now, having to move abroad in order to support a family I barely got to see, it would tear my heart out. I suspect this is because I'm a soft-handed ninny who's never had to deal with any major hardship before. But my parents are tougher than that. It's the rule they've always lived by: in the face of adversity, get back on the horse.

And that's what they did. They got on with it, speaking on the phone every week and exchanging long letters sent backwards and forwards in red-and-blue-striped envelopes. The set-up didn't seem unusual to me or Pete, because we didn't know any different.

Also, at the very least, we got a couple of pretty neat holidays out of it.

My parents made me keep diaries of these trips – thanks to which I'm able to tell you that we flew to Jeddah with British Caledonian (which no longer exists) in the smoking section (which has since been banned) and the in-flight menu included Lincolnshire duckling breast on a compote of lemon and orange (which doesn't appear on in-flight menus any more, because everyone flies EasyJet now, and the only thing they eat on planes are panic-bought WHSmith departure-lounge Haribos).

Three Excerpts from my 1987 Jeddah Diary

Sunday 12th April – Yesterday we caught a big cockroach and put it under a glass. When Daddy came home he killed it. We went to Daddy's office in the evening. We met lots of Arabs. They kept looking at me.

Tuesday 14th April – I had a tummy bug. Daddy told me that there are little bugs inside your tummy that help you break your food, and I have got some Saudi Arabian bugs that fight with our bugs and the Saudi Arabian bugs win. Then we killed a jumping spider.

Sunday 19th April – Yesterday when I woke up I had the mumps. I had a swollen face. Daddy said, 'You look like a monkey.'

According to the diary, the menu on the return flight included something called 'Raspberry Chicken'. This, I'm certain, is the reason why British Caledonian is no longer an operational airline.

With Dad working in Saudi, Mum was left in charge of the family. She was the one who took us to appointments, and taught us to read, and walked us to school, and decorated the house. Dad was earning all the money, but Mum did all the gruntwork. She had to be logical and organised and single-minded when it came to getting stuff done.

We lived about a mile and a half from Ashford town centre, and Mum didn't drive, so every Friday we'd go into town – me frantically walk-running to keep up with her absurd pace – to do the weekly shop. And then we'd walk home just as fast, except this time she'd have the handles of about 150 bulging plastic bags cutting into the palms of her hands. The woman was a machine. She was a Trojan. Nothing could stop her.

Heather Heritage was born in 1951, the second-oldest of six kids. Her father died when she was thirteen and she had to put her own needs to one side in order to support her family. She left school. She got a job as an egg-packer, walking the three-and-a-half-mile journey across the ridge of the North Downs twice a day until she eventually met my dad and moved in with him. You know the rest of her story from there. Tried for a baby, couldn't get pregnant, had a baby, baby died, had two more kids, raised them herself, one of them was a prick. It's been a life that's toughened her up beyond all measure. It's made her invincible.

One morning in the middle of August – the August after the wedding, the August after the move, the August after Herbie was born, the August after the fire – my dad phoned. My days of automatically answering with 'OH GOD IS MUM OK?' had long been beaten out of me, but in this case it was premature. Mum wasn't OK.

Dad told me that she'd woken up with breathing difficulties, and he'd taken the day off work to get her checked out at A&E, but he assured me that things were fine and that we didn't need to come to the hospital.

When Pete and I arrived at the hospital twenty minutes later, we peered through the window of Mum's ward to try and locate her. She was nowhere to be seen. It was only on our second parse that we noticed the tiny woman, utterly diminished, sitting in an armchair with a respirator mask over her face.

Mum.

It was awful seeing her like this – the sort of sight that makes your gut sink and your pulse race – but not a surprising one. Mum, you see, is Pete's mother in every way. She's just as stubborn, just as unwilling to entertain discussion. She wouldn't engage in conversations about anything; not even, for the longest time, the state of her own health. Whenever her weight loss was brought up, she'd wave the questions away.

Mum isn't someone you can simply confront about this sort of thing. You have to be patient, and carefully thread your concerns into a longer conversation, or she'll slam the shutters down. We put

Dad on her case, too, but he'd just sigh, 'Oh, you know what your mum's like,' in the way that only a husband in his forty-fourth unbroken year of marriage can. My best guess now is that Mum knew that something was wrong, but she was too scared to find out what.

Now it was too late for discussion. She'd been hospitalised because her breath was shallow and, although she was well enough to be discharged the same day, the doctors asked her back at a later date for a bronchoscopy to see what was up with her lungs. I spent the afternoon googling the terms on her discharge notes, hoping for a best-case scenario of chronic pulmonary disease, but fearing worse.

Her second hospitalisation took place a fortnight later. Mum went in for her bronchoscopy but things didn't go as planned. She reacted badly to the sedative and, on the way home, found herself gasping hopelessly for breath. Dad, seriously worried for the first time, turned the car around and rushed her back to hospital. That's where she stayed for three days, in a ward just a few yards from where Herbie was born.

Mum looked exhausted and shrunken during this stay. She was ashen-skinned and skeletal, permanently attached to either a nebuliser or a respirator, barely able to force down the sad little sandwiches brought to her every day, too tired to watch the TV shows we downloaded to her iPad. It was hard to reconcile this version of my mother with the one who shoulder-barged her way through my childhood. But it was really her. This was really happening.

I find that I have two stock reactions to situations like this. First, I try to learn as much as I can about the situation, because I often struggle to cope with the uncertainty of it all. Second, I cook like mad. So, while Mum was in hospital, I had Pete and Dad around every night, feeding them dinner just the way I did after the fire. Around a table, like a family.

I did this because I didn't know what else to do. Mum was always the caretaker of the family and, if she wasn't around, all I could do was assume her position as best I could. I'm not sure what the others thought of my determination to feed everyone – on at least one occasion, Dad spent the entirety of the meal grumbling that he was missing *The Great British Bake Off* – but it helped me get through.

The needing-to-find-out-more part was a little more troubling. I googled all the terms on Mum's medical notes whenever I saw them, in a frantic attempt to try and get to the bottom of the problem. And, every time I did, the answer gradually began to reveal itself. Then came a line from the bronchoscopy notes, in tiny letters at the bottom of a page that we all seemed to have missed in all the panic about her breathing.

Definite tumour.

Shit.

Once Mum and Dad were formally given the diagnosis, the task fell to them to tell me and Pete.

I only have my own experiences with my mum to go on here, so forgive me if I'm a little off base, but one of the cruellest aspects of cancer seems to be how it robs you of your agency. Your own body has decided to kill you, and there's very little you can do about it. Your identity dissipates, and people start addressing your disease instead of you. Once treatment starts you end up becoming a helpless bystander to your own life, to this awful back and forth between the illness and the medicine. So, with all this going on, the few things you can actually still control suddenly become very important to you. In Mum's case, the thing she could control was how she told people.

What a horrible responsibility. Telling someone you love that you have cancer – and that it's both advanced and inoperable – and watching all their shock and anger and sadness play out in front of your eyes, must be a huge thing to do. It must need a hell of a run-up. So, naturally, it took her a few days to bring herself to tell us.

*

When she told us – separately – Pete and I reacted in different, yet completely understandable, ways. Since I had a feeling the news was coming, I was already braced for it. I'd had time, privately, to come to terms and wail and gnash and stare off into the distance. So I went to visit her at home, and she told me that she'd been diagnosed with incurable lung cancer, and my primary reaction was to go off and cook her a billion shepherd's pies. She needed fattening up, Dad can't cook to save his life and God knows I really needed to throw myself into some mindless busywork.

But Pete found out in a much more complicated manner, and I have to take some of the blame for that. Although Mum had told me about her illness, she'd also told me not to tell Pete. This, she said, was partly because it was her duty, and partly because he was moving house and she didn't want to burden him any more than he needed to be.

Looking back, I should have just told him. It's always best to be upfront with Pete, and I should have remembered that. Instead, feeling trapped between knowing that Pete would want to know and wanting to respect Mum's wishes, I did just about the stupidest thing imaginable: I tried to cryptically engineer a meeting between them.

We're at Mum's now, I texted him. Are you coming over? Then, when that didn't work, We should try to see her as much as we can at the minute. He invited me to his new house. I pulled out because I couldn't take the prospect of sitting there trying to keep all this a secret from him. But then he asked what was going on. So I cracked. 'She's had results, but she wants to be the one to tell you.'

What an idiot. I was exacerbating a situation that was already quickly becoming dire. By handling it so ineptly, and letting slip that I knew about the cancer before him, I'd made Pete feel as though he'd been deliberately left out of the loop. It meant that the sadness of his reaction would be tinged with a streak of anger. Everyone had nothing but the best intentions, but we'd all independently conspired to make a complete meal of things. This whole nightmare could have been avoided if we'd all just been straight with each other.

Later I'd learn that Mum had expected me to tell Pete all along, even though she'd told me not to, because I normally can't keep my mouth shut about anything. The one time she wanted me to be a shit-stirrer, I'd let her down.

Our differing reactions pushed a wedge between us. It was all too raw to properly examine, and this resulted in a prolonged Cold War between us. Without the Wednesday Night Dinner Club to hold things together, we stopped arranging to see each other. Our texts became sporadic and functional. Communication, when there was any, was brokered remotely during lunchtime meetings between Robyn and Emily, who stayed friends throughout all this and couldn't really understand what the fuck was going on.

We've always had moments of frostiness, me and Pete, because we're brothers. We've been brothers for three and a half decades, and over that time we've developed a shorthand for pushing each other's buttons. It doesn't take a lot to make us fight. But this felt different. He was annoyed at me for not being upfront, and I was annoyed at him for not understanding the predicament I'd been put in. For the first time, the schism felt as though it could be permanent.

It was just a dark, dark, horrible time. A few days after Mum was diagnosed, our old neighbour died. She was Mum's closest friend, to the extent that we called her Auntie, but she'd been chronically unwell for years. Mum was ill and Pete was working, so Dad and I were the only two members of the family to attend the funeral. Before the service started, Dad took me to a tree in the grounds of the crematorium. He told me that the ashes of his parents had been scattered there, along with the ashes of my brother Paul. 'When I go, I'd be very happy to end up here,' he told me.

But things move on. Bad news is like a weird smell. When you first discover it, it overloads your brain and you can think about nothing else. But live with it for a while, and it fades away. The smell is still there, and you still get wafts of it from time to time, but you start getting used to it. It's like this with most strong emotions. When my son was born, for example, everything seemed debilitatingly profound for the first couple of weeks. 'LOOK at his TOENAILS!' I'd exclaim every fifteen minutes, wiping the tears from my eyes. 'They're so PERFECT!' But you can't keep that sort of behaviour up the whole time. You can't keep dragging everything to a halt in order to marvel at the fragile majesty of life, because then you'd never get anything done.

The same thing happened with Mum. Once we all knew the deal, once Mum was given her chemo dates and we all found ourselves with a plan to stick to, our baselines shifted and we cracked on. This is not a family of mopers. Dealt a shitty hand? Back on the horse.

Again, this was Mum holding the family together. This was all happening to her, so she got to set the tone. If she'd wanted to cry, we'd have cried with her. If she'd wanted to crawl into bed alone, we'd have sat at the other side of the door in silence. But Mum did neither. Mum cracked the fuck on. She went out. She did stuff. She was so thin that she struggled with the cold, but she was determined to get on with life as well as she could. No tears, at least not in front of us. No bargaining. Just defiant acceptance. Time had become finite, so a moment wallowed was a moment wasted. The dignity of her response was breathtaking. I've been proud of my mum countless times throughout my life, but never as proud as I was then.

As the effects of the chemo kicked in, along with the effects of her predominately cheese-and-cream-based diet, Mum's weight eventually started to increase again. This gave her the strength to pick Herbie up. To play with him. To chase him around the garden. Seeing her with Herbie is just the greatest. My mum, in traditional mum style, had pestered me for grandchildren for years. Now I can see why. She dotes on that kid like nothing I've ever seen. She can't leave the house without buying him a present. She rolls around on the floor with him. She sneaks him sweets whenever she gets the chance. My wife has had to scold her for giving Herbie sips of coffee. Mum is actively mischievous around him, and it's wonderful to see.

Herbie's grandparent situation isn't the strongest – Robyn's parents are out of the picture and Mum's future is uncertain – but we'll cope. We'll get back on the horse. It's going to be a lot of responsibility for my dad, when the time comes for him to be the sole grandparent of our child, but I have no doubt that he'll do great. Mum's teaching him well.

I dreaded seeing Mum in the chemotherapy ward for the first time. The thought of seeing her hooked up to a bag of poison in a gloomy room, surrounded by dozens of people all at death's door, was bad enough. What made it worse, though, was that David Bowie died on the morning of my first visit. I was convinced that his death would bring everybody down, the cruelty of cancer reinforced with every song played in tribute from every radio, including the one perched on the windowsill of the chemo ward, twelve times an hour for an entire day.

In fact, the opposite was true. After a few minutes of small talk as I entered the room and sat down next to her, Mum leant over and said, 'Did you hear about David Bowie?'

I nodded.

'Just goes to show, doesn't it?' she smiled. 'You can have all the money in the world, but if it's going to get you, it's going to get you.'

I'd got it completely wrong. Mum actually seemed lightened by the news. Cancer is such an equal-opportunities bastard of an illness that she didn't feel picked on any more. It doesn't matter who you are – an androgynous superstar or a former egg-packer – you still don't get any say in it. If it's going to get you, it's going to get you.

The next time I visited was the morning that Terry Wogan died. Pete had arrived before me, and in passing Mum had told him that she was having trouble seeing her television at home. Although our relationship had been in much better shape, Pete nevertheless took me to a side room to suggest a plan. If Mum couldn't see her TV, he said we should both chip in and buy her a bigger one. And we should do it today. Just completely *Ocean's Eleven* it. Leave the chemo unit while she was still hooked up to a drip, stop off at an electrical store, buy her a bigger telly, drive to their house, let ourselves in, box the old telly up, put the new telly in, clean up and leave them to discover it for themselves. I agreed, and went back to Mum.

Mum was still complaining about her television when I sat down next to her. This time it was the remote control. The batteries were dead or the buttons didn't work or whatever. I didn't really listen, because I knew we were about to buy her a new one.

Our plan went off without a hitch. Although Pete still managed to wind me up a little in the shop – he was rude to the guy serving us, partly because he didn't meet the standards Pete set for himself at work – I kept my mouth shut. We bought the TV. We drove to Mum and Dad's. We took the old TV down, we put the new TV up, we cleaned up and we left. Pete drove me home, and that was that. A thawing of our relationship. Better still, a thawing that Pete had initiated himself. What a thoughtful suggestion of his. What a generous, selfless thing to do. This was prime favourite-son territory.

A couple of hours later, Mum rang. She'd just got home and she wanted to express her thanks.

'You didn't have to do that!' she said.

'Listen, don't worry, it was nothing . . .'

'I'm so touched. I only told you once that I was having trouble with my remote control, and you went out and bought me a new one.'

I took a beat to try and unpack what was happening. Mum must have got home, seen the remote control, assumed that I'd bought it for her, and phoned me up to thank me.

'You do realise we bought you a new TV as well, don't you?'

The line went dead. After a while, she piped up again, audibly choked.

'This was very naughty of you.'

'It wasn't me. This was all Pete's idea.'

'Really? Pete did this?'

This was the perfect outcome. We'd done a nice thing, and we'd done it together, but in the end Mum had automatically assigned all credit to me because I was the favourite son. I got to be proud of Pete, but I also got to rub his nose in it a little bit as well. I couldn't have been happier.

But, at the heart of all this, there was still an underlying tension between the pair of us. We were butting heads a lot more than we should have done while our mum was so ill. Mum needed us, and we needed each other, but it felt as though everything we did made the other one unbelievably angry. The whole thing was turning into a tinderbox.

ANOTHER COLD WAR

In retrospect, the worst noise anybody could have made at the time was 'Haa'.

Any other noise would have done. 'Grr' would have worked. 'Hmm' would have worked. 'Plop' admittedly would have been a bit of a weird choice, but still preferable to 'Haa'. That's how bad a decision 'Haa' was. It wasn't even a noise. It was a magnifying glass, a laser. It was a bloodhound that sniffed out all the simmering awkwardness in the room, then tore its guts apart in front of everyone. Under no circumstances, at that particular time in that particular place, should anyone have attempted to break the uneasy silence with 'Haa'. But, hey, that's what happened.

Because 'Haa' forces everyone else to join in.

Because 'Haa' is the first syllable of 'Happy Birthday'.

Pete came to visit on Herbie's first birthday. Looking back, it could have gone better.

First, some context. To be a parent, especially the parent of a baby that's just figured out how to walk, is to be the guy tasked with bailing out the *Titanic* with a thimble. Whatever situation you ever find yourself in, your brain is constantly red-zoning with a million different directly competing information streams. There's a glass on a table that the baby can reach. There's a lit candle somewhere. There's a protruding cable that can't decide whether it's a tripping danger or a choking hazard. A kettle is boiling. Your kid has something in his hand, and you don't know where it came from, and he's pulling at your trouser leg because he wants to be picked up, and he's making the same noise he did three nights ago right before he had that ninety-minute screaming fit. Meanwhile, some idiot is telling you a boring story that you need to appear at least slightly interested in for the sake of basic social etiquette, your wife is signalling that you left the wet wipes at home again, and someone from your office keeps phoning up and leaving silent, one-second-long voicemails that you don't know are silent or one second long until you've gone through the thankless rigmarole of calling up your voicemail service. This is what you're dealing with, every second of every day. To be a parent is to know that one day your supraorbital artery will explode and kill you. And that's fine. I made my peace with that long ago.

But, in the moment, it's like walking into a migraine. All these little irritants coalesce and start to screech and vibrate and swamp you from the peripheries in, and I've found that the only way to stop it is to let off a safety valve now and then. You let it off by being a dickhead to someone who doesn't deserve it.

All right, someone who deserves it a bit. I'm talking about Pete. Pete deserves it. A bit.

So, it's my son's first birthday. My mum is the first one through our front door, laden with gifts. She's carrying an enormous box with a trike in it, and there's a cake balanced on top of that, and a helium balloon bobs a couple of feet above her head. Since her diagnosis, she's decided to buy Herbie a full lifetime's worth of presents while she still can. The trike, for example, is in addition to the giant sit-in Mini Cooper that she bought him for Christmas; the one with the 'HERBIE 1' number plate; the one that's the size of our living room;

the one we make her keep at her house because if we tried keeping it here one of us would have to sleep in it.

Pete is next through the door. Things have improved between us, although they're still a little uneasy. Pete grunts hello, thumps down on our sofa and proceeds to eat a pre-packaged, shop-bought boiled egg as though it's an apple.

So, a quick recap of all the pieces currently in play. We have my mother. We have a ton of presents. We have my wife. We have Pete, chomping on an egg – an egg that must have been boiled and peeled a minimum of forty-eight hours earlier – in the same way that a cartoon beaver eats a corn cob. We have a one-year-old boy who doesn't know what a birthday is but seems excited by all the attention. We have wrapping paper all over the place. We have four boiling hot cups of tea. We have a box containing a trike that needs to be assembled. We have a fragile-looking birthday cake. We have desperately limited space. And we have me, anxiously running through this list over and over again, parsing it for all the numerous things that could go wrong, an uneasy smile plastered across my face.

The next half an hour or so passes exactly as expected. Herbie is the centre of attention. There is all manner of small talk, and a weird moment of tension when my wife and I both try to Instagram a photo at the same time, which is possibly the most damning indictment of any marriage you will ever hear. The trike is slightly more difficult to put together than I expected. Pete, whenever the subject turns to anything even remotely adjacent to the subject of cycling, looks up from his eggs to tell us about his Ironman training. Individually, these irritants would pass most people by unnoticed, but I haven't had enough sleep, and everything is starting to vibrate.

Still, I swallow it down. I remember that Mum brought a cake, so I ask if anyone has a lighter for the candle. Nobody does.

'Use your hob,' suggests Pete, attempting to keep the globs of yolk from spilling out of his mouth.

I ask my wife if she knows where we keep the matches.

'Why don't you just use your hob?' asks Pete.

A dull screech emits from the back of my mind.

My wife doesn't know where the matches are.

The words 'Just light the candles on the hob' somehow elbow their way past clods of half-chewed egg and force themselves out of Pete's mouth.

This is Pete all over. He sees a problem, then he convinces himself of a solution. It's a trait that makes him a brilliant leader, but an infuriating brother. Regardless of how much he knows about the situation, he's found his answer, and it's the only possible answer in the whole world, and you're an idiot for not thinking of it first. The answer runs in a direct line from his brain to his mouth. This is how he'd win *The Apprentice*, by constructing an Escher painting of such impossibly broken logic that all the other candidates have aneurysms trying to reason with him. I should know this. I've lived with it for years. By now it should be water off a duck's back. But everything combined – the baby, the hazards, Mum's condition, the current iciness in my relationship with Pete – is nagging away and my head is starting to go full spin cycle.

'The hob.'

'It's an electric hob,' I remind him. There. Checkmate, motherfucker. I've diverted his reasoning directly into a dead end. My argument is a sycamore tree, and he is Marc Bolan. Because you can't light a candle on an electric hob, can you? And, with this line of enquiry hobbled, I now have a little bit of space to think about where I put the matches.

Except I don't, because now my son has clocked the cake and he's heading straight for it, which means that I have to start holding myself in a number of increasingly uncomfortable CIA stress positions in order to stop him from slapping it to the floor.

'Why don't you know where your matches are?' Pete asks as I unsuccessfully attempt to slot an uncooperative trike together while simultaneously waving a birthday cake around in the air in exactly the same way that people in old films wave television aerials around whenever the picture drops. 'Oi,' he says. 'Why?'

Screech. Vibrate.

'Pete,' I snap, 'give it a rest.'

That's all I say, but it's enough to unleash months of piled-up resentment. It's been five months since Mum first went to hospital, and all the unspoken annoyances between us start tumbling out in an unstoppable cascade.

I don't really remember exactly what happened next. Pete was definitely offended, I know that much. He said something – the exact words aren't clear – about how he'd spent his entire life putting up with my shit. And then I must have glared at him in return, unwilling to engage in a shouting match with him because I didn't really want to have a yelling match on my son's first birthday. I know I must have glared at him, because he bellowed, 'Oh, a dirty look. Well done.'

Screech. Vibrate.

Snap.

'Pete, why don't you fuck off?'

This bit definitely happened. I definitely told Pete to fuck off, because Mum told me off for swearing. But then Pete retaliated by saying that actually he wanted to fuck off anyway, but he couldn't because he needed to drive Mum home, which is something I couldn't do because I didn't even know how to drive a fucking car. Then I think I said something about how I'd fucking well book Mum a fucking taxi, because the last thing I wanted in the entire fucking world was to have him in my fucking house on my fucking son's birthday for a second longer.

This is where Mum butted in again, to drop her newly learned but nonetheless devastating trick. She didn't like to see us fight, she said. And this worked, because she's got incurable lung cancer and neither of us wanted her to die thinking that the family would fall to pieces without her.

So now there's an icy silence. An icy, completely impenetrable, completely adolescent silence. It's a brain-stem silence, the sort of silence that only a family member can instigate. It's a pre-eloquence silence. If your little brother is being a dick – and you're kind of being a dick, but clearly nowhere near as much of a dick as him, I mean anyone can see that – then all your learned behaviour and hard-earned coping strategies fly out of the window and you're back in the playground. You're so angry that you can't even think, let alone speak. Besides, what are you going to do? Have a punch-up? With your baby and cancer-patient mum in the room? Hardly. We both know that.

So silence it is. Silence punctuated by tentative attempts at small talk about the baby, addressed through the baby as though he's suddenly Mo Mowlam. The silence lasts, conservatively, for about eighteen hours. It's only broken when Robyn hands me the matches that were in the kitchen drawer just as they always had been.

In any normal situation, this is what would happen next. I would light the candles, initiate a big family sing-along of 'Happy Birthday', then I'd help Herbie blow out the candles, then he'd have a mouthful of cake and the sugar would cause him to run around the living room whooping for the next day and a half.

But what was the etiquette here supposed to be? What do you do if 40 per cent of the people in the room hate each other beyond words? You should probably just leave it, right? Even though your mum bought the cake, and you're worried that this could be the only time she ever gets to celebrate the birthday of a grandchild? It's probably still best to leave it, right? Best to wait for a better moment, when minds are calmer and the gesture would be better received.

So this is what I decide to do.

Except my mind keeps rushing forward ten years. 'Daddy,' my son asks, 'what was my first birthday cake like?' To which I would have no choice but to reply, 'We never found out. There was a match-based dispute that got out of hand and, well, look, Uncle Pete is dead now.' I couldn't do that to my son. Not on his birthday. Not on his first birthday. What sort of precedent would that set? The poor kid would be on *Jeremy Kyle* before he was in long trousers.

So my hand was forced. I struck the match. I dimmed the light. I lit the candle.

'*Haa* . . .'

Now, by no means was this a rousing rendition of 'Happy Birthday'. It was the sort of rendition you'd hear in Guantánamo Bay. It sounded like a school-assembly hymn, but at a school where none of the pupils had ever heard the 'Happy Birthday' song before, and they all had guns to their heads, and they were all de-tuned violins instead of children, and they were aware that a bomb would go off in a nearby shopping centre if it detected anything more than the absolute minimum level of enthusiasm. It's what 'Happy Birthday' would sound like performed by a shipwreck survivor who'd spent the last few months in the middle of the ocean clinging to a plank of wood and had just that second given up hope of ever being rescued. It was exactly as excruciating as it was interminable.

But you know what? It is impossible to sing 'Happy Birthday' to a one-year-old without realising that life is about more than petty disputes with your relatives. Somehow, if only by a little, singing the song was enough of a gut-punch to help us realise what arseholes we were being.

As he left, I begrudgingly apologised to Pete. He apologised back. Neither of us really meant it, but Mum heard and it made her happy. Pete wished my son a happy birthday and departed. After he'd gone, I realised that he'd accidentally ground an entire hard-boiled egg deep into our sofa with his arse.

We didn't speak for about a month after Herbie's birthday. To even think about Pete would cause my brain to seize up like a jammed gun, and I suspect it was the same for him. As usual, the red-hot diplomatic pairing of my wife and his girlfriend would meet every week in the local Muffin Break to try and figure out what had happened between us, and why we were so reluctant to see each other any more.

I suspect the reason had as much to do with embarrassment as it did anger. That was certainly the case for me. We'd both, the pair of us, lost our minds in front of three people who didn't deserve to see it. Over the years we'd fought countless times – physically fought – over nothing, but this time it felt different. Maybe we were better off apart, I thought.

Our lives had veered off in different directions, anyway. I had a kid to look after now, and that's where all my attention needed to go. Since Herbie was born, my priorities had shifted so dramatically that I found myself paring everything else down to the basics, cutting all unnecessary strife out of my life. At that moment, Pete was the walking definition of unnecessary strife. Life is just a series of hellos and goodbyes anyway, I told myself, and perhaps this was my cue to say goodbye to Pete.

Eventually, though, the Cold War ended. And the reason – not in any way she would have guessed, if she even guessed it at all – was Mum.

Mum has three brothers and two sisters. Maintaining a tight-knit family with that many loose threads is incredibly difficult, but they managed it. They managed it for over forty years. And then they didn't.

Out of the blue, Mum stopped talking to one of her younger sisters. We never knew why, but that's the way it was. Their relationship just broke down. There was an argument on the telephone one day, and then nothing. Radio silence. Maybe a brief, distracted conversation at a family wedding every six or seven years, but only ever conducted at arm's length. They could just about manage civility, but anything more than that was beyond them.

But when Mum got ill my aunt sent her a bunch of flowers as a peace offering. Mum, at that point still battered by the diagnosis, and struggling to cope with a chemotherapy routine that knocked her out of action every third week, couldn't quite bring herself to respond. Every time we saw her, we'd ask if she'd called her sister. 'No,' she'd always sigh, 'but I should, I know.'

To some extent, I can see her rationale. Why risk another fight? Life was too short.

Peacemaking lunches were arranged – brokered by their incredibly patient sister-in-law – but one or the other kept cancelling at the last minute. Eventually, their hands were forced when my Uncle Vince, the youngest of the six, flew back to the UK from Africa and essentially banged their heads together until they saw sense and agreed to have lunch.

And, slowly, things improved from there. They didn't exactly become inseparable after that, but they started to go out for lunch together without a third party to hold their hands. They're getting there. And that's great because they've still got so much ground to make up, so many bridges to repair from all those wasted years. But how heartbreaking that this is what it took to bring them back together.

We eventually found out why they fell out, by the way. It was because of their mother. When she died, one of them – and exactly who is a highly contested matter – thought that the other knew more about the circumstances of her death than they were letting on, and emotions began to flare up. An argument about their mum put a chip in their relationship, and the chip became a crack, and then the whole thing died for twenty years.

Sounds familiar, right? Who knew dickishness was so hereditary.

I couldn't let this happen to me and Pete. Neither of us could. Slowly but surely, and fairly unsteadily at first, we realised how stupid we were being. Neither of us wanted to lose the other, no matter how hard we fought. Neither of us wanted to waste our lives apart, only to crawl back to each other full of regret once something terrible had happened.

I wouldn't be Pete's friend if I wasn't his brother. I'd sneer at all his laddy interests. He'd think I was a ponce. I like nice quiet pubs; he only goes to places if they promise some sort of *Sky Sports* megatron. He can drive. I rely on public transport. He's several rungs up the property ladder. I'm on first-name terms with the letting agent. We like different things. We move in different circles. We behave differently. I'm eager to please. He doesn't care who he offends. My life is spent trying to mould myself into whatever situation I'm in while he breaks his neck trying to force the world to fit around his needs. I'm the favourite son. He's the disappointment. There is no way that we could ever be friends. We'd rub each other up the wrong way too often.

But we're not friends. We're brothers. And that's more important. We're bound together by something deeper than superficial interests. Our lives will always be tangled up in one way or another and, whether I like it or not, the relationship I have with Pete will be the longest of my life. Friends come and go. Parents get old and die. If I live to be ninety, I'll have a maximum of sixty years with my wife, and a maximum of fifty-five with my son. But with Pete? A full eighty-seven. We're both in this mess together, all the way to the end. He's always been there, and that isn't about to change.

We've clashed before, and I guarantee that we'll clash again in the future – over and over again, I guarantee it, about absolutely nothing – but we'll always find our way back. Yes, we're stubborn. Yes, we're miserable. Yes, we're petty and pathetic and able to wind each other up more than anyone else on earth. But what can we do? We're brothers.

And yet our life is now about more than the pair of us. Right now, I have my wife and son to think about. He has his girlfriend.

We both have Mum to care for; and Dad, if he'll let us. Life is tough sometimes. People come and go, whether you want them to or not, but you can't do it alone. You can't. Nobody is strong enough to do all this by themselves.

I'm lucky to have Pete in my life, and I hope he thinks the same about me. Our relationship is so stressful that I'm convinced it'll kill me one day, but what else is there to say? He's my brother. I love him.

Obviously I'd never tell him that to his face, but I knew the next best thing. A way for us to have regular contact. A way to let him have the upper hand. This wasn't anything I ever expected to do – it was something I'd been actively running from for close to twenty years – but the time seemed right.

'Pete, can you teach me to drive?'

PETER HERITAGE WRITES

It took a lot to ask Pete to be my driving instructor. Just by asking, I was making myself completely vulnerable to him. However, to prove my complete and total trust in him, in a final act of vulnerability I decided to let him address you directly.

'Write something about you teaching me to drive,' I told him. This is what he sent me, in an email written on the train he now has to take to work:

To: Stu
Subject: The best chapter of your book

Well, Stu's an idiot.

There are thousands of reasons why Stu is an idiot, but today there is a very specific reason. Today he asked me to write a chapter for his book, which is a terrible idea. As you've probably heard by now, I wasn't the sharpest knife at school, and I'm hardly going to say many nice things about him since he's writing a book called *Don't be a Dick, Pete*. So no doubt this will end up being a badly written chapter full of childish insults.

By now, you know that Stu thought it'd be good for us to do things together. I took him to watch WWE, which I secretly love. Not that it's a secret any more.

But he took me wine tasting, because he is a fucking ponce. I hate wine, and he knows it. He was just trying to wind me up. It worked.

The worst part was that, since it was 'his day', we had to go on the bus. This was for two reasons. One, because he was successfully trying to wind me up. Two, he is a thirty-five-year-old man who can't drive.

Which leads me on to something else he wants to do for the book. He wants me to teach him how to drive. And he wants me to predict how the lessons will go, hence why I'm writing this now. These are my predictions.

Prediction number one:

I'm going to be an awesome teacher. I won't be perfect, but I'll commit to it 100 per cent. I'm not teaching him to drive for this book, I'm teaching him to drive because he is A THIRTY-FUCKING-FIVE-YEAR-OLD MAN WHO CAN'T DRIVE, and I'm embarrassed for him. How's Herbie going to feel growing up when Daddy can't take him anywhere? Ashamed, that's how he'll feel. My nephew deserves better.

Prediction number two:

Stu absolutely won't commit. I'm ready to see this through to the end, and see him finally get his licence. But I don't think Stu sees it that way. Do a couple of lessons, have a massive argument because he crashes my car into a lamp post, write a 'funny' chapter . . . that's all he wants. He did have driving lessons when he was in his late teens. Off the top of my head, I think he took his test seven times, failing miserably each time. Then he gave up, and I think he'll do the same again now, before he even takes a test.

Prediction number three:

He'll have terrible coordination. This will result in, at best, near misses. I can almost guarantee that his feet will be all over the place. I wouldn't be too worried, except we'll be in my car. To be fair, I've relaxed a bit with my car over the years. I bought it from new, and wouldn't let anyone else drive it for years. But it's a few years old now, and starting to get a little tatty. Despite this, BMWs aren't designed for driving lessons. Basically, my car is too good for Stu. And it's certainly too good to be driven into a ditch, which I fully expect to happen.

Prediction number four:

We'll fall out, and it'll be his fault. Because he is a stroppy twat.

Prediction number five:

If (and it is a massive if) Stu takes this seriously, I actually think it could be a really good bonding experience. We're both busy people, and rarely do the two of us spend quality time together away from partners and family. I'd feel a massive sense of achievement in successfully teaching someone to drive, and hopefully Stu would be equally proud of himself. It would be something special, a brothers' bond overcoming adversity.

Alternatively, Stu will just be an uncoordinated journalist ponce who can't drive for shit. Either way, I'm never getting the fucking bus again.

Sent from my iPad

LESSONS

I don't get to dream very much. Sleep is far too precious a thing to waste on bullshit like dreams. My time isn't my own these days. I wake up at the crack of dawn. I work. I take care of Herbie. That's my day. Aside from the ten seconds before I wake up at 10 p.m. fully dressed and covered in my own saliva, there is no downtime whatsoever.

So when I go to bed, the last thing I want is to put up with an abstract fucking slideshow of that day's meagre highlights, randomly edited to include sporadic yet deafening howls of my subconscious sexual motivation. That's too much to deal with. I want oblivion. I want non-stop jet-black unconsciousness from dusk to dawn. Dreams are a luxury I can't afford. Dreams can piss off.

But when I do dream, it's often the same.

Now, let me preface this next bit by pointing out that I *know*. I understand that describing your dreams to people is an act of almost extravagant dullness. The only thing duller than describing your dreams to people is showing them photos of your baby. However, you only have to take a look at my Instagram feed to see that I'm not exactly dripping with qualms about that, either. So just go with it. It'll be over soon, I promise.

Anyway, in this dream I'm at the wheel of a car, and the car is careering through a residential street at some speed, and I don't know what to do. I stamp on all the pedals, but they do nothing. I yank and tug at the steering wheel, and it just spins uselessly in my hands. I'm sure that there has to be a secret button to press, or a sequence of motions that will bring the car safely to a halt, but I can't figure it out. I'm just sitting there, panicked and terrified and bracing myself for a crash that – although it never comes – I am utterly powerless to stop.

I've looked into this dream, and it appears to be a control thing. Most symbolic interpretations of the dream suggest that my inability to steer the car in an appropriate fashion hints at a deep-set discomfort when it comes to relinquishing control, and a tendency to obsess about aspects of my life that I cannot change. It's apparently telling me that I am not in charge of my own life, that I am impotent in the face of upheaval.

But I think that might be bollocks. I think that I have dreams about not being able to drive a car because I cannot drive a car.

I mean, I can drive a car in theory. I know that there are pedals and gears and switches and steering wheels and everything. Put me in a go-kart and I'll be up there with the best of them. Put me in the middle of a desert and point me in the right direction and, providing I'm in a car with automatic transmission, I'll be able to get you home. But stick me on a four-lane roundabout outside town during rush hour and I guarantee that I'll either bring us all closer to death than we've ever been before, or I'll just abandon the car in the middle of the road and bolt for the nearest bus stop.

I can drive. I just haven't passed my test. Because the thought of driving terrifies me.

When I was seventeen, my mum bought me a block of driving lessons for my birthday. I used them all, then took my test, and failed. So she bought me some more, and I failed. Then she bought me some more, and I failed again. I honestly don't know how many driving tests I failed. I stopped counting at six, around the time that we started eating wallpaper paste for tea because I was blowing the family's entire food budget on driving lessons.

In a car with an instructor, I was perfectly fine. We got on really well, which helped. We'd drive up to roadside cafés and eat lunch together. We'd stop off at his house and hang out with his family. If he didn't have any lessons after mine, we'd go off on long, looping drives around the coast. And, while I was still a little hesitant at times, I was driving. The problem wasn't my ability to drive.

But then test day would come, and I'd clam up. You know how, when someone is taking your picture, sometimes you suddenly don't know what to do with your hands, and you end up just swinging them around uselessly like two big balls of stupid ham? That's what my entire body would do as soon as the examiner closed the door behind him. I'd panic and hyperventilate, and wait to be put out of my misery, which would never take very long.

Things got so bad that, at one point, a co-worker at the café where I had a Saturday job pressed a temazepam into the palm of my hand. 'Take this right before the test begins,' she whispered conspiratorially. 'I passed my driving test because I was smashed on these.' I threw the pill in the bin because that felt like cheating, which in retrospect seems like a waste, and carried on failing until I finally got the message. I am not a driver.

But since we left London, the thought had been nagging away at me. Should I bite the bullet? I drew up a list of reasons in my head.

NOT DRIVING: PROS

- Public transport is convenient
- Public transport is better for the environment
- Cars are ridiculously expensive
- It's easier to change a baby's nappy on a train than it is in a moving car
- When a baby starts crying in a car, it just keeps crying. It cries and cries and cries, and everyone gets more and more tense until the driver loses their mind and deliberately swerves into the central

reservation just to get a moment of peace. This is slightly less likely to happen on a bus.

NOT DRIVING: CONS

- Cars are more convenient than public transport
- When Herbie gets older and needs to go somewhere, a car will be invaluable
- I'd eventually like to live somewhere that isn't walking distance to a train station
- Regular contact with Pete
- It'll be much less of a headache if I ever decide to take Pete to a vineyard again

By the thinnest of margins, driving just about wins.

Pete, crazy as it sounds, seemed like the ideal person to teach me. He's been driving for fifteen years, so he knows his stuff. He's such a goonish alpha male that his entire identity is wrapped up in the car he drives, so he'd be extra careful not to let me crash it. Plus, this is Pete we're talking about. Pete hates losing. If he taught me to drive, and I failed my test again, he'd take it as a violent personal defeat.

That said, part of me – a giant part of me, in fact, almost all of me – was hoping that Pete would refuse out of fear that I'd wreck his beautiful BMW. And that wouldn't be so bad. I'd have made a reconciliatory gesture, he'd have turned it down. Morally, I'd be the winner and also I wouldn't have to learn to drive. A win-win.

Sadly, Pete was aggressively up for the idea. In Pete's head, teaching me to drive would right a number of desperate cosmic wrongs, among them:

- My inability to drive
- My inability to properly support my family thanks to my inability to drive

- The fact that my testicles were tiny and internal, which is something that happens to men when they don't know how to drive a car
- The perception that he was somehow the lesser son, when really he's so competent that he can not only drive a car but also teach other people to drive
- The fact that I sometimes willingly go on buses, when buses are exclusively for the old, the weak, the stupid, the poor and the drug-addled

There would be no backing out, then. In a moment of emotional fuzziness, I'd asked to be taught to drive, and Pete had reacted enthusiastically. So that was that. I was going to learn how to drive.

And I immediately plunged head first into a state of existential dread.

One thought kept running through my head over and over again any time I went near a car: why hasn't everybody already died in a traffic accident? After all, a car is a colossally heavy lump of metal and glass that you pour explosives into and then turn into a missile. A motorway is basically just hundreds of two-ton time bombs catapulting around a few inches from each other. The potential for giant, screaming, blood-soaked, mangled-limb mass death seemed just too great. At any moment, you could misjudge your speed, and lose control, and die. You could sneeze at the wheel, and lose control, and die. You could try and remember the lyrics to 'I Wish' by Skee-Lo, and lose control, and die before you'd figured out the line that came after 'I wish I was a baller'. Worse, any of that could happen to the driver next to you, and they'd lose control, and take you out, and you'd be helpless to stop it.

Driving a car is so stupid and dangerous that the government pays millions of pounds in advertising every single year, just to remind people to concentrate really hard when they're driving so they don't end up killing themselves – and an entire family of strangers – with their stupid Vauxhall Mokka.

The more I thought about it, the more I became convinced that I shouldn't learn to drive. But Pete wasn't letting me off the hook. His texts were exactly as incessant as my reticence.

Have you got everything you need to learn to drive?

When are we going to get cracking?

Lesson next week?

There was only so long I could hold out. After all, this is the same Pete who talked me into doing a Tough Mudder despite my utilising the exact same avoidance tactics as now.

Lessons?

Bro?

Brother?

Bro?

Braaah?

I really should have tattooed 'Pete does not forget' on my forearm while I had the chance.

So I bit the bullet and applied for a provisional licence. By which I mean I spent three months trying to think of an excuse not to apply for a provisional licence, and failing to find one, and then finally sending off the form with all the resentment a human being can muster. I was all set to go.

Except for one thing. I didn't have any learner plates. This presented me with two options:

OPTION ONE: Go to the shop and buy a set of learner plates.

OPTION TWO: Use a complicated web of procrastination, self-deceit, genuine forgetfulness and debilitating fear to delay your purchase for a period of eight weeks until you find yourself in a supermarket with your parents and your dad says, 'Look, I've found the learner plates,' and puts them in your trolley and your entire world collapses around you because you realise that you can't buy yourself any more time.

I chose option two, as if you needed to be told. And, on top of that, I still had a get-out. This was all happening around the time that Pete was training for his Ironman, and commuting to London every day meant that the bulk of whatever free time he had left needed to be spent training. 'Listen, get the Ironman out of the way, then we'll think about the lessons,' I told Pete.

'It's fine. I've got loads of time to teach you. If anything, I actually need to train less in the weeks before the race,' he replied.

'No, no, this is important to you,' I told him in a fit of pure-hearted altruism. 'You do you, Pete. You do you.'

This bought me a few more weeks. Sucker.

Eventually, the deed could be put off no longer. Every stalling tactic in my arsenal had been driven into the ground. At a total loss, I texted Pete.

Fancy a drive this weekend?

OK. I've hurt my back, so don't crash.
Have you got Loser plates,
dicknose?

My anxiety dreams went into overdrive. In these dreams I wasn't just helpless at the wheel of a car, but I urgently needed to get somewhere as well, and I was late. It's hard to think of a more thuddingly literal way for my subconscious to manifest itself, short of me pulling up outside my primary school naked to find that all my teachers had been replaced by a laughing chorus of everyone I've ever fancied.

On the day of the lesson, I packed Herbie off to my parents. Pete arrived early – much earlier than planned; in fact, in a portion of the day I'd cordoned off expressly for panicking – in a bad mood. 'That,' he yelled, pointing dismissively at a cluster of toys piled up on a coffee table in lieu of a formal hello, 'is CHAOS.' Then he toppled over and crashed face down on my sofa, like a tranquillised bear.

'Nervous?' he barked.

The old me might have tried fronting this out, by puffing up my chest and trying to summon a droplet of fraudulent machismo. But I was starting to learn a long overdue lesson. This isn't the best way to deal with Pete. Instead, I decided to be honest.

'Actually, I am,' I replied, and to my happy surprise he didn't respond in the way I thought he would. That is to say, he didn't reply the way he does to all other signs of perceived weakness, by miming a two-pump wank and then jazz-handing an ejaculation. For once, he seemed to grasp what a big thing this was for me.

I was only partially correct. After we'd put the L-plates on the car, I said, 'So, for our first lesson I thought we might—'

'YOU DON'T GET A FUCKING SAY IN WHAT WE DO TODAY!' Pete shouted, veins jutting a full inch out of his neck. 'WHO'S THE FUCKING INSTRUCTOR HERE? DO YOU WANT TO BE THE INSTRUCTOR? BECAUSE IF YOU DO, YOU CAN FUCKING TEACH YOURSELF TO FUCKING DRIVE.'

With that, he pulled off. I asked him where we were going.

'I'M NOT FUCKING TELLING YOU WHERE WE'RE GOING!' he shouted.

I reminded Pete that this was only a driving lesson, and not some terrifying CIA rendition operation, but I still couldn't coax anything out of him.

A few minutes later, Pete pulled up in the almost-deserted staff car park of the local Matalan. This place had special significance for him. This Matalan was the site of his first ever Saturday job, his first experience in retail. It was here that he took his first unsure step on the expressway that would eventually lead to his coronation as King of Ashford.

The car park was in no great shape. It was gravelly and unmarked, save for some doughnut tracks left by bored kids some time ago. Happily, though, there wasn't much to crash into if I suddenly lost control.

I got out of the passenger seat. He got out of the driver's seat. We switched places. This was it. It was happening. There was no backing out now. Oh God. Oh *God*.

The old nerves, dormant since the late nineties, came surging back. What was all this stuff in front of me? A wheel, a gearbox. Three pedals, but I was buggered if I knew what order they were in. A speedometer. Another dial that I didn't understand. The indicator lever. Something else that looked like an indicator lever, but wasn't. What the fuck had I signed myself up for?

'Are your mirrors OK?' Pete asked.

They weren't, but I didn't know how to alter them. I flustered and fannied with switches and buttons for what seemed like an eternity, but nothing would move.

'Turn the engine on,' Pete said.

I tried to turn the engine on, but his ignition had some sort of intricate hotel-door system set up that I couldn't fathom. He had to turn the engine on for me. Pete actually had to lean across the dashboard and physically turn his car on for me. I had failed at literally the first step.

'Fuck,' he muttered under his breath. His next expletive would be louder, and come thirty seconds later when I couldn't adjust his seat to the position I wanted, which was bolt upright and pushed all the way forward until my nose was an inch from the windscreen, Miss Daisy style.

'You know how a gearbox works?' he asked once I'd contorted myself into the desired stress position.

'I think so.'

'Good. Then let's go, shall we?'

What? This hadn't been what I wanted at all. I was after a much softer run-up than this. This was a driving lesson, but that didn't mean I wanted to actually drive anything. That would come three lessons in, surely. Pete had cut me off before I could finish telling him what I wanted, but the rough schedule I had in mind was:

LESSON ONE: Sitting in the driver's seat, running my hands over the steering wheel a couple of times and nodding, the way I'd seen actors do in films in which people buy cars.

LESSON TWO: Turning the wheel and pressing the pedals with my feet. Possibly saying 'Beep beep' if I was feeling confident enough.

LESSON THREE: Switching the engine on, driving three feet in first gear in an abandoned car park, then bursting into tears.

But no. Pete wanted me to drive around five minutes into my first lesson, like a maniac. This lesson couldn't end quickly enough.

I depressed the accelerator and let up the clutch, and the engine revved out of control. The car lurched a foot forward and then went quiet. I'd stalled. I restarted the engine, and shot off so quickly that I almost careered into a skip. Pete, flinching and squirming, helpless in the passenger seat of his beloved BMW, muttered 'Fuck,' again and told me to park up.

My nerves already shot to pieces, I got my feet into a tangle and almost drove into a bush. He made me reverse out again. I did so too fast, without checking any mirrors, in the opposite way than I'd intended, and brought the car within a couple of inches of a lamp post.

It was hellish. I was ungainly and embarrassed, Pete was worried and irritated. I can't say if he was mentally running down the clock in his head. I certainly was. I just wanted it to be over, so I could go home, shrug, 'Oh well, I gave it a shot,' and wait for someone to manufacture an affordable driverless car.

Slowly, though, it came together. The acceleration grew a little less jerky, the steering less erratic. I actually managed to change up into second gear – which took me two whole lessons when I was seventeen – and I found myself happy to spend the hour doing little circles away from everyone out the back of Matalan. I was jittery, and drenched in sweat, but this was something I could just about cope with.

'Right,' Pete said after fifteen minutes. 'Public road, then?'

What?

This was a madness. It was a madness. I could just about avoid a skip in a car park that only contained one skip. What the hell was I going to do on an actual road, with parked cars and moving cars and children and dogs? I wasn't ready for that. That's crazy. I'd annoy everyone. I'd certainly kill the pair of us. But Pete had got it in his mind that we were taking this thing public, and Pete getting something in his mind is never good for anyone but Pete.

He jumped in the driving seat again, and took us to a nearby village. He showed me the path he wanted me to take – just a quiet stretch of country road, with no kerb or white lines to worry about. I'd drive down a few hundred metres, take a sharp right and park up; then he'd turn us around and I'd drive back. That would be our hour.

And you know what? It was OK. It was shaky, and it was hesitant – and I kept too far left, to the point where Pete was having palpitations about how close he was to the side of the road – but nobody died. And I went into third gear. Third! That took me a month when I was a teenager.

On the third pass, just as I was about to pull in, right at the very last minute, Pete told me to take a left. There wasn't time to argue with him – the sum total of my brainpower was being used up just keeping this thing on the road – so I took the next left.

He did the same thing at the next junction too. And the next. Suddenly the narrow country road had opened out to something more urban, with pavements and white lines and pubs. And children who could run out into the middle of the road at any point. My heart was pushing blood around my body so fast that I was dizzy. A car approached from a distance, the first I'd had to deal with. All I wanted to do was run away and hide in bed, but I had to concentrate. No slip-ups. I pulled into the side of the single-lane road. The car passed. Nobody died. We were really doing this.

Within minutes I had got the car into fourth gear – a first for me – and looked down to see that I'd somehow reached 50 mph.

'Do you want to pull in, or shall we carry on the pussy patrol?' Pete asked. And I didn't want to say it – of course I didn't, I'm an adult human being and not a teenage boy – but the words just came out.

'I . . . I guess we should carry on the pussy patrol,' I said.

'PUSSSS-AY PATROL!' he yelled.

Here's how my dad taught me how to ride a bike.

I was glued to my stabilisers. Absolutely glued to them. Why wouldn't I be? Stabilisers were just the sensible option. They were unobtrusive, they didn't hurt anyone and they stopped you from falling off. The question wasn't when I'd graduate to two wheels, but why anyone would ever graduate to two wheels at all. After all, what's the point of making life any more difficult for yourself than it needs to be?

There is a cricket pitch at the bottom of my parents' garden. A big, usually empty cricket pitch that, for as long as I can remember, has endured the threat of housing development. There used to be a big rusted metal pitch roller near our back gate, and when I was three I was climbing on it and slipped, and I got wedged in the frame, and the fire brigade had to come and cut me out of it, and years later an old man told my mum the story of the stupid boy who got stuck in the roller and my mum kept quiet, but that's a different story. Anyway, this cricket pitch was the perfect place to lose my stabilisers.

My dad knew that, given the choice of taking a chance or using stabilisers for the rest of my life, I'd never lose the stabilisers. So he offered me a compromise. Whenever I wanted to ride my bike, he'd run alongside and hold it upright. I agreed and, for what seemed like hours, that's what we did. I didn't need stabilisers. I had an adult male willing to bend over double and hold me up instead. In a way, it was actually better than stabilisers, because I could chat to Dad while I rode.

Then, inevitably, the ruse. I pedalled off away from my back gate the same as always, babbling on to Dad about nothing as is my tendency, and it took a little time to realise that he wasn't responding. I looked around, and saw him miles behind me, chatting to a neighbour. He'd tricked me. And it had worked. At some point, once he realised that I could stay upright, he let go of the bike and I carried on without him.

And then I noticed. And then I fell off.

This was Pete's plan too. Knowing that I'd shrink up and do as little as possible in the face of adversity, he forced me out into unknown territory as quickly as possible, not giving me any time to overthink things. It probably isn't how a qualified driving instructor would go about teaching someone to drive, but it was absolutely perfect for me. All his annoying qualities – his stubbornness, his single-mindedness, his tendency to dominate situations – had somehow conspired to make him a pretty good instructor.

We drove through another village. And another. And the terror slowly began to subside. I actually felt in control. This stupid missile, this dumb two-ton status symbol, wasn't beating me. I was taking it wherever I wanted to go. It was responding to me. *I was in control.*

The wheel, the gears, the speed. It wasn't like my dream at all. I had this, and it felt as though something was being banished.

We looped further and further out of town, towards the vineyard I'd taken him to by train and bus and taxi, the one he hated, the one that cost so much money. I could see Pete start to relax beside me, and his relaxation made me feel even more confident and comfortable. We started talking, actually talking instead of just swapping nervy instructions with terrified responses. We talked about Herbie, and Emily and Robyn, and our parents.

And as we spoke, I realised that I wasn't scared any more. I had no reason to be scared. I wasn't the same nervy boy I'd been when I was seventeen. I was a man, with a wife and a kid and a lifetime of experiences I might not have had if I'd stayed in Ashford my whole life. But now I was back. And I was in Pete's BMW. And I was driving.

I shouldn't have worried about fitting into my family again, because leaving Ashford was precisely how I got to fit in. The rest of my family, everyone who stayed at home, hadn't moved on without me. Not really. They moved along *with* me, separately but at the same pace, waiting until I was ready to rejoin them.

At the outer orbit of the journey, Pete suggested that we go and pick Herbie up from Mum and Dad's house. This presented a wealth of new challenges – traffic lights and roundabouts and roadworks and dual carriageways and speed. This was still only my first lesson, and I didn't feel up to it. But look at what I'd achieved. Look at what Pete had got me to do.

Impatient bloody Pete, barrelling through my insecurities just as he's barrelled through everything else in his life. 'Fuck it,' I said. 'I'm in.'

What was I doing? This was so unlike me. It felt, just a little, as though I was turning into Pete. A little of the bullish determination was starting to rub off on me. And he was acting differently too. Dozens of opportunities for piss-taking were going by completely unremarked. Had he suddenly discovered empathy? Were we becoming each other? Was he turning into me?

'PUSSSSS-AYYY PAAAA-TROL!' he yelled again, for no reason.

OK, perhaps not.

Still, it was hard not to get a bit emotional on the way to Mum and Dad's place. I was driving through Ashford, through the place I thought I'd left behind, past the town centre and my old school to the house where I was brought up, the house that burnt down, to see the people who raised me and the boy I was raising. And I was driving there. I was in control.

As we pulled up outside the house, I was beaming with pride. I'd been driving without a break for over an hour, and it was fine. I was sweaty, and adrenalin was pounding through my body, but I'd exorcised something. All those insecurities, all those times I'd sheepishly stared at my feet whenever anyone asked when I was going to learn to drive, were for nothing. I'd beaten them. I'd done it.

I walked in through the back door. Mum was in the kitchen, surprised to see me.

'What are you doing here?' she asked.

'I drove here,' I grinned, waiting to soak up the adulation.

'Listen, Herbie's just done a poo and it's gone through his nappy and it's on his trousers, and I don't have any spare, so that's why he smells so bad,' Mum replied as my shit-stinking son leapt up into my arms and started punching me on the chest.

Nobody cared. But then, why should they? It's just a bloody car, for God's sake. And here was my family behaving exactly like my family. Mum fretting about immediate practicalities. Dad in the garden, sneakily uploading proud pictures of his grandson to Facebook. Pete rifling through cupboards looking for something to eat. Me desperately clamouring for approval. It felt perfect. It felt as though I'd never been away. Everything had changed and nothing had changed.

POSTSCRIPT

These last couple of years have been a motherfucker. It's all happened. Life. Illness. Fire. Marriage. Baby poo. Imminent baldness. It's been a lot. But the load has been shared. With Robyn, with my parents. And with Pete. He's been a constant throughout it all. We're far too male to ever tell each other this, but I'm pleased he's been by my side. He's just as difficult as he's always been – just as loud, just as abrasive, just as incapable of traditional empathy – but the more time we spend around each other, the more driving lessons we have, the better we're getting to know each other.

Thirty years ago, the thought of him teaching me anything would have been ridiculous. Twenty years ago, it would have been a lost cause. Ten years ago, we'd have both been too consumed by whatever dumb shit we had going on in our own lives to concentrate. But now, with me thirty-five and him thirty-two, we've somehow glided to a place where he has the patience to teach me to drive and I have the temperament to let him. I don't think it could have happened until now. Pete would have lost his temper whenever I hesitated at a junction. I'd have lost my temper whenever, instead of saying 'left' or 'right' as we approached a junction, he mimed masturbating a water bottle and then aimed the imaginary ejaculate in the direction he wants me to turn.

(That's something he really does, by the way. He sits there with a half-empty water bottle on his lap and, whenever he wants me to go somewhere, he pumps it up and down on his groin, grunting, 'Uh uh uh, oh yeah,' and then noisily splatters invisible jism to one corner of the windscreen or the other. This is a real thing that he actually does, and I haven't deliberately crashed him into a tree yet, which is entirely to my credit.)

During one of our lessons, the one he unofficially dubbed See If You Can Drive Home Without Any Help From Me Because I've Just Bought A New Phone I Want To Play With, Pete told me that Emily was pregnant. Maybe he is ready after all.

I'm coming to terms with being back in Ashford, too. There might be better, more glamorous, more exciting places to live, but those places wouldn't mean the same to me. This is my home. I suppose it always has been.

And it's Herbie's home now too. Almost exactly two years after we moved to Ashford – two years since the fire, two years since I became a dad, two years since I had to insert myself back into the functioning chaos that is the family Heritage – we've just bought a house here. Pete's helping us move. He's hired a van and everything.

A CONVERSATION WITH PETE HERITAGE ABOUT THE PERCEIVED DISCREPANCIES CONTAINED WITHIN THIS BOOK

The following takes place during a driving lesson, three days after Pete has finished reading the final manuscript of Don't Be a Dick, Pete.

'I didn't help you move. The last line of the epilogue was bullshit. You didn't even ask me.'

'Yeah, because you were away on work. Listen, it was a better ending than: "Two Latvians helped us move because Pete was doing a presentation in Dublin." What did you make of the book, then?'

'It was all right. Most of it was quite funny. It's just been a bit of a weird experience, hasn't it?'

'You've been a very good sport about this.'

'Emily hasn't read the chapter about the strippers yet, so . . .'

'Is that going to go badly?'

'I dunno. You made it sound a lot worse than it was.'

'I don't think I did.'

'It's definitely one of those things you lied about.'

'Name one single thing I lied about.'

'You said I booked the hotel specifically because it was near a strip club.'

'That's because you fucking did!'

'No. You're a liar.'

'That's the truth. I could get that verified by so many people. You said you went away to a work Christmas party, and when you stayed in that hotel, you realised it was near a strip club.'

'Well, yeah. What do you think of the book?'

'I can't even tell any more. I've spent an entire year thinking of nothing but you, Pete. I'm done in. What else would you say was a lie?'

'Well, I was thinking about this, and I haven't really made a very good list—'

'You made a *list*?'

'I'll just run through what I've written on my iPad. You're going to have to fucking drive by yourself, because I won't be able to see what you're doing. OK. You got my Ironman marathon time wrong. I did it in four hours and twenty minutes, not four hours and thirty minutes. '

'OK, I'll change that.'

'Good. Oh, and the Herbie chapter is a bit bullshitty. You said I'd had him for fucking half an hour before he had a meltdown.'

'No, I said we went to see a film. We went to see *Jurassic World*, plus we walked to and from the cinema, and we had a Kentucky Fried Chicken. So it was a while. Where am I going at the end of this road?'

'Wherever you fucking want. Anyway, you called me when the film was over, and everything was fine. I remember saying, "This is a piece of piss, crack on, have something to eat." So that must have been well over an hour and a half.'

'Did the tantrum happen on our way back? It must have escalated quickly.'

'Yeah, he fucking turned into a little prick. He's just like his dad – he can turn into a little cunt at the drop of a hat. And Vinnie Jones isn't one of my favourite actors!'

'You said that one of your favourite films has got Vinnie Jones and Stone Cold Steve Austin in it, and there's a bit at the end where Vinnie Jones goes crazy.'

'Oh, that is a good film, actually. It's a really good film. Vinnie Jones just goes nuts and fucking shoots this woman. It's really good actually. I can't remember what it's called.'

'Google "Vinnie Jones goes nuts and fucking shoots a woman".'

'*The Condemned*. Anyway, I'm more of a Stone Cold Steve Austin fan, so I don't agree with that.'

'Do I merge here?'

'Yes. Now, the Christmas Day joke . . .'

'Which definitely happened, by the way.'

'Oh yeah, it definitely happened. But I think I told it funnier than how you wrote it.'

'You thought it was hilarious.'

'It's probably the funniest thing I've ever said. I think you were trying to light the Christmas pudding, and I said, "Give it to Mum, she's good at setting things on fire." So I think you actually did me a bit of an injustice about how good my joke was.'

'Sorry.'

'Another thing is that list of Danny Dyer films.'

'What? You love Danny Dyer films!'

'No no, I do. And I love Danny Dyer. But I've never seen *Borstal Boy*, *Dead Man Running* or *Pimp*.'

'Have you seen *Malice in Wonderland*?'

'No.'

'Have you seen *Severance*?'

'No.'

'Have you seen . . . what's the one where Gillian Anderson shoves a shotgun up a man's arse?'

'I don't know! You see, this is the thing, right? As much as I do love Danny Dyer, I don't think I'm quite the expert you make out.'

'By the way, did you see how well I just took that roundabout?'

'Yeah, really good, well done. Also, you said I was nine during the 1992 European Championship, when actually I was eight.'

'That's an important point. I'm sorry I said that.'

'And then the two bigger ones. There's your recollection of our argument in France, which is just fucking ridiculous. You were being a proper stroppy little bitch. I'll tell it from my point of view, shall I?'

'Sure, go ahead.'

'First, you were the most miserable fucking piece of shit I've ever known during that week. I had a lovely week hanging out with Mum and Dad and Herbie. You were the miserable shit who kept over-reacting to stuff. Second, you said we went to the supermarket "down the road"? Down the fucking road? It was at least forty-five minutes away. It was miles away. And it was right in the middle of a city centre, so we had to park up and pay for parking, and walk to the supermarket and walk all the food back, and it was horrific. And then we bought food for fucking nine people, and I was ready to fucking kill myself in that supermarket. Honestly. So that's the first bit of bullshit.'

'OK, what else?'

'Down the road. That's such a bullshit thing to write. You know it wasn't just down the road. It's like, for us, it's like going to fucking *Ramsgate* to go to the supermarket. Then you write, "Robyn came through the door, carrying the shell-shocked expression of someone who's just been through something." That's just wanky bullshit. It doesn't even mean anything.'

I drive around a roundabout into a housing estate. A car behind me beeps.

'You know what, Stuey, you're all right there. He's just being a fucking dick, so he can fuck off. Anyway, apparently the first thing I said when I walked through the door was, "Don't fucking shout at me." Nothing provoked me, according to the book.'

'What provoked you was that you had a bad time shopping.'

'No. Shut up. What happened, right, we had a McDonald's on the way back, because we'd been out for so long that we'd missed lunch. And French McDonald's have got chocolate McFlurries, which you can't get in this country. We sat in the car and we all said, "Don't tell the others that we had a McDonald's." And then Robyn – I don't know what happens with her head sometimes, it's like the Keep Your Mouth Shut button doesn't work. She comes in and the first thing she says is, "Oh, we just had a McDonald's." And your face, right? You're sitting on the sofa, and I could see your face.'

'Right.'

'Your face annoys me sometimes. You have this expression. You don't have to say anything, but I can see that something has really annoyed you. It's genuinely like someone has done something awful to you. Your unreasonableness with the McDonald's situation, along with your bitch bolshiness, is why I got angry and called you a cunt. Which you deserved. And then you were a stroppy mardy cunt for the rest of the holiday and I had a great time jumping around in the pool.'

'We were all waiting for you. Nobody had lunch because we thought we'd be considerate and wait for you. And you were out eating chocolate McFlurries.'

'I'm right and that part of the book is complete bullshit.'

'Saying that you're right doesn't make you right.'

'I know I'm right. Sometimes you just know. The book's bullshit.'

'The entire book is bullshit now?'

'Well, that chapter.'

'It wasn't even a chapter. You're getting your knickers in a twist about three lines, maximum.'

'Why didn't you write about me winning you that gym membership?'

'I don't know.'

'Let me tell the story now. There was a festival in Ashford, and a local gym was giving away free membership to whoever could do the fastest five hundred metres on a rowing machine, and I won that. And I also won their competition to see who had the biggest lung capacity. So officially I'm the best on a rowing machine in Ashford and officially I've got the best lung capacity in Ashford.'

'Well, I think it's probably more the case that you're the best out of the three people who went on a rowing machine hidden in the corner of a tent in their normal clothes in the middle of summer.'

'The next bit was the argument on Herbie's birthday. Your recollection of it isn't incorrect in some senses. The argument went how you said. But the difference was, you were just being a moody fucking cunt beforehand. Sometimes, when you're stressed—'

'Which I was.'

'When you're stressed, you just get really snappy about stuff. I wasn't even in a bad mood.'

'You seemed like you were in a bad mood.'

'No, I wasn't in a bad mood at all. But I wasn't going to take any of your shit. So you were being a dick and I told you. And that's it really. Your book gets a lot more negative towards the end.'

'Is that a bad thing?'

'Well, I'd have thought that it should start off bad and then be all, "Aww, they're brothers, they love each other really," by the end.'

'No. First, those chapters set up the happy ending where you teach me how to drive. And second, things really have got a bit worse since all the Mum stuff happened.'

'Yeah, you're probably right.'

'And I know I haven't been dealing with the stress of it very well lately. With Herbie and with Mum and everything. Everything gets on top of me too quickly, and I don't know how to handle it. I know it doesn't make me fun to be around, and I know I need to work on that.'

'Maybe this is a flaw with me. If I think you're being a dick, then I don't give you any concession for that. Whereas if I'm in a bad mood, you probably deal with me better than I deal with you.'

'I don't deal with it better. I deal with it differently. I'm not as keen on confrontation as you. I'd rather put my head in the sand and wait for everything to disappear.'

'Yeah, I don't mind a row. I think I'm OK with the book. The thing is, I'm going to have a kid soon, and they're probably going to read this one day.'

'Well, maybe. Let's not discount the possibility of this book sinking without trace when it comes out.'

'I don't think it will for our family. It'll be around. But some of the bits that are closest to the bone are the bits I find the funniest. I liked hearing from Craig and Mike.'

'They think the world of you.'

'I'm surprised you didn't write more about Emily's pregnancy, though. Since it's a book about me, and me knocking Emily up is the biggest thing that's ever happened to me.'

'Well, yeah, but I'd pretty much finished writing the book by the time you told me.'

'What you did write about it was a lie as well. I didn't tell you on a driving lesson. I told you in your house, in front of everyone.'

'Yeah, I know, but it sounded more brotherly the way I told it.'

'I told you in front of Mum and Dad, and Mum and Dad didn't believe me.'

'So if there was a chapter about you finding out you were going to be a dad, what would you want to be in it?'

'Well, the chapter about Herbie basically sounds like I'm going to be a shit dad.'

'But if I had to rewrite that now, based on how you are with Herbie and how you are with Emily, it would be a completely different chapter. You're going to be a great dad.'

'Yeah, I will be. I still find Herbie difficult sometimes. Like, when I picked you up today, he wasn't interested in me.'

'To be fair, though, all you did was shout at him and swing him around by his ankles. And he's got chickenpox.'

'He could have still given me a hug, though.'

'It's different with nephews.'

'Especially when they hate you.'

'Herbie doesn't hate you.'

'I think I'm going to be a better uncle than you, Stu.'

'Why?'

'I'm going to show more interest.'

'I'll be around all the time. I'll be Cool Uncle Stu.'

'If anyone's going to be the cool uncle, it's going to be me. The thing is, if I have a poncey little kid who wants to read books, then you're going to be the favourite uncle. If Herbie grows up like a proper little boy and wants to play football and watch wrestling—'

'Wait a minute. A *proper little boy*?'

'Yeah. I don't mind what I have, but I'd quite like a girl. I'd like to be able to tell Mum and Dad that they're going to have a granddaughter.'

'I dunno. I saw a little girl being changed once. It must be so weird to clean a girl's bits?'

'Oh, don't say that.'

'Baby balls are weird too, but at least I understand them.'

'Yeah, I like having balls. We need to go and pick Emily up soon.'

'How do you think people will react to the Bang Folder section?'

'The Bang Folder was brilliant.'

'And you did it all on a regular mobile phone, not a smartphone?'

'There wasn't even Facebook back then. It was so much harder, because you'd meet a girl, and you wouldn't be able to remember what she looked like. The amount of times I met girls and just hadn't got a clue what they looked like.'

'Oh, someone I know told me that her brother had a Bang Folder too. I wonder if loads of people have got Bang Folders, and I'm just too innocent to know about it.'

'Did he actually call it a Bang Folder?'

'I don't think so.'

'It ain't the same thing if it's not a Bang Folder. You've just got to send that one-word text – "bang?"

'Where are we going?'

'Wherever you fucking want. Oh, when I pooed myself, you said it was the day before I picked Emily up.'

'It was, wasn't it?'

'No, it was the day after. It was definitely the day after. My stomach was bad because I didn't have dinner the night before.'

'Really? So you picked up Emily from the airport, this girl you'd spent thousands of pounds trying to win over, and then on your first day together you fuck off and do a race?'

'Yes. And she stuck around. And the next thing we know I'm doing an Ironman and she doesn't see me for six months.'

'And now she's pregnant.'

'That strip club chapter is going to give me so much grief.'

By this point, the lesson has ended and I've parked outside Emily's gym. Emily enters the car, and I start driving us back to my house.

Pete: What do you make of the book, Emily?

Emily: I haven't been allowed to read the chapter about the stag do yet. From what I hear, Pete's been withholding information from me.

Me: I don't think I wrote anything that would come as a surprise to anyone who knew Pete.

Emily: It wasn't a surprise. But back when the stag night happened, I asked Pete if you all went to a strip club. He said, 'No, we were all too drunk, so we went back to the hotel.' If he'd have said, 'Yeah, 'actually we did,' then at least I'd have thought, 'Oh well, it's a stag do, fair enough.'

Me: I didn't go to the strip club.

Emily: That makes it worse.

Pete: Yeah, you're not helping here, Stu. What lane are you in, you fucking mug?

Me: Almost everyone else went, though.

Emily: Well, I suppose that makes it better. So long as it wasn't just Pete and some poor souls he forced along.

Pete: And I was still the best man. When you read the chapter you'll realise that I catered for everyone. I catered for those who wanted to do the theme park, I catered for those who wanted to drink, and I catered for those who wanted to see some tiddies.

Emily: I hate it when he says 'tiddies'. It's creepy. It's old-man creepy.

Pete: Old men don't say 'tiddies'.

Emily: Perverts say it.

Pete: No, it's a gangsta thing. Tiddies, motherfucker!

ACKNOWLEDGEMENTS

This book was a full-blown team effort from start to finish. First and foremost I'd like to thank Rosemary and her team at Square Peg for somehow chiselling my initial vomit-puddle of words into something approaching a printable work. It's been a pleasure to work with people who care so much.

Next are the moral support people: people like Tom Williams, my colleagues and editors at the *Guardian*, and Robyn and Herbie. My god, especially those last two.

Then there are those who helped out with the meat of the book: most notably Mum, Dad and Emily. Craig and Mike, thanks for sending me all those photos of Pete. I'm sorry we couldn't print any of the ones where you could see his testicles.

However, there are two people without whom this book wouldn't even exist. The first is my agent Antony Topping, who throughout this process has been my biggest ally, cheerleader and bully, depending on what I needed to hear most at the time.

The second, and most important, is Pete. Good Lord, what a tremendous sport you are, Pete. I'm proud to be your big brother, and I have no doubt that you're going to be a brilliant dad to little Tyson.